BEAUTIFUL ON THE OUTSIDE

BEAUTIFUL ON THE OUTSIDE

A Memoir

ADAM RIPPON

GRAND CENTRAL PUBLISHING
New York Boston

Certain names have been changed.

Grand Central Publishing
Hachette Book Group
1290 Avenue of the Americas, New York, NY 10104
grandcentralpublishing.com
twitter.com/grandcentralpub

First Edition: October 2019

Grand Central Publishing is a division of Hachette Book Group, Inc. The Grand Central Publishing name and logo is a trademark of Hachette Book Group, Inc.

The publisher is not responsible for websites (or their content) that are not owned by the publisher.

The Hachette Speakers Bureau provides a wide range of authors for speaking events. To find out more, go to www.hachettespeakersbureau.com or call (866) 376-6591.

Unless otherwise noted, all photos are courtesy of the Rippon family.

Library of Congress Control Number: 2019944321

ISBN 978-1-5387-3240-3 (hardcover), 978-1-5387-3239-7 (ebook),
978-1-5387-1768-4 (signed edition), 978-1-5387-1769-1 (signed special edition)

Printed in the United States of America

Book design by Marie Mundaca

LSC-C

10 9 8 7 6 5 4 3 2 1

This book is dedicated to my haters.

You're not that cute, your hair is uneven, and you look dusty.

Thank you for being my motivators.

BEAUTIFUL ON THE OUTSIDE

The Winnie Cooper of Pittston, PA

The first time I went ice skating I absolutely fucking hated it. I was about five years old and had begged my parents to take me to Montage Mountain, a small ski resort in Scranton, Pennsylvania, where we lived. At the bottom of the mountain was the field for the Scranton Red Barons, the local minor league baseball team. In the winters they would turn the field into an ice skating rink so those who didn't want to risk their lives on the bunny hills of the mountain could instead risk their lives on this makeshift pond, with at least fifty people who would be wearing knives on their shoes and had no idea what they were doing.

My parents brought me there because I was begging to go to a rink, any rink, and this is the one they chose. I had gotten the idea to go skating from one of those giant tins of popcorn that you usually only grab at CVS when you need a last-minute gift for some random office Secret Santa or when you're running late to your aunt Gail's Christmas party. You know the ones—they are divided into three compartments inside for regular, caramel, and fluorescent orange "cheese" popcorn. Hey, I'm not above it. I've given one or two in my day, and everyone loves a giant popcorn tin. On the outside of this particular tin was an idyllic Victorian scene of all these people skating happily on a frozen pond. After someone gave it to my dad for Christmas, it was around the house and always filled with cookies or snacks of some kind.

Not only did I love whatever was inside that tin, I also loved what was on the outside. There was one woman on the tin that I was infatuated with. She was gliding across the lake on one skate, the other one dangling in the air behind her. She wore a long black coat, a matching bonnet, and a white muff. It was the muff I was fixated on, and the first time I saw it was maybe the first time I knew what love was. I wanted to glide as effortlessly across ice as this mysterious and fabulous Victorian woman, and I knew that a white muff was essential to making that happen. For the record, this is the only time in my entire life that I ever needed a muff but not the only time I wanted one. I wouldn't be too proud to wear one today—it's just that I've never really encountered the right muff.

For a couple of months I pleaded with my parents to go ice skating. I would say, "Wouldn't it be really fun for the whole family to go to a rink? I think it would be a really good time." That's me—selfless to the end. Eventually, my parents agreed to take my younger siblings and me to Montage Mountain. I had this perfect vision of what skating would be like in my head and I knew exactly what I would be wearing. I had this one fleece jacket with huge toggle buttons, sort of like the coat that Paddington Bear wears. I would wear that, blue jeans, plastic rental skates, and, of course, a muff. The muff would obviously be the key to my success.

None of this ended up happening. The toggle coat was really more of a lightweight fall jacket that was not suitable for the Scranton winter, especially on an outdoor ice rink. My mom nixed it immediately. And the muff? Forget it. "We're not going to get a muff," my mom said. "You don't need a muff. Where do you even buy a muff? You're going to wear mittens. You need to have your hands free if you fall. You're going to wear mittens and this ski suit and we're going to go skating." Fall?! *My poor mother*, I thought. She didn't know who she was dealing with.

The sleeves of the ski suit had elastic around the cuffs, so I couldn't even fit my hands in the opposite sleeves and pretend I was wearing a muff like I had planned to do as backup. But as my parents' green Chrysler Town & Country minivan got closer to Montage Mountain, I convinced myself to get over it: *I don't need any of that stuff. I'm still going to be amazing.* My blue ski suit had green lightning bolts down the side that I felt gave off the vibe that I would be going very fast. Even though I wasn't dressed like her, I could still saunter across the ice just like the popcorn tin lady.

My mom laced up my skates and we went onto the ice with all the other families out for a day of frosty fun. I took one step with the confidence of someone who had been touring with the Ice Capades for thirty years and immediately fell over. I was wet, cold, and absolutely devastated. I sat in the middle of this makeshift pond, with the wind stinging my eyes, and stared up into the dark winter sky asking God to teleport me to the warmth and safety of the couch in our living room. The whole time we were out on that drafty fake lake, all I wanted to do was go inside and sip on a Swiss Miss hot chocolate—another fantasy that wasn't to become a reality that day. After that fiasco, I never wanted to go ice skating again. My dreams of being the world's next "popcorn tin lady" were over.

Her elusive muff is a reminder that a lot of the major events of my childhood revolved around whatever outfit I would get to wear. For example, another one of my grand dreams was to host a talent show on the back deck of our house. As I planned it in my mind, I would coax my two younger brothers into performing their talents, which, at the time, probably would have been something like naming every species of dinosaur, singing the first verse of "Till There Was You," or maybe they would have stuck to what they knew best and shown off how they were able to stick their heads through our fence and not get stuck (which they were able to do at least 70 percent of the time, and it was honestly impressive). I knew that, no matter what they did, I was going to be the star of the show, and that's all I was concerned about. I was going to wear a white turtleneck shirt and these red plaid pants that my grandmother's sister bought for me. While this is not something Ryan Seacrest would normally wear, I was convinced it was the fanciest thing I owned because of where it came from.

We called my grandmother Nana and her sister Nono. Nono spent a lot of time with my family because she had no children or grandchildren of her own, and she was a star of my childhood. For some reason I thought Nono was the chicest person on earth. I remember her having fur coats and a maid, but that might be a fiction I concocted to make Nono seem famous. She drank canned Donald Duck orange juice just as I imagined everyone in Hollywood did. Every time I saw her it was like looking at a movie star or Princess Diana or someone else whose job it was to be professionally glamorous.

I got this whole idea for a talent show from an old episode of *Barney & Friends* where the purple dinosaur had a talent show for all the kids on the program, including a young Selena Gomez. I wasn't just going to be like Barney hosting the talent show; I was also going to be like Selena Gomez, showing off my own considerable talent. Naturally, I was going to tap dance. Granted, I had never taken a dance lesson, and certainly not a tap dancing lesson, in my entire life. But I figured if I could get on my plaid pants, grab the microphone from our karaoke machine, and drag the entire family out onto the deck that the ability to tap dance would just flow through my body like a gift from above. Unfortunately, the world would have to wait to witness the Gwen Stefani of Scranton, PA, because the Rippon talent show was not meant to be.

My plan was that I was going to put it on when everyone in the family was visiting my house for a birthday party or a barbecue. But every time one of these events occurred, there was always at least one Rippon child having some sort of meltdown—maybe my brother was crying or my sister shit her pants. It was always something. Even worse, I could never find my plaid pants. My mother stored them away somewhere in case I needed an emergency Easter outfit and she didn't have the decency to tell me where they were.

One of the biggest meltdowns of my early years had to do with another costume. It was Thanksgiving week, and everyone in my preschool class was asked to choose if we wanted to be a Pilgrim or an American Indian. Well, I went to school in the early '90s when the teachers called them "Indians." Sorry—we didn't know better at the time and hopefully they've updated their curriculum. If they haven't, they'll definitely be hearing from my lawyers. I'll stick to American Indian for the rest of this story.

When the class was selecting which one they wanted to be, I was having my daily cry in the mud room (more on that later) so I missed the roll call. I just assumed everybody was going to be a Pilgrim. I was shocked to discover that in my class of thirty, only four people were Pilgrims. I was one, and all the cool kids were American Indians. Everyone else was making a vest out of brown craft paper, and they got to wear a feather headdress. It was the kind of themed costume I could only dream about.

The teacher showed us that the Pilgrim costume we were going to make was a giant collar and a hat with a buckle on it. When I found out I was going to be stuck as a dowdy Pilgrim in this stupid hat, my heart sank. I got home from school and sobbed to my mom. "You have no idea what they're going to make me *wear*," I blubbered through my tears. The Thanksgiving party finally came, and I spent the whole day crying again because all my friends were basically wearing haute couture vests crafted from paper grocery bags with Bob Mackie–inspired headdresses, and I was stuck in a blue cardboard collar and a hat that wasn't even stylish in the seventeenth century.

Outfits weren't the only cause for meltdowns when I was that age. Every day at preschool was hard for me. I went to Step-Up Preschool and on the drive there, I would cry. We got into a sort of routine where my mom would be driving me and I would sit in the passenger seat of the car (it was 1994 and apparently five-year-olds were still allowed in the front seat—I don't know; ask my mom) repeating, "Tell me a joke. Tell me a joke. Tell me a joke," over and over as I rocked back and forth like Meryl Streep in a movie where she cries in the shower. I hated that car ride to school because I had this irrational fear that my mom would drop me off, forget about me, and I would have to live at my preschool my entire life. I thought if I could laugh, then I wouldn't be so anxious about going to school. If I could just think about something else for a second, I would be OK.

My mom kept a joke book stashed on the dashboard of the car and she would read me a different joke each day. It had to be a new joke, because if she would repeat one, I would say, "Mom, you already told me that one. How am I supposed to think it's funny if I already know it?" Even at five it was important to me to keep hearing fresh material.

There was a mud room at the school where all the kids would leave their jackets, boots, and Power Ranger backpacks before going into the class. I would sit in the mud room by myself and cry for a bit. Only once I was done crying could I enter the classroom for a day at school. I would take my seat like nothing had happened. I was perfectly fine. It was my first acting gig, and if I didn't deserve an Oscar, I at least deserved a Golden Globe.

Crying wasn't the only way my anxieties manifested themselves—when I was little, I also had crippling superstitions. I thought I had to abide by these arbitrary rules that I set for myself, but even when I did, they didn't make my life any better. As I got older and deeper into my professional skating career, I became superstitious about being superstitious. If something started to get into my mind like, "Every time I enter the ice from this door I skate really well," I would go out of my way to eradicate it. I would deliberately use a different door every time or walk all the way around the rink to make sure that I wasn't getting hooked on using the "good" door. This might sound crazy, but as you will learn, I *am* crazy. I do those things even now and I need to tell myself that it's just stupid, crazy stuff that I made up in my head.

Also, I had a severe case of perfectionism and nothing could cure me. I always had to have absolutely perfect grades or I wouldn't forgive myself. Once, there was a science test that I was worried I hadn't gotten 100 percent on, and I wanted to do something dramatic. I had seen a rerun of *The Wonder Years* where Winnie Cooper got a test back and she was nervous about looking at the score. She ran home from school, closed the blinds, and locked herself in the closet. She had a flashlight in the closet and she turned it on and then opened the folder with the test inside, shutting her eyes tightly. When she finally opened them and looked down at the grade, it was the perfect score she wanted.

I was going to do the exact same thing and it would give me a perfect grade, because if it worked for Winnie Cooper it had to work for me too. So I ran home, closed the bedroom door, closed the blinds, and ran into the closet. The door to my closet was always open, so I had to scrape it along the carpet to get it closed and it took a ton of effort. Then I was in the closet and falling all over my clothes, and things were falling off their hangers onto my head. I sat on the top of the hamper and it creaked under my weight because an eleven-year-old should not be sitting on a hamper to check his grade for a science test, but for the full effect of this ritual, it had to be done. I didn't have a choice.

Finally, I turned the light on and I put my hand over the grade so I still couldn't see it. Then I took my hand off the grade but closed my eyes, just like Winnie Cooper. I thought to myself, "This is going to be a one hundred. I absolutely know it." When I opened my eyes to look, instead of a one hundred I saw a ninety-nine. I immediately started bawling. I went through all that fuss with the closet and I still didn't get a one hundred. Winnie Cooper had no idea what she was talking about. This would be my first bad experience of being in the closet, but as I would later learn about myself, not my last.

Because I was always a crying, nervous mess at school, I never felt like any of my teachers really liked me. That all changed in second grade when I had Mrs. Lucarelli, a good Italian woman who loved the tuna hoagies that the cafeteria served every Wednesday. Near the beginning of the year, Mrs. Lucarelli said she needed a volunteer for a very special job. Everyone raised their hands, so I raised my hand too. Mrs. Lucarelli called on me rather than any of the other thirty kids. "Adam, here is some money. Go down to the cafeteria and get me a tuna hoagie." Not only did I do it but I wanted to be the best tuna-hoagie retriever that Our Lady of Peace had ever seen. If Uber Eats were a thing in 1997, I would have been determined to get five stars.

I must have done a good job because every Wednesday it was my job to go down and get Mrs. Lucarelli's hoagie. That was my first taste of being a teacher's pet and I found it intoxicating. I mean, first of all, how could you not love all this wonderful, high-strung, overachieving, daily mental-breakdown mess? Second of all, I finally felt for the first time that I had a friend in class.

It's not like the other kids were mean to me; it's just that none of them really wanted to play with me on the playground. In fifth grade I would brag to my classmates that I was only forty pounds. Why? I don't know. It was a stat that guaranteed me to get picked last for every recess kickball game. But I didn't want to play kickball; I wanted to jump rope and hang out with Sarah, the only girl to comfort me in preschool during my mud room crying jags, which will always make me think of her as a goddess who saw through my shortcomings.

Eventually I did make another friend, Alex. We just sort of found each other because we were the misfits of our class. I was a skinny, short kid with full-size adult front teeth in a child-size head, and Alex was a husky boy who was missing half of his pinkie finger, but to me he was the coolest person I'd ever met.

He was the yin to my yang. I think maybe no one knew what to do with either of us, and then we found each other.

Alex was the only classmate who would invite me over for playdates and to hang out at his house. He had a Nintendo and we would play *Super Mario Bros.*, and even though I was awful, it was the best time I had ever had. He also had an air hockey table in his basement, which really blew my mind. It was nothing revolutionary, but he was always nice and sensitive and made me feel like I belonged somewhere.

The time Alex and I spent together always seemed special, because it was so rare for me to have someone who wasn't related to me to hang out with. Once, I went to Alex's house and his mother made us that childhood staple: grilled cheese and tomato soup. When my mom came to pick me up later, the first thing I said to her when I got in the car was, "Alex's mom made the best soup. It was delicious." I went on and on about this soup for days, asking my mom to make it for me again because it was so heavenly.

My mom finally got so interested (what could this gourmet family recipe be?) that she called Alex's mom and asked her for her soup recipe. "It's just Campbell's soup from the can. I don't know why he loved it so much," she told my mom. So my mom got it for me at the store and made it one afternoon. I thought my mom must have made it wrong because it wasn't nearly as good as it was at Alex's house.

Even though I wasn't Mr. Popularity in grammar school, it was a school rule that if someone in the class was going to have a birthday party, then everyone had to be invited. In fourth grade, just before I turned ten, one of the girls in my class, Anastasia Davenport (if that's not her drag name, then maybe it should be mine), decided she was going to have her birthday party at the Ice Box. It was a brand-new skating rink that had just opened in nearby Pittston, Pennsylvania, a town just as glamorous as its name implies.

At first I wasn't excited about it because of my experience at Montage Mountain and because, once again, there would be no muffs. But when we arrived at the rink, it was totally different. It was inside, so even though it wasn't warm, at least it wasn't freezing cold and windy.

But the real reason I was willing to give skating another chance was because a year earlier I had watched figure skating for the first time on TV, during the 1998 Olympic Games. (My mom says we watched the 1994 Olympics together, but I was four and must have been in a blackout because I don't remember a thing.) My mom had invited her friend Andrea to come over and watch the games. I had never met Andrea before, but I heard a lot about her. If this stranger was coming over just to watch something on TV, it meant the event had to be something special. I can't help but get excited about an occasion.

I got even more excited about the Olympics when, on the afternoon of the big day, we were in the drive-thru at McDonald's and the announcer on the car radio said he had the results of the women's individual figure skating competition and if you didn't want to spoil that night's prime-time coverage of it, then you should turn off your radio now. My mom heeded that prehistoric spoiler alert and I thought to myself, "Wow, this is going to be so dramatic when we finally find out who wins!"

Once Andrea arrived, I thought we were all going to watch the competition together and, when it was over, have our own medal ceremony. This was just a few months after the holidays, so I found some Christmas ribbon and cut circles out of paper to make gold, silver, and bronze medals. I loved watching Michelle Kwan battle Tara Lipinski, especially because it was being billed as this supreme artist against an up-and-comer, but I fell asleep halfway through and my mom had to tell me who won in the morning. I was happy for Tara, but mostly I was upset that I didn't get to perform the mock medal ceremony with my homemade medals in my living room.

Because of all this, I was willing to give skating another chance as long as it wasn't at Montage Mountain. When I got to the rink, I was skating around with the kids in my class. I wanted the ice to be really worn out, full of the cracks and divots that professional skaters hate. Twice during the public skate they cleared the rink so the Zamboni could cut fresh ice, and I didn't like that. When the ice was smooth, it was fast and furious, and I was already too much of both. Once the ice got sufficiently bombed out, I learned that I could go slow enough to move around and start to have some fun.

There were some local girls who I had never seen before skating at that rink, and they knew a few simple jumps and how to do spins on one foot. During a normal public skate the figure skaters have to skate in the middle because the rest of us laypeople have the perimeter of the rink to be messy train wrecks and fall all over the place. I remember watching these girls in the center and being completely enamored. I thought they were the coolest thing ever, and though the kids who were cool at school never wanted to hang out with me, I thought maybe these girls might.

These master skaters didn't know who I was. It was a fresh start. They had never seen me cry in the mud room or try to impress the teacher with a hoagie delivery. It was like in a movie when someone moves to a foreign country and changes their name. Better yet, it was like a classic rom-com where the heroine takes off her glasses and gets her braces removed (either from her legs or her teeth, but maybe both) and the audience realizes there was a beauty hiding underneath the whole time. This was my version of that.

I was feeling kind of brave, so I skated into the middle—or more likely crawled or slowly glided, because I was really bad at stopping. I went up to a girl who was doing the single-foot spin and asked her how to do that. "I don't think you can, but I can teach you how to do a two-foot spin," she said.

In that moment I was sold. It was the first time someone my age offered to teach me something, and they were excited about it. Several of the girls took me on as their project for the day. I remember them telling me I had to go over to one of the dots painted under the ice that hockey players use (I still have no idea what they mean), and I should practice spinning in that dot. They were all helping me do a two-foot spin in the middle of the ice. Who knew where the rest of my class was? Who cared? I was where the action *really* was.

Two of those girls were Kitty and Jocelynn, who were already honing their skills with figure skating lessons. They would later become my friends when I started skating all the time. I just thought they were totally amazing, and them teaching me how to skate felt like Mariah Carey and Whitney Houston taking a break from dueting on "When You Believe" to give a young singer a voice lesson. When the informal lesson was over and we had to clear the ice, one of the girls said, "You should come back; it would be really fun." I knew, at that moment, that I would certainly be back, if not only for the skating but for something I'd never felt before that day—the warm Swiss Miss–hot-chocolate glow of acceptance.

Victory at the Holiday Inn

After having so much fun at the Ice Box during Anastasia Davenport's birthday party, I started plotting different reasons and scenarios of why my mom had to take me back to the rink for another public skate, especially because she was going by herself already. My mom actually started dabbling in the art of figure skating before I came along. She was a dancer her entire life, and before she had kids she even ran her own dance company. She worked with and choreographed for all the dancers in her company as well as did some gymnastics choreography on the side. This one family she worked with had one daughter in skating and another in gymnastics. She did such a good job on the one girl's gymnastic routines—I come from a long line of overachievers—that they asked her if she could choreograph their other daughter's ice skating programs.

"Oh, I don't know anything about ice skating," she told the girl's mother.

"It's easy," she told my mom. (Note to that lady: Choreographing an award-winning ice skating routine isn't as easy as you think.) "It's not strict like a balance beam routine. You'll be fine!" She assured my mom that this would be a walk in the park, but like on ice. She wanted my mom to choreograph a show program, which didn't have any required elements, so my mom agreed. She thought it would be smooth sailing, but little did she know the seas would be mighty.

My mom showed up at the rink at the appointed time. Immediately the girl's skating coach gave her the stink eye. Who was this confident woman standing at an intimidating five feet two inches—I also come from a long line of statuesque Irishmen—who didn't know nothin' 'bout birthin' no babies (she would learn, as she later had six of them) or figure skating? When my mom first showed up at the rink, this coach snidely offered to give my mom some skating lessons, and to call her bluff, my mom agreed, so she learned how to skate for free from a professional skating coach. The Rippons are not just overachievers; they also love a bargain. There's an old Irish proverb that goes something like, "Every time a Rippon gets a deal, an angel gets its wings."

My mom is no Dorothy Hamill, but she could do some turns, spins, and even a jump or two. Her signature move was the Mohawk Half Flip, which is the trick she would perform when she wanted to show off. It was nothing crazy, but my mom did it with flair and with her arms over her head like any true ballerina on ice would. Misty Copeland would approve—I'm almost positive. But for years after that and through my childhood, my mom would go ice skating once or twice a week just to clear her head and have some alone time. At this point she had four kids, one of whom was still reliant on jokes to get to school and out of the car between anxiety attacks, so an hour or two on the ice alone was meditative and necessary.

After the skating party, every time my mom would go to the rink, I would beg to join her. Often she would relent and it would be just like the birthday party, where I would take off and attempt tricks I had seen on TV. I'm sure I must have looked like a hot-trash disaster because eventually some of the *real* figure skater girls would come over, bring me to the center of the rink, and try to teach me things. After years of trying every all-American sport, I finally found something I loved and my mom knew it. I wanted to skate more than anything in the entire world.

I didn't have a very good track record (HAHA—I crack myself up) when it came to following through on sports thus far. First I tried to play soccer. As anyone who has been to a junior league game will tell you, when seven-year-olds play soccer, they all run in this huge clump around the ball from one side of the field to the other. I was getting so tired from running the whole time that I thought, *Oh, I'll outsmart the team. Wherever they run, I'll run to the opposite side, so I'll already be there when they get there.*

I thought this was a brilliant strategy, but my young and still-developing brain didn't see the glaring flaw in what seemed like the perfect crime. If I was always going to the opposite side of the field, it's just as much running as every other panicked seven-year-old was doing with the exception of being in the clump. Finally, the coach yelled at me in the middle of play, shouting, "Adam, get in the game!" I was shocked that he didn't appreciate the strategy I had. "Adam, you are so smart. Avoiding the clump the entire game helped us win! You're a hero," was the reaction I was going for. After getting yelled at, the only thing going through my head was, *I don't want to be here anymore.*

Next I tried baseball, which was a pretty big deal because my dad loved baseball. He used to play when he was younger and it only made sense that his son was going to be the next Babe Ruth. He had an autographed Mickey Mantle baseball card that was his prized possession. I remember seeing this card, framed in our dining room, and knew that we were never allowed to touch it. It was our family's version of the Hope Diamond.

Baseball was pretty fun, but I was really small for my age and I didn't have any friends on the team. I always had to play in the outfield, and the ball never seemed to travel that far, which led to a lot of "me time." Whenever the ball did come my way, I was always so deep in thought that I usually didn't even notice. How was I supposed to pay attention to the game when I was thinking about important things like how on earth dandelions and the cotton ball weeds that you can blow are the same flower? When

I was at bat, I always thought it would be my time to shine and show why I deserved to be the MVP of the season. But whenever I got up to the plate, I inevitably struck out.

Once, though, I got hit by a pitch. I cried a little bit, but then the umpire said, "Take a base." And I was like, "What?" I found out every time you got hit by a pitch, you get to go to first base, a mythical castle that I had never visited before in my, up to this point, very tumultuous sporting life. The next game, each time I was at bat, I tried to lean in close to the plate so I'd get hit by a ball again, literally taking one for the team, and I wouldn't have to strike out anymore. I finally felt like I was in good graces with my entire team because they could always count on me to make it to first base now, but my dad wasn't a fan of my new trademark move. He yelled at me and told me that if I was going to play baseball, I had to play it right.

I was over baseball and was just trying to get through the season. One day at home before a baseball game I asked my mom, "What do people look like when they faint?"

Her immediate response was, "Adam, I swear to God, if you pretend to faint in the middle of the game so that you can go home, you're going to be in very big trouble."

"Oh, I wasn't going to do that," I said, faux aghast. "I just want to know what people look like when they faint. I'm just curious." But *of course* I wanted to pretend to faint, like some Southern belle who had just gotten the vapors because a mouse ran through her legs. I could totally see the whole scenario in my head, my little body collapsing into the dust of the outfield, the coach and my parents rushing to see if I was all right, being carried back to the car and then put softly into bed without having to endure another awful baseball game. Another foolproof plan. My mom killed that fantasy right there in our kitchen on what I thought would be the Saturday I wouldn't have to play baseball.

Then I tried tennis. I started taking lessons right before going to Anastasia's ice skating party, and my mom made me keep going even while I was annoying her to go back to the rink. What I loved most about tennis was getting a red Powerade from the vending machine at the end of practice. I worked hard and tried to do everything the coach asked, but red Powerade was my light at the end of the tunnel. There was nothing like opening a cold one after practice. I remember the coach once asked us, "Who is the best tennis player in the world?"

The eternal teacher's pet, I said, "You are!" But he really wanted an answer. He told us if we were truly into tennis, we would start watching it on TV, we would learn who all the players were, and we'd start wanting to train harder and harder to be like them. That's when it hit me, right there on tennis court 2 at Birchwood Tennis & Fitness Club. That's when I realized I wanted to be a figure skater. If I was going to start watching a sport on TV and finding out who the best was, I imagined myself staring at Michelle Kwan, not Martina Navratilova.

Finally, for my birthday, which is November 11 (set your calendar reminders and tell all your friends), my parents signed me up for group lessons at the Ice Box. There were maybe about a dozen kids in the class, including my brother Tyler, who started skating with me. The lessons were for beginners of all ages, boys and girls. We learned the basics: how to skate forward and backward, how to do a two-footed spin, how to fall and get up, and how to skate on one foot, which really threw me back to my favorite popcorn-tin-that-had-been-repurposed-into-a-cookie-tin lady in our house. I worked harder than anyone else in the class. I did all the extra practices that were allowed, I would endlessly drill the elements we were learning, and I listened in on all the higher-level classes and collected all the intel I could like I was Don Lemon about to break a story on CNN. At the end of the six weeks, I had drastically improved. I like to think that maybe I would have been able to land a triple jump at this point already had I not been weighed down by my very thick fleece pants and matching Old Navy fleece tech vest. I guess I'll never know.

I moved through all the levels that they offered at the Ice Box very quickly, and I just wanted to skate all the time, but there were only a few times each week that the rink allowed figure skaters on the ice. On Monday nights it was "club night," where adult members of the local figure skating club could skate, and Wednesday nights were when the kids could come and figure skate. I started showing up on Monday nights because I wanted to skate so much. I had to promise all the adults that I wouldn't skate around too fast or get in their way—a promise that I wasn't always able to keep. I won them over by being able to talk shop about all the different famous skaters we would watch on TV and give them my opinions on how they would do in their next event. And also by begging. It was like *The Art of the Deal* but without Russian collusion, just Russian skaters.

After three months of lessons and a few pairs of fleece pants, I was making a lot of friends at the Ice Box. That's how I got roped into the Keystone State Games in nearby Mechanicsburg, Pennsylvania (yet another town just as glamorous as its name suggests). It was the annual statewide competition, and every year since the Ice Box had been open it had won the "club trophy," which means that collectively, at the end of the four-day-long event, they had earned the most medals. They signed me up to do three different events and even got my mom and my brother Tyler to compete as well. Anything so they could get that sweet, sweet victory. That's a motto I continue to live by.

There are two tracks in skating governed by two very different groups. There is the recreational track, for those who don't have dreams of Olympic glory. The skaters who choose this track are just skating for fun. That track is governed by the Ice Skating Institute, or ISI. Because it's recreational, they have all sorts of competitions for anyone who wants to participate. There's a category just for footwork, there's one that is an "entertainment" category that is like jazz dancing on ice, there's a category for people who want to skate with their friends, and there's even a family skate category where moms and dads can do programs with their children. You can also use props in ISI, and a skating program with elaborate homemade props is something you need to see at least once in your life. I know it's starting to sound like two ice skaters stayed up late one night binge drinking while creating these categories, and maybe they did. Who am I to question the creative process? They also make all the groups small enough so that everyone will win a medal or a ribbon for placing.

The other track in skating is the competitive track, which is overseen by US Figure Skating, or USFS. They are the ones who govern the national championships, send skaters to international competitions, and oversee the selection of the Olympic team. I knew that was the one that was prestigious, so I wanted to compete in that track too, even though there were no precious points for the Ice Box if I did.

There are only four competitors in each ISI category and everyone wins. There's first place, second place, third place, and the participation trophy, much hated by Fox News anchors. For the USFS competition, there could be as many as eighteen competitors and only one winner. It was the first time in my sporting career I actually felt competitive because this was the first sport I actually thought I was good at. The people at the Ice Box were mostly skating for fun, so they had no idea why I would want to stress myself out with this competition.

I signed myself up for two USFS competitions on top of the three ISI events the Ice Box signed me up for. Suddenly, I had five routines to figure out. My mom tried to help me do one of them, and even though I had been skating for only three months, I thought I was an expert. She tried to show me a move she thought would go nicely with the music, and the reaction I gave her was the same that Randy Jackson would give a bad singer on *American Idol*. It was a no from me, dog. My mom asked one woman, Debbie, the only coach at the rink who had students in the USFS categories, if she would be my coach.

"Are you turning into one of those crazy figure skating mothers?" was her response.

"No," my mom said, a little annoyed. "Adam thinks that a flip is jumping to the left and a lutz is jumping to the right. He's teaching himself these tricks and he's doing them wrong and I'm afraid he's going to get hurt. I just want someone to show him the right way."

"Well, you sound like one of those moms, and if I had a nickel for every mother who thought their kid was going to the Olympics, I'd be rich," she said. Debbie was also fully booked. She was the highest-level coach at the rink and had all the best skaters. She didn't have time for someone who just started.

Instead, my mom hired another one of the coaches at the rink, this very eccentric woman named Valerie. She talked about her "energy" and "being connected to the earth." Every lesson, before we could start skating, Valerie had to cleanse the energy around me. It was hocus-pocus I wasn't ready for at that age but now would be all about. You pay skating coaches by the minute, so this wasn't my mom's favorite part of our lessons either.

Between Valerie doing some choreography and me just inventing things, I finally got all of my programs together. At that age, each of the programs is only about a minute long, so my mom bought this CD that included fifty famous TV theme songs. They weren't famous to me, because I had never heard of any of these shows, even on Nick at Nite. *Bonanza*? Never heard of it. *Car 54, Where Are You?* I couldn't be bothered to find it. *Mission: Impossible*? Isn't that a Tom Cruise movie? She thought I could just use the music on there for years and years to come. It was another Rippon bargain. I didn't really care, as long as I had something to skate to.

I didn't have a skating costume to wear, and it's not like they sell them at Dick's Sporting Goods. My mom was still getting magazines for dance costumes from when she ran a dance studio, so we ordered something from that—this thin black shirt that zipped halfway up the front and a pair of black stretch pants that were so big on me they flapped in the breeze when I would skate fast. I was a vision.

My mom, Tyler, and I drove about three hours to Mechanicsburg. The competition was four days long, which meant it would be my first stay in a hotel. All I knew about hotels was what I learned from TV and movies, particularly *Pretty Woman*. I thought every hotel room had three living rooms with a Steinway grand piano in each, a dining room, and a giant Jacuzzi bathtub that you could dunk your head in while listening to a yellow Walkman just like Julia Roberts.

Imagine my dismay when we pulled up to the Mechanicsburg Holiday Inn and checked into a room with two full beds and a dirty bathroom. (The hotel has since been torn down, which is one way to get rid of a dirty bathroom.) *This is a lot different from* Pretty Woman, I thought.

The day of the ISI competition I did several of my ISI programs, including an entertainment program set to the theme from some mythical sitcom called *Dennis the Menace*. I liked that program because I got to roll around on the ice for a section, but I was upset that my costume was only a T-shirt and overalls from Gap Kids. I thought it was reckless of my mom to think it would be enough. I was scared I would lose to a bitch who brought props. I also did a footwork program to the theme from *Hawaii Five-0*, which I hated because there weren't any jumps in it. I fell during that competition, so I came in third out of four skaters in my age group.

When the results came in, I was so disappointed that I started crying. I felt horrible because I was standing with my friend Marci Mateo, who had just come in first. "Are you all right?" she asked me.

"I'm just so happy for you," I lied to her through the tears. She skated to "Be Our Guest" from *Beauty and the Beast* and performed her whole routine while holding a serving tray and dressed as a maid. Even without my fall, how was I to compete against that level of theater?

The USFS competition, being *so* prestigious, consisted of two parts over two days. The first part was called "compulsory moves," where you have to do very basic elements with no music. I was at the level "no test," which meant exactly what it sounds like—I hadn't tested to advance through any levels yet.

When the event was over, the referee would post the results on the wall in the hallway leading to the locker rooms. This piece of paper taped to the wall held my destiny. I remember hearing a girl scream that the results were up, and I ran into the hallway to see where I would place in this group of fifteen other skaters. The gods were in my favor—I had placed first.

I went to find my mom to tell her I was Mr. Keystone Games "No Test" Level Compulsory Skate 2000, and she said, "No, you didn't win. You must be reading it wrong." She didn't think that with four months of training I could beat out kids who had been doing this for four or five years.

I kept shouting that I had won and my mom said, "Adam, stop screaming. You're going to upset whoever the real winner is." Then she saw the score and realized I was right. I decided in this moment of glory I would forgive her for doubting me.

The next morning I woke up and was very excited not only because I got to compete again but also because the Holiday Inn had a free breakfast buffet. At ten, my favorite restaurant was Old Country Buffet. You could have pizza and make your own ice cream, and I just thought it was the coolest thing in the world. (Now I don't even like to be within a ten-mile radius of one, but I didn't know then what I know now.) At the breakfast buffet I had that classic culinary pairing of watermelon and bacon. It was the same winning breakfast I had the previous day when I won the "no test" competition. It was truly the breakfast of champions.

Back in the room, while we were waiting to leave, my mother

closed herself in the bathroom for a while. Tyler and I thought nothing of it and continued bouncing on the polyester floral bedspreads. Then I heard my mother crying quietly on the other side of the door. "Are you OK?" I asked through the closed door.

"Yeah, everything's fine," my mom said, flushing the toilet and coming out. I would find out much later that is where she found out she was pregnant for the sixth (and final) time. But she had to stay focused. Her now-growing uterus would have to wait because we all had a full day of competing ahead of us.

For my freestyle program in the USFS competition, I was doing a routine to the theme from the show *The Wild Wild West*. Yeah, I had never heard of it either. The most difficult jump I had in my program was a single lutz jump. During the six-minute warm-up period (which is when skaters get to practice in a group before they each compete), I tried my lutz and fell. Being dramatic, as I always am, I thought, *Now I'll finally see if I can pull it off under pressure*.

During my routine, I landed the lutz jump and proved I *could* pull it off under pressure. As I was skating, I started to go through the rest of the program really quickly in my mind and decided that I could add more to it. I was skating really fast and finished my whole program in about thirty seconds. Then I just stayed in the middle of the ice and started adding jump after jump without listening to the music at all. Suddenly, when the music stopped, I stopped. I thought to myself, *I think I've done enough*, as if there were a spotlight trained on me and my performance moved the entire audience to tears as roses rained down around me.

It was nothing like that, but I did win. After the State Games my mom and I started taking my skating a little bit more seriously. She saw not only that I enjoyed the skating but also that there was a competition aspect to the sport, so it might be worth pursuing better coaching to help me improve.

I was spending so much time at the Ice Box working on my

skating that my mom got a job there to make extra money to pay for the coaches, equipment, and rink time I'd need. She started doing promotions for them, because she thought she could help improve their group lesson program. Since she had run a dance studio, she figured running a skating program would be similar, and she started to get them more people for their classes.

Then she convinced the owners that they should do something called an "early bird" package, where skaters could get ice time if they showed up between 6 and 8 a.m. before work or school. They told her if she could get ten people to buy this, they would do it. She got twenty-five. Then they said they didn't have anyone to open up in the morning and let the people in, so this mother of five, with one on the way, volunteered.

Since we would be the first ones in every morning, that meant my mom had to "cut" the ice. One of the college kids who worked at the rink had to teach her how to drive the Zamboni. She says now that she was terrified, a five-foot-tall, five-months-pregnant woman trying to maneuver a hulking $100,000 piece of equipment around the ice rink.

But if you thought being pregnant would stop Kelly Rippon, then you didn't know Kelly Rippon. Soon, running the early bird skate and the group lessons wasn't enough for my overachieving mom. Next she took over the freestyle skating times and the hockey program. She went from making some posters to essentially running the whole rink. She said it was to make money for my skating, but I think she also liked being back at work and having her talents appreciated.

I used to love those early mornings at the rink, especially when there would be a snow day. We'd go in early to skate and then we'd huddle around the TV near the wooden picnic tables in the Ice Box lobby. I'd watch WNEP 16 with my two friends Danni and Emily, and we'd wait for each of our schools to come up saying that it was cancelled. "Please say Our Lady of Peace," I would plead with the well-coiffed local news anchor.

Danni, Emily, and I all went to different schools, so the only time we got to hang out together was at the rink. One morning each of our schools had been cancelled, so we all got to have a few extra hours of ice time. It might have been so snowy it was too dangerous for school buses on the road, but our parents' cars would be fine, right? Right!

When the three of us were together, we'd find old cassettes that skaters had left at the rink with the music for their routines on them. We'd pick one at random and we'd take turns making up routines on the spot. One of us would serve as the judge (I was always strict but fair) while the other two would compete. One day, we rustled up some tapes and Danni and Emily were going to compete for me.

We were all standing on the ice. As part of the rules, Emily had to turn her back so she couldn't steal any of Danni's interpretive moves. Danni skated around the corner of the rink and did a jump of some sort and fell. Immediately she started screaming, but I thought she was laughing. It was so sweet that she was such a good sport about inevitably losing the interpretive dance competition and could laugh at her mistake. By laughing she let Emily know the door was open for her to win, which wasn't a great strategy. Then I realized she wasn't laughing—she was crying. "Emily, I think something's wrong," I said to her as we went to go check on Danni. It turns out she had broken her leg.

Emily and I ran to get help from one of the adults at the rink. They called the ambulance and told us not to touch her in case it would hurt her more. We got our winter coats and bundled them around Danni so at least she would be warm while we waited for the paramedics.

Eventually, Danni would be fine. She came to the rink a few weeks later, though she couldn't skate with a cast on. Emily and I both got her gifts to make her feel better. I gave her one of my Beanie Babies that was a sheep. I took a Popsicle stick and snapped it in half and taped that to the sheep's foot with medical tape so it would have a broken leg like hers. I meant it to be sweet, but looking back on it now, it probably wasn't helpful to have a reminder of her injury stare at her in the form of a bean-filled lamb.

This was the first time any of us realized this sport could actually be quite dangerous, but it didn't stop us from skating or pushing our limits. In six months Danni was back with us, trying to take the gold in the interpretive snow-day championships once again.

Not everyone at the rink was as nice to me as Emily and Danni. There was one girl who always teased me named Eliza (that's her real name, and she knows who she is). The figure skaters took the ice after the youth hockey team practiced and there would always be some of them straggling around as we got ready. She would say, "Hey, Adam, don't you think all the hockey players are hot? You're looking at the hockey players, aren't you? You *love* them." She was clearly trying to shame one of the few boys in figure skating for being gay, which, yeah, real original, Eliza.

I would say, "No. I don't know," and it was the God's honest truth. I might have been attracted to boys back then, but it's not like any of these boys were going to wind up in a Calvin Klein underwear ad. They were a bunch of goofy teens from small-town Pennsylvania. Even at that age, I knew I could do better.

To make it even worse, all of these boys were always telling Eliza how beautiful her eyes were. She wore pounds of eye shadow and so much mascara that it looked like two tarantulas stuck to her forehead. I had no interest in these boys who always said they loved her eyes when no one had ever seen them.

Around that time I was doing more local competitions in all of the great hot spots of figure skating: Harrisburg, Hershey, Philadelphia. I joke about it now, but I was honestly having the time of my life, placing pretty high in competitions doing the thing I loved the most in the world. It was great.

When we were in Philadelphia, my mom prepared me to get

onto the ice, stood by the rink door, and held my water bottle—all things a coach would normally do—because Valerie was afraid to travel, so she hadn't come with us. It was only a two-hour drive, but alas, there was no energy cleanse that would get her to make the trip. When my mom was looking around, she saw a brochure for a woman who was giving skating seminars and lessons in the Philadelphia area. She didn't have any Olympic-caliber athletes but she had tons of experience, and my mom thought that she would focus more on my skating and less on my chi.

Her name was Sofia and my mom called her to set up a time for us to meet. As soon as we walked into her rink, the Skatium in Havertown, Pennsylvania, I could feel my heart beating faster in my chest. When my lesson was over, she approached my mom and said, "He's such a nice boy. It's just too bad he's fat." My slight frame had been concealed by my Old Navy tech vest and the crash pads I had shoved into my underwear before my lesson so that if I fell, I would be able to get up immediately without any pain so as not to show this Russian woman any sign of weakness. I would eventually learn this is something all Russian coaches say, whether it's true or not. I think "You look heavy" translates directly to "How are you?" in Russian.

After the session, she and my mother decided that Sofia would be my coach. Eight months into my skating career I had a championship under my belt, a real coach, a mother who worked at the rink and would drive me anywhere, and a whole host of friends in the "industry." I was finally being treated like the star I was already in my own mind.

The Price of Shame

Things with Sofia got very serious very fast. I was spending a lot of time with her, I was thinking about her every day, and I had to do everything she said. It sort of sounds like I'm describing an ex-boyfriend, but if he were a Russian woman in his sixties.

My mom would drive me down to work with her every Wednesday and Saturday. I had a deal worked out with the school where I would be absent on Wednesdays. My mom, my infant brother, and I would drive down to the Philadelphia suburbs Tuesday nights, stay over in a hotel, and return Wednesday evenings after my lesson.

We would meet Sofia halfway between our house and hers on Saturdays at The Rink at Lehigh Valley in Allentown, Pennsylvania (whose claim to fame is having a Billy Joel song about it). The caliber of skaters at this arena was so much higher than at the Ice Box. I remember one girl named Laura Wetzel (no relation to the Wetzel's Pretzels dynasty, unfortunately), who I always wanted to see there. She looked like Anne Hathaway, always had her hair up in a bun, skated to music from Cirque du Soleil, and never took the ice in anything less than a full skating costume. She even brought her own box of tissues onto the ice to clean her nose when it would run from being in the cold instead of stealing toilet paper from the bathroom like I did. She was just so classy.

The Rippons couldn't really afford that level of class. Always loving a deal, my mom would put a bid of forty dollars on

Priceline for a hotel (this was around 2000, when you could still do that) when we would make the trip all the way to Philadelphia on Tuesdays. She would start at the five-star hotels and see if anyone accepted. Then she would move down to the four-star hotels. We once had our Priceline bid accepted at a Hilton, which made me feel like I was Queen Elizabeth II, even if just for a night. Usually by three stars we found a place for the night, either at a Holiday Inn or a place called the Adam's Mark hotel (no relation to me, Adams Rippon).

I remember one night my mother drove to Philadelphia in a torrential downpour. It was raining so hard we couldn't even hear the radio or my mom yelling at me that I wasn't reading the MapQuest directions we printed out at home correctly. She was such a stud the whole drive down, and because of the weather, it took us almost four hours rather than the customary two. When we finally pulled into the parking garage of the Adam's Mark—which was the winner of the forty-dollar Rippon hotel bid that night—it was the first time we didn't hear rain pelting the roof of her Ford Expedition. We both breathed a huge sigh of relief that we had made it.

Then, while she was pulling into a parking spot, she hit the gas instead of the brake and the car rammed right into a giant concrete pillar. It ruined the whole front of the car. She had just driven with the confidence of Dale Earnhardt Jr. through all the rain, but in the end, she forgot all about the parking. Years later I would follow in my mom's footsteps and crash into my garage on a night I got home from practice really late, smashing the entire passenger side of my once beautiful Volkswagen Jetta.

Sofia really helped improve my skating dramatically though. She made me do hundreds of thousands of skating drills to improve my technique and make me a great skater. It wasn't just the jumps and the fun things to watch (and perform!) but all of the mundane shit of making me as adept as possible on the ice. I'm grateful she made me do it then, but while it was happening, I would have rather pulled my eyeballs out of their sockets.

Training with Sofia wasn't all shits and giggles though. Sometimes it was just the shits. My mom always used to keep bacon in the fridge and just throw it in the microwave for a few minutes and have a quick, easy breakfast. She was trying to get six kids ready in the morning and while it wasn't the ideal breakfast of a bowl of Kix with a glass of orange juice and a glass of milk like in the commercial (the kind of breakfast I assumed only very wealthy people got to indulge in), it did the trick. One day, before leaving to meet Sofia for an early Saturday-morning lesson, I had some microwave bacon, but something felt off.

That bacon wasn't sitting right in my stomach, so in the car on the way to the rink I told my mom I needed to use the bathroom. "Adam, can you wait? I don't want to stop," she said. I told her I could. Then, when we were about ten minutes away from the rink, I told her again that I needed to go to the bathroom. "Just relax. We're almost there," she said.

"Mom, it's going to happen right now!" I shouted from the back seat in a panic. She looked at me in the rearview mirror. She could tell I was serious and also that it was past the point of no return. When we locked eyes, it wasn't her son looking back at her–it was the picture of a boy who was about to poop himself. When I told my mom that I was going to poop myself, she looked worried for me but she was also laughing, and I was laughing too, but also shitting.

My mom pulled into a gas station so we could figure out my poop situation, which by this time was running down my leg. Luckily, as a prepared mother of six always does, she had another pair of pants in the car for me but not another pair of underwear. Then, with poop pooling in my sneakers, I had to waddle into the bathroom and clean myself up. I remember holding my pants, now heavy with my own shit, like Marie Kondo does when she wants to find out if something sparks joy. They didn't spark joy, so I thanked them and threw them away.

It was the most humiliating moment of my young life, but because I'm a champion, I picked myself up, cleaned myself off, and was still five minutes early to the only lesson I never had the chance to wear underwear to.

Even though I was only in class four days out of the week, I was always an excellent student. Part of the reason was because I was still obsessed with getting good grades like Winnie Cooper in her closet. The other was that I knew if I started to slack off in school, my parents wouldn't let me skate anymore, and I was not about to let that happen.

After the first year of skipping Wednesdays at school, I wanted to start training even harder. This was the first time I had real goals of elements I wanted to master and things I wanted to achieve. At eleven, I had this timeline of how 2010 was going to be my first Olympics and I was going to win a gold medal. Then I would go to the 2014 Olympics and win another gold and be the most decorated American male figure skater of all time. I didn't do any of that, but, girl, I still wrote a book.

It was also clear that I needed some more professional help, not mentally but athletically. My mom was buying these VHS tapes where a skating coach would teach the audience at home how to do certain moves. The problem was the coach was left-handed, so she always took off on her left foot and landed on her left foot. I'm a righty, so whenever I would try to do what she taught me, I would do it in the wrong direction.

The only thing getting in the way of my Olympic dreams was a pesky little thing called my formal education. When I was about to enter the sixth grade, my mom asked the principal at Our Lady of Peace if I could skip Tuesdays *and* Thursdays. That was when Our Lady of Peace said, "Peace, lady!" to this part-time student with double gold medal ambitions. When this happened, I begged my mother to be homeschooled so I could focus more on skating.

Around this time my mom had a talk with me about skating. She said if I was going to take it seriously and do everything I needed to get to the Olympics, she would treat it seriously too. If I was just going to do it for fun, then she would treat it like it was fun. The next day, like a serious skater, I woke up early so I could skate before school, but when I woke my mom up, she said, "We can't go to the rink right now. I have to get everyone up, I have to make all their lunches, I have to comb your sister's hair. There's a lot I need to do."

By the time she was finished with her routine and everyone was suitable for my dad to drop them off at school, there was only twenty minutes left for her to take me to practice. One morning I said to myself, "Oh, this won't do." The next day I woke all of my siblings up at 6:15 and told them it was 7. I got them all ready and fed, made everyone's lunches, and even combed my sister's hair. I gave her two pigtail braids and pinned them up in the back so she had a crown of braids. She would be the belle of Step-Up Preschool. Then I sat them all down in front of the TV and told them they could watch *Rolie Polie Olie* until they had to go to school. They loved it.

Then I woke my mom up and said, "Mom, everyone's ready. You can take me to the rink now." That is what a serious skater would do, right? She loved it too, so that became what we did every morning.

Even though I proved I was serious to my mom, my parents didn't really see eye to eye about my skating career. My mom saw that I was talented and obsessed, but my dad didn't want me to be taken out of school or, God forbid, homeschooled. He wanted me to have a "normal" life and not miss out on things at home with the family.

I felt my dad wasn't a huge fan of me skating. Just to be clear, it wasn't that macho, "No son of mine will be a sissy figure skater" shit. My dad is actually an artist himself. He didn't think it was necessary for me to be doing all this traveling or to be putting this huge strain on my family. I remember he told me once that he had a chance to play baseball with some minor league players and he was totally out of his depth. "It's a lot harder than you think to make it," he explained. He was probably trying to temper my expectations and help me avoid disappointment the way I think he felt that day he played baseball with the minor league players. Despite what he said, I never thought I wasn't *going* to make it. I could at least try.

Though I didn't realize it at the time, my parents were fighting a lot. I remember once my mom opened up the front door and threw the cordless phone out into the dark winter night. The handset was lost in a snowbank and we didn't see it again until spring when all of the snow finally melted. This just seemed normal to me. Didn't all families wait for spring to come to see the flowers bloom and find their cordless phones from winters past?

Despite my dad's objections, my mom started homeschooling me. I got all of the same textbooks the kids in the public school had and I had to complete a certain amount of work each year. At the end of the school year, I'd take my whole portfolio to the woman who lived next door to us, a principal in a neighboring town. She'd make sure I was learning everything the state of Pennsylvania said I should be and would sign off on my progress.

I was mostly left alone to read the books and figure things out on my own. If I needed help, I would ask my mom. I loved math in school, but when I was homeschooled, I had trouble with it because I didn't have anyone to actively go over it with me and explain it, and my mom wasn't much help. Eventually a nice woman named Emily would be my math tutor and would help explain fractions and decimals and all of those wonderful things I now figure out on my iPhone calculator. I always loved our math lessons because when she said I did a good job, we got to play the Michelle Kwan computer game, which was actually my true motivation for getting any math finished.

Since my dad wasn't a huge fan of homeschooling, he left my mom in charge of it. She liked to get my work together after a month or two and slowly build the portfolio up. Every so often she would say, "Let's get everything together."

"Yeah, OK, Mom," I would say on our way out of the house. Inside I would be thinking, "Fuck, I didn't do any of the work." I would do a month or two of work in five days of complete and total panic. Everything was rushed and at the last minute. It wasn't a great choice, but it was my choice. This is what sixth, seventh, and eighth grade looked like for me. I'm confident Winnie Cooper wouldn't have done the same if she were in my shoes. The only thing we had in common now was being in the closet.

Later, when I was in high school, I would do online classes instead. After a couple of years of homeschooling and all of that cramming, I was afraid that I was going to turn out stupid. I wanted someone to hold me accountable a little bit each week. That's how my mom and I found the online classes, which we didn't know existed before.

These had a lot more structure, and I had to do online meetings with teachers once a week. Still, I was cramming a lot of work into a little time. Take science, for instance. I was supposed to read a chapter a week and then take a test. So on a Saturday I would read chapter one in an hour and take the test. Then, in the next hour, I'd read chapter two, go take the test. Then chapter three, go do it. Then there's the master test, which is based on chapters one, two, and three. I had just read everything earlier that day, so I didn't even have to study. Take the master test and then, boom—I'm done with the whole first unit of science for that semester. It was time management at its finest.

After that I was less paranoid about not knowing anything. I think I turned out all right. There are plenty of people who aced AP World History who are still Holocaust deniers, so it's all a toss-up, really.

I homeschooled myself on the express plan. I graduated from high school *on time* (class of '08), which was the first miracle I ever performed. I've always been a little paranoid that people would think I'm dumb, so it's led me to a life of Googling everything so that no one would ever be able to think anything other than that I am a genius. It's also led me to WebMD for every little symptom I ever have, which is the curse to the blessing of Google.

The only reason I was homeschooling was because I was serious about skating. The best ice time available for training was during school hours when the ice would be the least crowded, and I was always working with a coach that was 150 miles away from my home. When I was thirteen, training with Sofia ramped up again. I was now working with her Monday through Friday, which meant that I moved closer to Philly to live with my aunt and uncle, who didn't have any children of their own but did have six cats.

I would take the bus from Scranton every Monday morning, stay with my aunt and uncle all week, and then take the bus back to Scranton after my session on Friday. Let me tell you something about the Scranton-to-Willow Grove route on the Greyhound bus: It was no luxury liner. Often the bus was empty enough that I could put my skating bag on the seat next to me and no one would bother to sit there and I could sleep—or pretend to sleep—and everyone would leave me alone.

Sometimes, however, the bus would be packed and I'd have to give up my buffer seat. Since I was doing all of this traveling alone, my parents got me a cell phone so I could get in touch with them if I needed to. I was passing one particular trip texting with my friends and zoning out on the phone as all thirteen-year-olds do.

"Can I ask you a question?" the guy sitting next to me said. He was over six feet tall with a heavier build, sandy-blond hair, and one eye that was a little lazy. He smelled a bit like mothballs but not dirty. "You don't need to say yes, but can I please use your cell phone? I'm getting off at the next stop and I forgot to call my ride and I don't have a phone." I told him that it was fine and handed over my most prized possession, my LG flip phone.

"Yeah, I just got out," he told the voice on the other end with a beaming smile. "I'm almost there. I'll see you soon. I love you and can't wait to see you." He hung up the phone and handed it back to me and then said, "That was my girlfriend. She's coming to pick me up because I just got out of prison." I'm not going to talk shit about him though. He said thank you and wished me good luck when he got off. He couldn't have been nicer, but it did feel like it was almost the second time that I would shit my pants while traveling for skating.

Soon I could mostly cut the bus out of the equation. Using her connections at the Ice Box, my mom found Sofia some more students in Pittston. My mom also started a hockey program at the rink and was booking a ton of rooms at a local hotel, so they would give Sofia a free room on Monday nights. On Mondays I would train with Sofia at the Ice Box and then she would drive me back to my aunt and uncle's near Philly. I would train with her all week and then after my lesson on Saturday I would return to my parents' house.

Though I wasn't at home a lot, I was still a part of the family—well, at least according to most. At school my youngest brother's class had to draw a picture of their entire family. When he showed his drawing to my mom and pointed out who everyone was, my mom asked, "But where's Adam?"

"Adam's not in the family," he told her. "Adam's the babysitter."

It's true—I would babysit them on the weekends when I was at home, but none of us knew anything different. It was all kind of normal to us. My mom spent a lot of time alone with me at practice or at competitions, but she never missed a school play or a dance recital. She was always there when the other kids needed her, so no one was resentful. But most of my siblings were so young when I started skating, so they were used to it.

Around this time, I competed at the Middle Atlantic Figure Skating Championships at Chelsea Piers in New York City. After the event, one of the judges approached my mom and me and said that I would be a good candidate for a particular young international skaters' program. She handed us a brochure and explained that this was a program where young skaters can get some international competition experience before US Figure Skating sends them to the marquee competitions.

My mom took her advice and filled out the application. She told Sofia, who loved the idea. Sofia was always DTF: down to fly. A few weeks later we got a call informing us that I was assigned to go to a competition in Luxembourg. What I didn't know at the time was that my parents were on the verge of divorce. Instead of going to Europe just for the competition, we went for a whole month. Now I think that my mom thought this was going to be the last big hurrah of my skating career—I'd get to compete internationally, we'd have a trip to Europe, and if she couldn't keep me skating after the divorce, at least I would have had that experience. Also, my mom had never been to Europe before, and frankly, I think she needed a bit of an escape. Without even knowing it, I was on the Eat, Pray, Divorce European tour.

We started in Amsterdam, because my dad had a cousin who lived there. We stayed in his partially finished basement and I'll never forget our stay. I remember my uncle *really* wanted me to hang out with this one neighborhood girl and insinuated with a wink that we were going to "do whatever kids do." I was thirteen. Maybe he just really wanted to get me laid or something, I don't know, but it felt so weird that he kept pressuring us to hang out. Was he trying to pimp me out? Was I getting into an arranged marriage at thirteen? These were real thoughts that filled my racing mind.

We were there for a week before I went to Luxembourg. Now, looking back, I'm like, "I didn't skate for a whole week before a competition?" If my mom let this happen, she was definitely going through it. Anyway, at the competition, even without training that week, I skated perfectly. It was the first time I ever landed a triple jump in a competition, and I won. Sofia flew out for the event, and when it was over, she was crying, my mom was crying, I was crying and in Europe. It was amazing.

My mom got us Eurail passes, so we were going to go all over France and Italy after the competition. We had these two huge suitcases that we had to lug on and off all the trains, and we had no real itinerary. We would get to our destination, wherever it would be that day—it was a total shit show. It was a coin toss whether or not we booked a hotel for that particular city for that particular night. I remember a few times she called my dad in Pennsylvania and had him make arrangements for us online. This trip was clearly run by a thirteen-year-old who just narrowly got out of an arranged marriage and a mother of six who was about to go through a divorce, but we made it work.

When we were in France, the hotel workers went on strike, so we were alone in a hotel with this other American mother and her son who was about my age. The boy and I started chatting, and we discovered we had the same video game for our Game Boy Colors. He said, "Do you want to go up to my room and play Pokémon?"

"Yeah," I said. "If it's OK with my mom." It was, so we went up, and I was playing the video game a little bit with the other boy. We decided to take a little break to watch some TV. One of my favorite things about hotels in Europe is that when you turn on the TV, there's always a channel that's just soft-core porn. So we just ended up watching soft-core porn together, and our conversation quickly drifted from Pokémon strategies to boobs. We couldn't look away. We were both completely hypnotized. Even as a closeted thirteen-year-old, I still had an appreciation for a nice rack.

We shut it off right before our mothers came to the room, and just like that, it was time for me to leave my new friend and for my mom and me to go to bed. The next day, when we were on an overnight train lying in our separate bunk beds in the same cabin, my mom asked, "Was everything OK with you and that boy when you went upstairs?"

In my mind I was like, "My mom knows I watched porn." But then I said, "Yeah, it was fine. Why?" as my porn-watching heart raced.

"I'm going to tell you something, but don't get worried," my mom said, which made me freak out even more. But then she told me that when she was downstairs talking to the boy's mother, she told my mom that she was getting divorced from her husband because he had just come out as gay. She also told my mom that she was from the year 4623. She was a time traveler from the future and she said that she knew exactly who I was and that I had a big future ahead of me and that everything was going to be OK. I totally believe that I'll still be famous in three thousand years, but I'm not sure that lady really was from the future. She was wearing a purple nylon tracksuit from the '80s. If anything, she was from the past! I will never forget that lady or the boobs that connected her son and me forever.

Shortly after we got back, our parents told all of the kids about the divorce. Of course, like every mom and dad about to break up, they told us it wasn't our fault, but at the time I took it very personally. I feel like it had to do with my skating. Both of my parents always told me that wasn't the case, but I still look back and think I'm a big reason why my parents got a divorce.

Strangely enough, I never really talked to my siblings about the divorce. As the oldest and self-appointed bagged-lunch maker, I felt like I had to be the leader. If I was strong and didn't get upset, then no one else would get upset. It was something we all had to get through, and get through it we did.

It felt personal when I was young, and everything that was

going on felt directed at me because a lot of time it was my mom going away with me to a competition, my mom driving me to Philadelphia. My mom was spending a lot of time with me alone, and there were five other kids to take care of. I also knew how my dad felt about my skating schedule and that my mother was the one shouldering all the costs for lessons, equipment, entrance fees, and all those luxury forty-dollar rooms from Priceline's finest two- and three-star hotels.

Once my parents divorced, we were to spend the week with my mom (while I would be away training) and the weekends with my dad. With everything going on, I would always feel out of place when I would get home for the weekend. I wanted to be anywhere else other than my dad's house.

My relationship with my dad suffered. I felt responsible for my dad having to find a new house, like this was my fault. Looking back I know that it wasn't, but my little old self didn't see it any other way. I felt guilty being home. I pulled away from my dad. I felt that he thought all this skating stuff would slowly pass and now was the time for me to be home. When a young teenager has made up their mind about something, it's hard to convince them otherwise. If it were easy, I would go back in time and tell myself that I didn't need to use a full can of Axe body spray every time I got out of the shower, but I can't change the past. I can only learn from it.

My dad did try hard and would always say that we should talk more, but I never followed through and we drifted even further apart. One Christmas at my dad's house, all of my siblings got what seemed like all of the presents they ever could have wanted: books, video games, DVDs, Barbies—whatever they desired. When I unwrapped my presents, I got one double XL sweater vest from a store called Five Below, where everything is either five dollars or less, and forty CD cases. No, not forty CDs, just the jewel cases they go in. I guess my dad thought I needed to bring my music for skating routines to the rink so I could really use a boatload of cases. It felt like a slight, but it really made me think that we just didn't know each other anymore. What Christmas gift would you give someone you didn't know well? Maybe not forty jewel cases, but maybe a double XL sweater from Five Below.

When my dad first got his own house, he didn't have beds for everyone so we all slept on air mattresses. Mine had a hole in it (probably from when my brothers and I would deflate it and use it as a medieval catapult) and I would inevitably wake up on the floor by the morning. When he finally bought mattresses, he only got five at first, so I had to sleep on just a box spring. It was basically a wooden box with a thin piece of fabric over it. My father's house was older so the living room was small, and instead of a couch he had these two giant overstuffed chairs. Three of us could sit in them at a time, but they were impossible to sleep in. Trust me—if I could have gotten off of that box spring and slept on a couch, I would have done it.

My dad explained that I wasn't there very often so I was to get the last mattress, which, as an adult, I totally understand. Also, he was now a single father of six children trying to get a life together—of course the transition wouldn't be seamless. But at the time it always seemed like my dad and I were slighting each other. Our relationship now is fine, but we've both had to work on it. I'm really grateful we made it through because I have a really good dad. I'm really proud of him, and I think Adult Adam is a lot more understanding of what he was going through than Child Adam ever was.

With all the transition at home, my skating schedule wasn't any calmer. I was going to different rinks at different times every day. All the running around became a little too much for my aunt, uncle, and their six cats. I had arranged for transportation to and from the rink through Sofia and some other skating friends, but my aunt understandably liked to know where I was all the time. One day our ice time got canceled at one rink so Sofia took me to another rink, which meant my drop-off changed a little. My aunt hated things like that, and I think they all added up after a while.

My mom knew this situation would come to an end soon and started mentioning it to some of the other parents around the rink. I was really lucky because when I needed a new place to stay, there was a family who offered their help right away. My mom and I became really close with the Collins family, who welcomed me with open arms. They lived in Bethlehem, Pennsylvania, and their daughter Michelle was a competitive skater like I was, so they totally understood the drill.

I had become a part of their family so much so that after about a year of staying with them, they had their basement redone and basically built a guest room for me. It had a bed, a dresser, and a desktop computer. That's where I lived. It didn't have any windows, but I didn't need them. I had a desktop where I was able to play *The Sims*, and they had every expansion pack. Who needed windows when you could just sit in your room and try to get your Sim to make whoopee with all the other Sims in the neighborhood? My mom told Debbie Collins, "Oh, this is way too much for him. This is above and beyond."

"Well, we just love Adam and we were going to do it anyway," she said.

If they didn't love me before I moved in with them, I did everything to prove my worth once I got there. Before I went to stay there, my mom said, "You need to help out with everything. You need to say, 'Thank you,' all the time. You need to offer to get everything. You need to offer to put things away. When no one's in the kitchen, you need to go and clean it. You need to know where the vacuum is. You need to know where the mop is. You need to know where all the cleaning supplies are, because that's your job. If you're staying in someone else's house, you need to be respectful and know how to do everything."

Luckily for both my mom and Mrs. Collins, I already loved to clean. Both of the Collins kids went to regular school, so I would sleep in a little bit and when I got up from my basement lair, Mrs. Collins would be out driving them to school. She would come home and there'd be no dishes anywhere, the counter would be wiped off, and the living room would be vacuumed. I did that every day because it is what my mother told me to do. Well, that and I love vacuuming, a guilty pleasure of mine still to this day. If you don't know the joy of leaving perfect tracings on the carpet from a vacuum, you are a monster and I pity you.

Then, Debbie would come home and I would sit with her and pretend to do homework, but I would just have my science book open to the same page and I'd chat with Debbie. At first my mother was paying the Collins family some rent each week for me to stay there, but after a bit they told my mom not to worry about paying. I was already paying them in free cleaning services and plenty of entertainment.

Though living with the Collins family was great, after a while I stopped skating at the rink that was closest to their house. It was kind of Sofia's fault. OK, fine. It was totally Sofia's fault. She didn't always get along with the other coaches and skaters at the various rinks we skated at. Sometimes everything would seem fine and then I would turn my back for just a second and she'd be yelling at a coach for some reason or another. When she did that, I felt the same sensation I felt when I shit myself in my mom's car: panic, embarrassment, and fear of the unknown. Now it's one of her traits that I love the most (seriously, she needed her own reality show), but back then it sometimes got her into trouble.

There was this girl at the rink near the Collinses' house who wasn't the greatest, and she would always blare her music so loud that no one else in the rink could think straight. Seriously, it was like she was pregaming before a night out in Vegas. After months of this, one day once her program ended Sofia walked up to her and her coach and said, "If you turn the music up really loud, it doesn't make you skate any better." Then she just walked away. That was all it took and that was the end of that rink.

Being coached by Sofia is kind of like being coached by Brandi Glanville from *The Real Housewives of Beverly Hills*. You like her, but at any moment she can throw her wine in Eileen Davidson's face, and in those situations I was Lisa Rinna and couldn't believe what I had signed up for.

After that I moved out of the Collinses' house and moved in with Sofia and her husband, Carl. She didn't tell Carl that I was moving into their house. I just showed up one day and started living in the room upstairs that they used for storage.

At first Sofia would just put a fitted sheet on the sofa and I would sleep on that, but eventually she decided to redo the room, move out the clutter, and replace the sofa with a pullout couch. Just like at the Collinses', I had a little home away from home.

Carl met Sofia because he was her English teacher when she first moved to the US, and he was still a professor at a local university. He was sort of a weird guy. He was really quiet and super nerdy. One time after I first moved in, I was sitting in the living room and Carl yelled for me from upstairs. At first I thought it was a mistake and I was hearing things, but no—he was really yelling for me. I started walking up the stairs but not before Sofia came barreling past me holding toilet paper. As I slowly put two and two together, I realized Sofia had saved me from seeing a sixty-year-old man sitting on the toilet with his pants around his ankles, asking for toilet paper. I'm still very grateful. Carl was actually a really nice guy—he was just a stereotypical nerd with huge glasses and pants that were too short and hiked up too high. I can't be more thankful that he just let one of his wife's random students live in his house for about three years.

Sofia didn't just not tell Carl about my moving into the guest room; she didn't tell him about anything. She kept a lot of secrets to herself. She told me crazy things from her past she didn't tell anyone else, like how she had defected from the Soviet Union. I still think about the insane things she would share with me. She had a ton of spice to her, and I always had a front-row seat to her shenanigans.

There was one time that Carl went away for a trip and Sofia decided to have all the windows in their house replaced. Not only that, she added a front room onto the house, sort of like a little entryway where the front door used to be. Carl came back from his trip while the contractors were still there, and he was furious. I remember Carl looking at me and asking me what was going on, and I decided that it would be best if I just acted like Helen Keller and pretended I couldn't understand him. They had a huge fight but then Sofia told me, "Oh, don't worry about him; he'll get over it."

And she was right. A few months later, Carl told her, "You were right about the windows and the new room. I love it now."

I grew to fit into Sofia's family pretty well. We would practice in the morning and then go to this one farmer's market and get vegetables and things and bring them back to the house so that Sofia's mother, Svetlana, who was exactly 194 years old, could make us the most delicious soups and Russian meals. Like at the Collinses' house, I helped clean up and I gave everyone their tray of vitamins every morning. I felt like I was at home.

Once, when I was about fifteen, Sofia decided that I should know how to drive. "If you lived in Russia, you would already have a license," she told me. According to all the stories she told me about her past, if I lived in Russia, I wouldn't already just have a license; I would have a mortgage and child-support payments by now too. She took me to the parking lot of a closed-down Aldi supermarket in her teal Nissan Altima and put me behind the wheel. The car was facing one of those little strips of grass and trees that are used as decorative dividers in a parking lot.

I had never driven before, and being the conscientious rule follower that I have always been, I was worried about breaking the law. I was waiting for some undercover cop to come rushing over and arrest us both. So when I stepped on the gas, I stepped on it kind of hard and went right into this little green patch and ran over this thin, dead tree that was still standing there long after the supermarket had closed. Let me say that one more time. The first time I drove a car, I ran over a tree. The car was fine, but I was shaken, as anyone who had just driven over a tree would have been. "It's fine," Sofia said. "It's no problem."

"Sofia," I yelled at her. "I *ran over* a *tree*." In my mind I was thinking, "The police are going to come to this parking lot and lock both of us up for even trying this, and they're going to take away Sofia's teal Nissan Altima and then we'll have to ask Carl to drive us to the rink every day." I didn't even try to get my license until I was twenty-two, but I'll get to that later.

Another time we were in that teal Altima we were driving down to the University of Delaware. They have always had an excellent figure skating program, and Sofia had worked there when she first moved to the US. We would go down periodically so I could skate with really good skaters.

On the way, we stopped at a convenience store and Sofia came back to the car with a six-pack of beer. I thought she was just going to have it later, but she opened one and put it in the car's cup holder. I remember being stuck in traffic and Sofia was just drinking a bottle of beer right there in the open. A guy in a truck next to us saw her, and he was shaking his finger at her like, "Lady, you can't be doing that!" I was terrified. I'd never had anything to drink in my life so I had no idea what it was doing to her. All I knew was all the "Don't drink and drive" commercials I had seen on TV. I didn't want to know what my brain looked like on drugs, and I didn't want to know what Sofia's looked like either.

Afterward I told my mother about the incident and she asked Sofia about it. "It was very hot out and I was thirsty," she said to my mom very reasonably, as if my mom were asking something outlandish.

"But it's beer!" my mother told her. "You can't drink beer while you drive."

"Oh, it's not bad," Sofia told her. "I'm Russian. We don't get drunk on beer. It's fine."

Sofia also loved to play fast and loose with US Figure Skating. When you get assigned to international competitions, USFS pays for your travel, and they used to give us the freedom to book our own tickets and then reimburse us. USFS would give us a limit for what my coach and I could spend on travel. Sofia would get the full amount from USFS and then go to a Russian travel agent friend of hers and get cheap plane tickets for both of us and then pocket the difference. It wasn't against the rules, just a loophole. Soon after we started traveling, USFS changed the way that they dole out money for travel not just for us, but for everyone. While I realize others may have been taking advantage as well, I was convinced Sofia was such an operator they had to change the rules. I feel like some of Sofia's wheeling and dealing has since rubbed off on me. For better and for worse.

For instance, when I was in my twenties, I bought a black Canada Goose winter jacket. It was the most expensive thing I ever bought for myself. It was so expensive I rarely wore it all winter. The next winter I decided I wanted the same jacket in red, so I used an old trick Sofia told me about. I bought the red jacket online and when it arrived in the mail, I returned the black jacket (which was still in mint condition) and told them they sent me the wrong color. Then I just kept the red one. Yes, I know it's wrong and I would never do it now, but Sofia coached me well in all sorts of matters.

When I was with Sofia, I first qualified for the national championships. I was fifteen, and because it was my first year, I was in the novice category. I came in second, which was great. The next year I was in the junior category, and I placed eleventh, which wasn't amazing. The following year, at seventeen, I placed sixth, so I wasn't really improving that much.

Even though Sofia was my favorite person in the world, and a bit of a mother figure to me, things could be contentious between us. The year I placed sixth at nationals, we were in the arena and they were playing a montage of one of my favorite skaters, Shizuka Arakawa, the Olympic champion from Japan, on the Jumbotron.

Sofia pointed up to the screen and said, "You skate just like her."

"Really?" I asked her, totally flattered by the comparison.

"Yes. Like a girl," she said and then walked away from me.

We would also get into screaming matches during practice. She would ask me why I was doing something and I would talk back to her. She would get me so mad that sometimes I would skate away with my gloved hand over my face, saying every cuss word I could think of under my breath. Oh, if those gloves could talk. I would never talk to any of my coaches like that in the future, and if a student of mine ever talked to me like that, they'd get an eye stinkier than the pair of shit-stained fleece pants I abandoned in a gas station bathroom.

It was like we were friends rather than coach and skater at this point. I also think she kind of knew that she couldn't help me advance as a skater much more. When I wouldn't place well at a competition, she would say, "See? You need to go someplace else."

But at the same time, she once charged me for "shame." When I placed poorly at that last national championship we went to together, she charged my mom an extra $500 for her time there because of the shame of being associated with me as a skater. It was a real diva move. Before there was a Barbra, Mariah, Celine, or a Whitney, there was a Sofia. My mom said that was the final straw in our relationship. She paid the shame surcharge but wasn't going to pay Sofia ever again.

When my mom broke the news to Sofia, she said, "I don't think that's Adam's choice; I think that's your choice."

Then my mom made me tell Sofia myself that we weren't going to be working together anymore. I was seventeen and this was a person who I had known for six years and had been living with for three, a woman who almost killed me in a teal Nissan Altima more than once. It was one of the hardest things I had to do. We both cried because we knew it was going to be the last we'd see of each other for a while and that things would never go back to how they were. We hugged and she gave me a duffel bag filled with all the little random things I had left at her house. I cried the entire way home, but I knew I was doing the right thing.

When I think of Sofia now, I think of someone who was my best friend but also a huge bitch. I mean that as a compliment. I think of someone who was super creative and somebody who would say things just to get her way. As an aspiring diva, I am a huge fan, except when she was saying things to *me* in order to get her way.

There is something about having a Russian coach, and I've had a few. They're so hard to get along with, they yell at you all the time, and they are crazy, but there's this overwhelming feeling that they'll protect you and not let anyone else mess around with you. I still feel that way about Sofia. She was like a momma bird who took me under her wing and protected me. Granted she would boot me out of the nest so I could learn how to fly, but she was a momma bird nonetheless.

Sofia taught me a lot of technique, but I don't think she knew how to train an elite athlete. She worked me hard, but I would train a thousand times harder later in my career. When I was older and training for a competition, I would go through my program four thousand times in a row to make sure I got it perfect. With Sofia, I might go over it once and not even all the way through. She focused on the details of helping me become a good skater, but I wasn't yet training like a good competitor. I would learn that in very short order, thanks to another crazy Russian.

Showdown at the Salad Bar

When I was fifteen and living with Sofia, I was finally making some friends. I had friends here and there before, but up until that point, I trained alone, I competed alone, and the person I spent the most time with was a sixty-year-old Russian woman who could also make me cry with the snap of her fingers.

That all changed when I went to a high-performance camp in 2005. Because I medaled at the 2005 national championships in the novice category, US Figure Skating invited me to a week-long training camp at the Olympic Training Center in Colorado Springs. I had already met most of the other kids at the camp during the national championships earlier that year. The national championships take place over a week, and the novices always compete first. We all hung around for the rest of the week because you want to see what the older skaters are doing and who is going to be your competition for the next year. During that week, of course, the kids congregated together, and it was the first time in my life that I realized I could make other people laugh (besides myself).

I was always shy when I was younger, but when I got to HP camp (as we called it), it was like someone flipped a switch and suddenly I was Dick Van Dyke. I was the center of attention, a total charmer, an entertainer who was funny but also a little bit (OK, mostly) obnoxious.

While we were at HP camp, there were plenty of other Olympic teams also using the training facility. One day, in the cafeteria, one of my teammates dared me to go over and sing for a table full of volleyball players, who were all about five years older than us.

I didn't hesitate for one second about whether or not I should take this dare. I saw it as an opportunity. I walked over, stood in the middle of the cafeteria, and started singing Alanis Morissette's "Ironic" to the amusement and confusion of the entire cafeteria. Why? Why not! "Ironic" was the only song I knew all the words to, and if I was going to look like a fool, I was at least going to know the lyrics.

During our week at camp, we also took a group trip to see the Colorado Springs Sky Sox, the minor league baseball team. At the field there was a "talent scout" who set up a booth where you could go and record a video to see if you had any talent. I'm not sure exactly who this person was scouting talent for, but I knew for certain I had talent to spare. All of my friends and teammates egged me on to go and record a video. I sang "Ironic" again, this time with interpretive dance, because the first time I did it in the cafeteria it killed. Even though we were in Colorado Springs, I was going to treat this like I was auditioning for the cast of *Saturday Night Live*. I got into the booth and recorded a video that looked like it was shot in a basement, but I felt like Judy Garland screen-testing for *The Wizard of Oz*.

After the video, our team captain, Ryan Bradley, said, "Hey, Adam. Go see if you can throw the first pitch."

I had no idea how I was going to do it, but I told him that I would figure it out. I left our seats and went down closer to the field to see if I could scope out what was going on. Turns out the same person who was in charge of the first-pitch talent was the lady from the talent-scouting booth earlier. Maybe this is what she was scouting for?

I asked her if I could throw the first pitch, and she told me that I was in luck—the girl who was supposed to do it (some local beauty queen or something) hadn't shown up and if I wanted to do it, the job was all mine. The stars had aligned in my favor.

The announcer gets on the microphone and says, "Welcome to the mound [the name of the girl who was really supposed to be doing this] to throw the first pitch." I walked out, wearing two polo shirts with both collars popped, to a smattering of applause and the utter amazement of my team who couldn't believe I finagled my way out there. I threw the first pitch and it was just as bad as when I was pretending to faint to get out of baseball games when I was a kid and the ball dribbled toward home plate. That didn't stop me from waving triumphantly like that local beauty queen who didn't show up and taking a bow before leaving the field.

The point was I had friends. Now when I went to competitions, I wasn't just concerned with how well I was going to do on the ice but where Juliana was and what she was doing. Juliana was this girl I had a crush on, and I just wanted to be around her and her whole friend group. I wanted to go out to dinner and catch up. It's not like we were partying and smoking cigarettes behind the arena, but it still affected my performance, and that is part of the reason I didn't do so well at my second and third national performances. I skated badly because I wasn't focused. Skating wasn't my focus because I was finally popular.

After one of those low-ranking times, Sofia said to me, "You like having friends, don't you?"

"Yeah, of course," I told her.

"Well, they're not going to be your friends if you don't skate well," she said.

She wasn't trying to be mean. (Trust me—when she was trying, it came out a lot worse than that.) But she was right. If I stopped qualifying for competitions, I would never see them because the group of us lived all over the country and only came together for skating events.

This was a small but contributing factor to my decision to

leave Sofia and get another coach. I was doing well with Sofia and glad to have friends, but I knew if I wanted to be in the Olympics, be the best in the world, and keep my new posse, then I needed to focus and work even harder.

In my last year with Sofia, I dedicated myself to my training. I bought a binder at CVS where I wrote down my goals for every day and how every practice went. I stole my mom's five-pound weights from home to work out every day. I did everything I could so I could be my best on the ice, but at the end of that season, I knew I still needed to do more.

After going two hours south to Philadelphia, my mom and I thought about going two hours north to New Jersey. There's a decent-size community of competitive figure skaters there, just outside New York City. Living in Hackensack, New Jersey, isn't as glam as living in Manhattan, but being a small-town boy from Scranton, it felt like I was truly living in the big city.

I went to skate a session at a rink that a lot of the major skaters at the time were using. I wasn't trying to attract a coach or anything; I was just trying to get a feel for the rink. One of the older coaches there, who I knew from competitions, saw me skating alone and came over to ask where my coach was. "Oh, I'm not working with her anymore," I said.

A little bit later, he came over again and told me that another coach at the rink, one who had two world champions on his roster and who had just coached someone to Olympic gold in 2006, wanted me to come over onto the ice where his skaters trained and skate for him. I did and it was a little bit of a tryout and a little bit of recruitment. His name was Nikolai and we agreed to begin working together. If this really famous coach was even just slightly interested, I needed to take this opportunity. Within two months I packed up my things and moved, full-time, to Hackensack (another town with a sad Billy Joel namecheck).

Shortly after I started working with Nikolai, I improved dramatically. He was a totally different coach than Sofia and I was working like a dog. Before, I would skate for a few hours in the morning and a few hours in the afternoon. Now I was skating from, like, eight in the morning straight through until six in the evening like it was my job. It *was* my job.

I elevated my game so drastically so quickly, and it was one of the most exciting times of my entire life. I went to bed every night and couldn't wait to get to the rink in the morning. I remember being like, "This is wild—like, I can't wait for tomorrow. I'm living my dream." I got so much better that I started to think that I could actually achieve something great with my skating. I, little Adam Rippon from the Ice Box in Pittston, Pennsylvania, was on the ice every day training with champions. It was the first time in my career that every time I got on the ice I was the worst—and by a lot. Even that motivated me and made me eager to improve.

The first few months with Nikolai were insane because I was still living at home with my mom. I would get up early every day, make all of my siblings' lunches, help my mom get them to school, and then we would drive up to the rink. She would make calls for work from the rink all day, and when I was finished, we'd drive all the way back home. I don't know how she did it every day, but she did. Her goal was to have dinner as a family every night, and for those first few months of going back and forth to New Jersey, we did.

Eventually Nikolai let me move into an extra apartment he kept for his out-of-town students to crash in, which meant my mom didn't have to drive me down every day. The apartment was in a complex not far from the rink. At the time, Nikolai was also coaching the world silver medalist, a Japanese skater named Daisuke Takahashi, so he was staying in the apartment too. He didn't speak much English, but we would sit around and watch anime in Japanese and I would just sit there and stare at the cartoons, having no idea what was going on. I would think, "Yeah, I'm just watching anime with my *roommate*, Daisuke Takahashi. No big deal." There were moments like that where

I felt like I needed to pinch myself. He even let me borrow his bike when he would go out of town, which I crashed into a bush once and needed to explain to him why his bike had a million scratches on it. I also needed to wear long sleeves for a few weeks because it looked like I had been mauled by a bear.

When the people in the apartment complex got to know me, they'd sometimes ask, "When is Nikolai coming back?" I would tell them I had no idea. They would claim he was behind on the rent.

Regardless of whether he was paying his bills or not, he was doing his job for me. My competition placement was just beyond. I went from being sixth at nationals the year before to winning almost every competition I entered the next year. I won the Junior Grand Prix Final, which is one of the biggest trophies in skating at the junior level. I won junior nationals. I won junior worlds and I hadn't even been on the junior worlds team the year before—not even close to it.

At the time, I was just skating differently than anyone else on the junior circuit; I was skating like an adult. I was doing the same jumps as the other juniors, so the technical aspect wasn't extraordinary, but the interpretation was. The skating quality was there. That whole season, I made only one tiny mistake. I easily beat people who were trying things that were harder than what I was doing because everything I did was just that much better at that time. (Thank God I'm not a junior now. Their programs are harder than what I did at the Olympics!)

This was the first time I realistically thought I would go to the Olympics. When I won the Junior Grand Prix, I thought to myself, "I actually could do this. This is what other people have done. These are the steps they have taken so they could go to the Olympics." The goal started to become even more tangible.

For something that once felt like *Mission: Impossible*, I was now doing *Mission: Possible*. I was the Tom Cruise of junior figure skating. I didn't need to spend as much time with Nikolai on the ice once we had been working for a few months, because I was doing everything I needed to do on my own. It was good that I was self-sufficient because Nikolai started spending more and more time in Japan with his other students and not as much time at the rink in New Jersey with me.

Though I was working hard, I had found a good balance between training and spending some time with friends. I was also living away from home on my own for the first time. Well, at least I was during the week. But that didn't mean my mom was taking a back seat to all the fun.

Every day my friends and I would go to a coffee shop near the rink for lunch, and I would get a drink and a salad. It cost about seven dollars. My mother got my credit card statement and she saw that I was spending the same amount in the same place at the same time every day. She told me that I should stop getting my salad and I should pack my lunch and take it to the rink to save money. Yeah, because that is what all the cool kids do—sit with their PB&J and Capri Sun in a brown paper bag at the picnic tables at the rink.

I kept going to the coffee shop every day. One day, I show up with my friends, and my mother is sitting there in the coffee shop waiting for me. My jaw dropped, and for once, I couldn't think of anything to say.

"Hi, Mom! What are you doing here?" I asked, knowing I was getting caught red-handed.

"You're not supposed to be eating here every day," she said, staring at me like she was either going to turn me into stone or transform me into seven dollars so she could eat a salad on the two-hour drive back to her house. Thinking about it now, I realize how much it must have meant to her that she spent forty dollars in gas and four hours of her life to keep me from spending that seven dollars every day—money must have been tight.

This wasn't just a little crazy—it was absolutely nuts. My mom drove all the way out to New Jersey to teach me a lesson. Even if, at the time, I would have rather recrashed into a bush while riding Daisuke's bike, I'm grateful my mom was tough on me. It reminded me to stay focused and to remember all the sacrifices everyone was making for me at home. Skating can be fucking expensive.

My mom will spend any amount of time to make a point though—a quality that as an adult I admire, but as a child I loathed. Once, she thought that my group of friends was too gossipy. I'm not much of a gossip, because as a good Catholic schoolgirl I feel guilty talking about other people. Also, I got made fun of so much as a kid that I'm pretty sensitive to it. Whenever the talk turns to gossip, I tend to deflect it by just talking shit about myself, which comes very naturally to me.

Anyway, these girls were a little bit gossipy and my mom didn't like that. I was at home one weekend and my mom says, "There's something I watched that I wanted you to see."

She puts on a four-hour PBS documentary about the Salem witch trials. When it was over, I said, "That was great, but why did we have to watch that?"

"I just wanted to teach you the power of a lie. I wanted you to know what gossip can do to people," she said. OK, Mom. Got it.

I felt it was a little extreme to think that some rink gossip would lead to someone being called a witch and getting thrown over the bridge on Midtown Bridge Approach outside the rink, but in both instances, I got the message loud and clear. To paraphrase something my brother once said, it's not that I was afraid of my mother—I just knew that she didn't care if we liked her or not. She didn't want to be our friend; she wanted to make sure that we learned the right lessons in life, even if that meant a financial ambush at a coffee shop.

While my mom was trying to make sure I was staying focused, Nikolai wasn't an escape from any sort of craziness. There is a fine line between being motivational and manipulative, and I felt

Nikolai crossed it. For instance, he had one skater who was about twenty, and she was really inconsistent. He started dating her. It seemed to me that when she wasn't skating well, he would break up with her so that she would get this "I'll show him" mentality and start skating well again. Then he'd get back together. But this woman was doing really well, so obviously, whatever he was doing, it was working.

He never did anything as outrageous with me, and there was a more uplifting side to him. Sometimes he would say the perfect thing where he lifts you up so you feel like you can do anything, and you go out there and you're perfect. And he's like, "I knew you would be." That made it all worth it. He had so much power that if I just looked into his crystal ball, I would believe anything he said.

There were plenty of other messy parts to Nikolai as well. The first time we went to an international competition together, he showed up with his hair slicked back, looking like James Bond in a designer suit. My mom told me later that she saw him the night before totally drunk, pissing on the hotel wall. I don't know how he pulled it together, but he always did.

One time Nikolai insisted that we all skate on a Sunday afternoon, which was kind of weird. Usually my mom would drop me off Sunday evening for my week of skating, but since we had this "important" session, she drove me down early and decided to stay to watch me practice, the first time she got to watch since she was driving me to the rink every day.

Nikolai didn't show up to the rink for at least an hour after he was supposed to. We're all there for him to work with us, and we're skating around just waiting for the coach to make his appearance. Finally, he came into the rink wearing dress clothes, which is a little weird to start with. We were all able to figure out what he had been up to when we saw he had dried barf all over his shirt.

He'd been drinking all day! He went to brunch and had at

least two bottles of champagne, kept drinking, threw up, came in still drunk with dried puke on his shirt, and started coaching us like nothing happened. Then he took his life into his own hands (literally) when he grabbed my mom's boob. Well, I don't know if he actually tried to grab her boob or if he just went to grab her arm and missed and ended up on her boob, but either way, there was hand-to-boob contact. My mom never let any of Nikolai's antics bother her, but when we left the rink that day, my mom was really upset. She wouldn't tell me why, but I pressed her about it and she finally told me what had happened.

The whole next week I gave him the cold shoulder at practice. He finally asked, "What is wrong with you?"

I told him about what had happened with my mom, which he didn't remember at all. I said, "You can be nasty to me and call me a piece of shit, but you cannot ever touch my mom or say anything bad about her." He felt awful and called my mom and apologized. Not that it made it any better. I think he was forgiven for his bad behavior so often because he was this genius coach. But if he was going to grab my mom's boob, I was going to make him feel awful.

I remember once he took the whole team out to dinner at a Japanese restaurant and was pounding shots of sake all night long. When we were done, he said, "I'm going to drive all the skaters home." He couldn't have even stood up to use the urinal in the bathroom much less get us all home in one piece.

Luckily one of us had her agent there and he said, "Actually, I'll take them home. You guys meet us there."

Nikolai and his friend, who was equally trashed, got in their own car and left after we did. When they finally got home, they were even more wasted. Nikolai said they got pulled over by the cops and talked their way out of it. I don't know if that's true or not, but I know for sure this whole thing was the biggest scandal I had witnessed in my young life. No wonder my mom would do crazy things—she knew I was dealing with (and in the care of) a crazy person.

There were a ton of completely nuts times, but there were also a lot of stupid-teenager fun times too. Once, we all went to Connecticut for Fourth of July weekend because the rink we work at was closed for the holiday, but the rink in Connecticut was open because apparently they have no patriotism up there or something. There was one Russian skater there for a brief stay who was twenty-two, so we convinced him to go buy three cases of Smirnoff Ice. It was just as easy to convince a twenty-two-year-old Russian boy to buy alcohol for underage kids as you would think. He came back not only with the booze but also with some fireworks.

About seven of us sat in the parking lot of the rink playing with fireworks and drinking Smirnoff Ice. I don't think my heart had ever beaten faster, and I don't think it was from the Smirnoff Ice. I'm such a paranoid person that the whole time I thought either we were going to get caught or I was destroying my body or both. Still, that is one of my favorite memories.

At the time, I thought, "I'm growing up. This is what being an adult is like." When I was in Hackensack, it was also the first time I skated with a group where I was the only white Irish Catholic person, because I was the only person Nikolai trained that competed for the United States. Everyone else skated for other countries, and they traveled all the time. Being in that environment, I was introduced to the larger world in so many ways, and I'm still grateful for it. This is when I went from being a small-town kid to a real-world person.

Not everyone at US Figure Skating saw it that way. Some of them felt his behavior was just too controversial. Someone from USFS told me at one competition, "I'm glad it's working out for you, but keep your distance."

What was I going to do? Go to someone else and end up being a worse skater? I was doing better than I ever had in my career, and I felt like I couldn't take that risk. Whenever a student would leave Nikolai, he would talk about how they were stupid and didn't know what they were doing. When I talked to the other skaters about leaving, some of us were afraid that Nikolai, who was well regarded and well connected within the skating world, would tell the judges we were shitty and our marks would suffer. No one had ever seen him do something like that, but it was a fear some of us had.

I just really wanted to impress Nikolai so much because, no matter how well I was doing, I always felt like I was his worst figure skating student. He mostly trained ice dancing couples, and his only other two students were Daisuke and Miki Ando, who was the female world champion. I felt like he didn't need to take me on, so I was really doing everything I could just to prove that I was worth the time.

My attitude changed one day at practice when Nikolai told me that he was bored of working with Daisuke and was going to work with another Japanese skater.

"You're gonna just replace him?" I asked Nikolai, skeptical that he would get rid of the reigning world medalist.

"Yeah. I'm bored," he said. "He wants to do his own thing. Whatever. Let him do his own thing. I'm just going to work with somebody else."

I thought to myself, "If he does that to Daisuke, then I could be next. He could turn on me at any moment."

Now, I realize that coaches need to keep their roster packed with the best possible students not only for themselves, but also for the athletes. It's letting the athletes know they can't get too comfortable and that they need to be working all the time. Is someone really going to be that good if she isn't literally training to win a competition every day? Some people can't handle that pressure, but a good competitor can.

My problem wasn't that I didn't want to work hard enough; it was that I wanted to work too hard. Nikolai was in Japan more often so he wasn't training with me as much. Because of his comments about Daisuke, I thought I wasn't getting any attention and I was on my way out the door. Yes, it's as ironic as my performance of Alanis Morissette at HP camp.

I said to Nikolai, "You're not helping me, and I need help this year if I want to go to the Olympics," which were a year away.

"It doesn't matter. You have time," he said. But it didn't seem like I had time, and those comments made me feel so unimportant. I was putting pressure on myself to go to the Olympics right away. (Little did I know that I would eventually get there—it would just take ten more years.)

Finally, I knew I needed to leave. Nikolai would never do my choreography. He told me he thought I was good enough and that I could just figure it out on my own. But I was nineteen; I didn't feel like I was qualified.

I remember I called Nikolai when he was in Japan and told him that I didn't feel like he had enough time for me and that I was going to start working with another coach. What he said I'll never forget: "You have no idea what you're doing. You're going to regret this phone call." And hung up.

I felt like I was doing the right thing, but I also felt like maybe I had just fucked myself. Was he going to tell the judges to give me bad scores? Was he going to tell other coaches that they shouldn't work with me? It didn't matter at that point. While I knew he probably wouldn't do that, I had other reasons for feeling that I shouldn't trust him with my career.

It was time to move forward and focus on the next event.

I told my mom I thought I needed a choreographer to smooth things out, and she got in touch with David Wilson, a choreographer in Toronto. I went up there to work with him and just fell in love with the rink, the people who were working there—everything.

It was important to me to train with the very best again because it pushed me that much harder. I ended up working with two-time Olympic silver medalist Brian Orser. At the time he was also training Yuna Kim, who would become a world champion the next year.

I moved up there in December 2008, about a month before national championships. Because of all the drama of getting ready and relocating, I didn't skate that well at nationals and placed seventh. It was my first year at the senior level, so seventh wasn't bad but definitely not good enough to make the world team, which was my goal. I do love drama, but not when it messes with me getting my crown.

Instead of going to the world championships, I went to the junior world championships again, since this was my last year of eligibility. Usually when a skater wins junior worlds, they become more successful and go to senior worlds, but when you're from a big country like the United States, that doesn't always happen. But a lot of times junior world champions won't do that 'cause they don't want to lose their title.

I didn't have to worry about that, because I went to junior worlds and I won again, still the only person to win back-to-back world championships. It was the perfect way to end a crazy season of moving and changing coaches, especially with the 2010 Olympics one year away. The next season, which would determine if I went to the Olympics, I got off to a great start and medaled at one of the Grand Prix events. The ISU Grand Prix of Figure Skating consists of six invitational events: Skate America, Skate Canada International, Cup of China, Internationaux de France, Rostelecom Cup in Russia, and NHK Trophy in Japan. These events are among the most prestigious in the sport. Skaters are invited to compete in only two of the six events, and the six skaters with the top combined scores from their two Grand Prix events are invited to the Grand Prix final.

Because I medaled in one of my Grand Prix invitationals that year, I thought I had a small chance at making the Olympics if one of the skaters above me had an off event. Sadly that didn't happen, but I did end up an alternate on the team.

Not going to the Olympics in 2010 was a blessing in disguise, though, because instead, I went to the Four Continents Figure Skating Championships, which is one of the major international skating competitions, and I won. Also, during Olympic years, the world championships are held shortly after the Olympics, so a lot of the top skaters will skip that year because they're still recovering from the Olympic Games. A few male skaters dropped out, so I went to the world championships and placed sixth, which was unreal. I had just placed fifth in America, but now I'm sixth in the whole world.

I don't want this to sound like the Adam Rippon Wikipedia page, which, honestly, is really worth a read. (I've spent a few hours there myself.) The point is that whatever was happening in Toronto was working. A large part of that was because of Yuna Kim herself.

Shortly after I arrived, I started to have a huge crush on Yuna. We were perfect for each other. She is this shy, beautiful, timid Asian girl, and I, too, am a shy, beautiful, timid Asian girl. Well, at least that's how I saw myself.

We became boyfriend and girlfriend, and kidding aside, it was the perfect relationship for both of us at the time. I was harmless to her skating career because I would want nothing to harm her, and I wasn't going to make any demands on her time and attention that a boyfriend who was outside of the sport and didn't understand the schedule might. I was not a distraction at all.

Even though we saw each other at the rink every day, we were still texting all the time and making mix CDs for each other—all the silly things that teens "in love" do. We went out on dates every weekend, but it was, like, dinner and a movie and home by 9 p.m. because we were training the next day. Our favorite place to go together was the riverfront in downtown Toronto. I know you're wondering (you perv), but physically things didn't really escalate beyond making out. It was all very chaste and sweet and supportive.

Yuna ended up winning the 2010 Winter Olympics. Still to this day, watching her win gold from my apartment in Toronto was one of the coolest things I've ever experienced. This was the first person I was very close to that I was watching achieve her dream. Everything was perfect. It was amazing.

I sent a text from my BlackBerry, saying, I love you and I'm so proud. That night I got one text back from her, and it was a smiley face emoji with one tear. That was the language we had with each other: emojis. We knew how we felt toward each other more than we used words to express how we felt. We didn't really use our bodies to express how we felt either. All we had were emojis, and for a twenty-year-old boy still in the closet, it was perfect.

After the Olympics were over and I was having my great season, there was some strain in the relationship and we started to fight a bit. Yuna went home to Korea. I emailed her all the time and I didn't hear from her for weeks. Finally I got a long email back and I could tell that we weren't on the same page.

Her excuse for breaking up was that she didn't really want to speak English anymore because it made her too tired. It was the international equivalent of staying in to wash her hair.

The breakup was for the best and we have no hard feelings for each other, but at the time I was devastated. "What does she mean she doesn't want to speak English anymore?" I thought. "She's going to have to speak English in her *life*." But no, she didn't. She could stay in Korea and never have to say, "Hi. How are you?" again if she didn't want to. (I've run into her a few times since this all went down and we're on good terms, but we've never talked about our relationship.)

She came back to Toronto later that summer to train, and I pretended like she didn't exist. Just as the relationship fizzled, so did my skating. At first I was killing this new season. I beat two of the medalists from the 2010 Olympic Games in my first event of the season. With that came new pressure that I wasn't used to or ready to deal with. I was expected to do well; I wasn't an underdog anymore. Everything hit me all at once. I was coming to terms with not making the Olympics, and though I had started the season strong, I ended so weakly. I was so in my head. I just needed a new perspective and I thought the best way was to leave Toronto behind.

There was a coach in California at the time named Frank Carroll who I really wanted to work with and who was highly recommended to me. I went there for two weeks, but he was still contracted with Evan Lysacek, the reigning Olympic champion, who hadn't decided if he was going to keep skating or not. Frank recommended I work with a coach named Rafael Arutyunyan who was also in California. However, he was in Georgia (the country, not the state) visiting his family for the next three weeks. During these years, I felt like everything needed to happen *now* or it wasn't going to happen at all. The trip did not go as planned. According to my timetable, I'd be moving to California to work with Frank, or at least with Rafael, his recommended replacement. But I needed to get going with training for the year so neither of them was really an option.

I had already booked a trip to Detroit right after I worked with Frank so the choreographer Pasquale Camerlengo could give me two routines for the next season. In an ideal world I would be leaving there and going back to California, but, sadly, this is not always an ideal world. When I got to Detroit, it was the same story as in Toronto: I just fell in love with the rink, the skaters there—everything. It felt like the perfect place if I couldn't yet work with Frank or Rafael. I started working with husband-and-wife team Jason Dungjen and Yuka Sato, who also coached the current national men's champion, Jeremy Abbott. Yuka and Jason had to talk with Jeremy to see if he was OK with one of his competitors training with him, but he graciously thought it would be good for both of us.

The important part about Detroit was it was the first time I was among a whole group of elite skaters. It wasn't just Yuna and me, or one or two others.

It was the first time I got a really solid group of friends who were all around my age or older, people who knew exactly what I was going through and that I wouldn't go out late and go to parties—something I never enjoyed doing. If we hung out, it was going to watch a movie and getting home by 9 p.m. because we all had to train first thing in the morning. It wasn't like I was disappointing people by always turning down invitations. Still, it was like being at summer camp with thirty people who all wanted to be Olympians. These guys just knew. It was this group of friends that would change my life forever.

The Intimate History of a Three-Day Boyfriend

My first crush on a boy was on Brad in the fifth grade, though I certainly didn't know it was a crush at the time. It was the early days of the internet and he would print out porn pictures from his dial-up connection and bring them into school in a Lisa Frank folder. It was mostly just titties and stuff, but a few of the boys in class, Brad, and I would go to a quiet part of the playground, open up the folder, and look at these pages of porn. Hell, if you told me now, as an openly gay adult, that you had a Lisa Frank folder full of boob photos, I'd probably be just as excited about it now as I was then.

There was one picture in particular of a girl sitting on top of a guy, but his whole body was obscured. The only thing you could see was his dick. I thought it was so big—considering the only thing I had to compare it to was my fifth-grade-size dick—that there was no way this could be a human penis. The woman in the photo was holding it with two hands, and I remember I said to Brad, "What's that?" convinced it was a pole she was holding to help stabilize herself from falling over due to the weight of her extreme breasts.

"That's a dick," he said.

"Oh," I answered, a little confused.

"Is that the part you like the most?" he asked.

"No," I said, almost reflexively.

He didn't say anything for a moment, and then he said, "OK."

But in my mind, I knew what my real answer was.

Every day I would go to school and there was one thing I wanted to do and that was look at porn with Brad. Looking back, I don't think it was the porn I really wanted, but to be with Brad, to have this deep sexual secret with him that no one else knew about. He told us all that we should go home and move the skin on our penises really fast and it would feel really good. The first time I did this, I did it to completion and had my first orgasm. I thought I was going to have to be rushed to the emergency room because something had gone terribly wrong. It was a sexual awakening. I felt like I was living in an episode of HBO's *Real Sex*, maybe even the episode I accidentally recorded over my parents' VHS wedding video.

The one thing I didn't want was to be gay. My family was always accepting of gay people, I knew gay people growing up, and I certainly worked with some in figure skating. But I always thought, "That's not me. It just can't be me. I can't be this thing that people made fun of me for when I was little. I can't be this thing that I know isn't accepted in my area." Even when hate isn't directed explicitly toward you, you can feel it in the air, like some corrosive mist that you can't wash off.

I also had some irrational fears about coming out. I always thought that once I did, I would get beaten up, which has never happened. I also worried about losing my family. I had heard plenty of stories about people coming out losing everyone close to them, and then being alone. That's what is so scary about having a secret—you never know how people will feel about it until you finally tell them.

Growing up I always had these massive crushes on girls, and they were almost always these beautiful, outgoing people. Basically it was like an early form of diva worship. I think that's what made coming out even a little bit harder because I had legitimate feelings for other girls, and in my mind, being gay meant you thought girls were disgusting. I told myself, "I don't think they're disgusting. I don't know—maybe I'm not gay." If I'm being 100 percent honest, the reason I wasn't having sex with the girls that I had dated was because I thought I was being a good guy. I didn't want to pressure them or make them go too far.

I would go so far as to watch straight porn all the time, as if it were some kind of test. If I could get off watching just two women having sex, then I had to be straight. But, come on. I was twenty years old. I could get a boner if the wind hit my pants.

There was definitely gay porn in the mix too, but I would tell myself, "I just think that humans are beautiful. Everyone's a little bit gay." I mean, am I wrong? Everyone *is* a little bit gay—it's just that I was a lot bit gay. Like entirely gay.

I finally realized this when I met Scotty. He was a choreographer working with one of my friends in Detroit. He was about five years older than me, tall, funny, and with a smoking body. He was also openly gay.

He spent some time with my group while he was in Detroit, and he was flirting with me hard-core. I was also definitely flirting back, even though I wasn't sure he knew that I knew that we were flirting. Being gay is so hard!

Before this, when watching gay porn, I would think I was just bi-curious, that I was "just a sexual person," even though I hadn't had sex with anyone in my entire life at that point. (I love going back and listening to the reasoning of me in my early twenties.) So, when I started flirting with Scotty, I realized almost all at once that I might be more than just bi-curious. That was the deeper realization.

Once I came to that conclusion I knew exactly what had to happen going forward. I knew I really wanted to physically do things with Scotty, and this was the first time I'd felt this way. There wasn't really an option. The seas parted and I knew I had to come out.

I really came out to myself within the same period. I hadn't really done anything that warranted me needing to come out, because

I was just training and doing my thing. I thought, "This is just something I'm going to deal with later in life. I'll figure it out, but I don't need to think about it right now, because I'm training. I'm skating. A relationship shouldn't be a priority. Any of these feelings of wanting to do something are just a distraction right now. I don't need to do anything."

I was almost twenty-two, and at first I felt a little embarrassed not only that I had lied to myself but also that my friends and family would feel like I had been lying to them. Everything I had done up to that point was honest. I imagined I could be straight. I had just so badly not wanted to be gay that I never said it out loud. I barely even thought it to myself.

After I met Scotty, who was a former Mormon, he told me about his struggles coming out and how he had triumphed over them. If he could do it and be OK, then I could certainly do it too. Once I realized I was gay, I really felt the need to put it out there in the world. I didn't want my friends and family to think that I was being dishonest or lying to them.

The first people I told were two of my very best friends, Douglas and Bianca, who are also really close with each other as well. I used all my miles from my competitions the past year and got a ticket to go visit them at Bianca's house in California. I told them about Scotty and all the flirting and stuff. Then I said, "I think I'm gay."

Bianca's mom overheard and said, "Adam, you've been carrying around a messenger bag since you were fifteen. Like, *we know*. This isn't breaking news. Thank you for telling us, but this changes absolutely nothing."

Another best friend of mine, Ashley Wagner, was performing at a show in Toronto, so I made the short trip from Detroit to Toronto to visit her. I told her one night about things that were happening, and of course, she was nothing but supportive. After telling Bianca, Douglas, and Ashley, I thought my work was done. I figured the news would sort of filter out from them and I was essentially done coming out, at least to my friends. I was right and that is exactly what happened. Turns out most people weren't surprised. I wasn't putting on as good of a show as I thought.

I still had to come out to my family, and of course, my mom was first. She had traveled to California because I was performing in a show there. Between the matinee and the evening show, I texted her. There's something I need to tell you, Mom. Can we meet in the parking lot?

I wanted to come out to everyone in my family in person, especially my mom. I felt like the news was big enough that it warranted a face-to-face interaction. I always imagined with my mom it would be a quiet and beautiful moment, like in a Lifetime movie. But this was the earliest I could see her and the only time we could steal away during the event. So, I told my mom I was gay in the parking lot. We weren't even sitting in a car—we're just standing in the middle of this huge parking lot outside the Toyota Sports Center. The glamour is astounding.

She told me, "You were inside me for nine months. I know." And that was it.

Still, I have five siblings and a father who needed to hear the news. I thought they deserved to hear it from me and, again, that I should do it in person. I didn't want to do something dramatic and just stop dinner and be like, "Hey, everybody. I'm gay," like I'm Ellen DeGeneres on the cover of *TIME* magazine. I decided I would be more under the radar and come out to each of my siblings and my father separately. It turned out the only thing more dramatic than one big announcement was six small announcements.

None of my siblings really cared. When I told my brother Brady, we were playing video games. He said, "OK. That's cool. Can we go back to playing *Dragon Ball Z* now?"

The only one who had a crazy reaction was my sister Dagny, who was fourteen at the time. I told her I was gay and she immediately started crying. I thought, "Oh shit. She hates me. This is going to be a problem."

Then she said, "Adam, I'm so happy. I've wanted a gay brother for so long." Yeah, maybe not the problem that I thought it was. Being gay was actually helping my sister live her best life.

My father's reaction was somewhere between those two. I was a little bit nervous to tell him and couldn't quite find the right moment to pull him away from the rest of the family. Then I saw him go outside to leave and I knew it was then or never. I told him at the last minute, right before my mom was going to drive me to the airport to fly back to Detroit. He was standing outside his car about to get in. He told me that nothing would change between us and that he was still proud of me. He told me that being gay can be a hard life and that he loved me very much. I knew where he was coming from, but it couldn't be harder than knowing you were gay and keeping it inside. I didn't take any offense to what he said. I think he was just trying to fill up the silence. He had never had a son come out to him before and probably didn't know how to react. At this point I had *plenty* of practice coming out.

As every gay person knows, coming out isn't an event; it's a process. Everyone's initial reactions were great, but things with my mom got a little bit strained. My mother had a lot of gay friends who were dancers with her when she was younger. This was the height of the AIDS crisis, and she saw them treated badly and discriminated against. She didn't want that for me in my skating career and wanted me to keep the news confined to my personal life.

It's like she was saying to me, "Adam, you can be gay, but just wait. Can you just wait?" It didn't matter to her whether I was gay or straight, but she didn't want me to get hurt.

As I was telling people close to me, the feeling was so liberating that I wanted it in all aspects of my life, both personally and professionally. The freedom was intoxicating, and I knew I wouldn't be able to go out and show everybody who I was and what I was made of in a performance unless I shared this part of me too. Being gay didn't seem like such a big deal to me, but I knew I would feel like a fraud if I didn't tell everybody.

Plenty of people today would probably say, "Adam, you were coming out in figure skating. It's not like it would have been a huge shock." I've also heard a lot of people say that they feel that skating is homophobic for a sport that has its fair share of gay people. I don't think it's so much that it's blatantly homophobic as it's trying to push this message that figure skating is for everyone. Boys who skate get teased so much that they're not even willing to try it, or even if they do and like it, they don't continue. I think that when there are out athletes, sometimes the backlash is, "See! They're all gay. I don't want that. I'm gonna get made fun of in school for that."

When there are other single skaters who are straight men, it seems like sometimes there's a huge push behind them because that's the image of inclusivity that the figure skating community wants. It's not an overt homophobia, where gay skaters are punished, but a softer and equally insidious version of it.

It's like when Johnny Weir and Evan Lysacek were competing against each other. The narrative would be "the artist versus the athlete." Even though Johnny wasn't out when he was competing, it's like they were saying one is gay and one isn't. They're both great skaters and Johnny is just as much of an athlete as Evan, and Evan is just as much of an artist as Johnny. Hopefully one day we'll get to a place where it doesn't matter and everyone can be who they want and skate how they want and no one will care.

Ironically, in the months following my coming out, I never acted more straight. I think I was putting on armor because I felt like now that I was out, I needed to kind of protect myself and say to the world, "I'm not like one of *those* gay guys. Yeah, I'm gay, but I'm normal. It's just that I like guys. I'm not, like, oh, frilly, frilly froufrou."

I started dressing a bit differently and buying all my clothes from PacSun. I still love a PacSun moment, but I was trying to dress like a skater, but not the kind of skater I was. Like a skater punk. It was all about Vans and baggy shorts and oversize T-shirts. I started to wear baseball caps because I thought that is what all the hot straight guys do. I was dressing like a California boy, though I had certainly never lived by the ocean in my life.

I used to have really long, curly hair and I cut it all off. I looked like Shirley Temple, and I don't know how I thought this gave off the impression that I fucked girls, but I did. When I chopped off all my hair, I felt like I was letting go of my past. I only kept my hair long because I thought the judges liked my curly hair. I was doing what I thought they wanted to see, but I wasn't doing anything for myself. I just couldn't do that anymore. Shirley Temple had to take a seat, and her gay understudy was finally ready for his lead role.

I also got my ears pierced at Claire's (grown men can still go there even if it is only meant for people who like JoJo Siwa). I don't know why I thought that was butch at the time, but that is what I did. The next time my mom was visiting me, she saw the new look and the earrings and she freaked out. She didn't care what I did with my ears—she was just worried about what the judges were going to think. She wouldn't even be satisfied if I just took the earrings out while I was skating. When I was at a competition I would often stay at the same hotel as the judges, and even if that sweet bling wasn't in my ears on the ice, she thought they might see it in the hotel lobby and that would affect my scores.

She said, "I am not gonna think that you take skating seriously, so I'm not gonna leave here until you prove to me that you're not going to wear your earrings. And you're gonna put Neosporin over the holes all the time while I'm here." Even though I was twenty-two, I put Band-Aids on my ears until my mother left. Knowing my mom, she really wasn't going to leave until those earrings were out and I had Neosporin dripping from my earlobes for at least forty-eight hours.

About a year after that first encounter with Scotty, he came back into town again and was staying with my friend Jeremy. When I saw him for the first time, he said, "We should hang out a bunch while I'm here."

"Yeah, that sounds amazing," I told him.

Over the course of that week I saw Scotty a lot, and we were always flirting and holding hands and cuddling. It was so cute that it was almost enough to make Hello Kitty want to throw up.

One night we went on kind of a date to a gay establishment. It wasn't a bar; it was more like a theater full of gay people where some gay movie was showing. I couldn't even tell you what the movie was about, because I was so infatuated with Scotty and what was happening between us. Yes, we were at the movie, but we were holding hands, and we were kissing a little bit. All I could think, with a potent cocktail of excitement and dread, was, "Fuck. This is full-on gay shit." It was my very first gay kiss, and there was no turning back now. When I kissed Scotty, I thought for the first time, "This feels correct."

At the end of the movie Scotty said, "If we were in Los Angeles, I would invite you back to my place. But, you know. I'm not home."

Naïve and with no game at all I just said, "Yeah. That really sucks." He was staying with my friend Jeremy the whole week, so I never thought we'd have the chance to do anything physical.

A few days later he called me and said, "I have to leave early in the morning. Do you want to come over to Jeremy's house?" Bingo! It was game time.

I couldn't get over there fast enough. I decided to play it cool and bring pizza and beer—which I didn't even like—to spend time with Scotty. We were watching the 2012 Summer Olympic Games with Jeremy and just hanging out. Jeremy said it was cool if I wanted to sleep over (a true wingman if I ever met one). I said I would take

Scotty to the airport the next morning. He had a very early flight and I told him it was on my way home, but I knew Jeremy was aware that I lived in the total opposite direction of the airport.

Jeremy went upstairs to bed and we were staying downstairs in the guest room, so there was a little bit of privacy, and I was certainly going to make good use of that privacy while we had it. We had sex. Full-on, the whole nine yards. Scotty was leaving in the morning and I had no idea when I was going to get it ever again. If I learned anything from skating, it was how to use my time wisely, and it finally paid off. It was like getting your wisdom teeth taken out. Are you going to do all four at different times, or are you just going to rip them all out at the first opportunity you can? I hope, for the sake of your mental health, that you would choose the latter.

Afterward I was glad I wasn't a virgin anymore, but I didn't really feel different. I do remember feeling grateful. I thought I was lucky that my first time wasn't some sad groping underneath the bleachers in high school or fumbling around in a steamy car with someone I really didn't like that much. I thought, "Oh my God. I'm so fortunate to do it with somebody who's so nice and smart and talented." When we lay there after everything was done, Scotty joked and said for the rest of the time he was there we should say that we're fake boyfriends. He was leaving in three hours, but my heart exploded.

We barely had any time to sleep before we had to leave for the airport around 4 a.m. I pulled up to the departures area and we were saying goodbye and sneaking in some last kisses before he left. He took out his phone and started typing. "I'm writing you a message, but you have to promise me that you won't look at it until I go inside," he said while giving me a wink.

I promised, but in the flush of just losing my virginity and being in love for the first time, I would have promised him $10 trillion that I certainly didn't have.

We got out of the car and I hugged him goodbye one final

time. He went inside and I got back in the car, dying to see what sort of romantic note he had sent me while we were making out in the car.

Thanks so much for a great week, it read. You're a really nice guy and I had so much fun hanging out with you. I know we were pretending to be boyfriends, but I have to break up with you now. ;)

That was it. That was the end. I could feel my heart drop to the floor of my Subaru Outback. I couldn't believe it was real and I didn't think it was necessary at all. I get it, dude. You're leaving and you live halfway across the country. I knew we weren't going to be boyfriends for real. I knew we were pretending the whole time. I wasn't thinking this was something more than what it was. I felt like that high school girl under the bleachers that I was so grateful not to be four hours ago.

It was sort of like getting fired from a job when you know you're about to quit anyway. The worst part was I would have been fine if he would have just left, but now that he had to go and unnecessarily break up with me, I felt used.

I started the car and began driving back to my house. I saw a twenty-four-hour diner next to the highway, so I pulled over and went in. I wanted to be alone, but I was hungry. I also have never turned down an opportunity to be dramatic in public when one arises. I got breakfast by myself and ate it while thinking and processing. I thought of the million bitchy, witty, and sassy things I could text back to Scotty to make myself feel better. I never sent any of them. What was the point?

I was eating my omelet and just letting everything that had happened in the last week soak in. It was then that I realized that Scotty had given me something that would last a lifetime. It was herpes.

Just kidding. He didn't give me herpes. But he did give me the courage to fully be myself in the world for the first time. He gave me the ability to be honest to everyone in my life about my sexuality. If that is a disease like herpes, well then, I'm glad I got it. (But seriously, I never got herpes.)

The Words of Someone Weak

Things were going great in Detroit, and for the first time I had a supportive group of friends around me, I was out of the closet, and I was no longer a virgin who couldn't drive. (Take that, Cher Horowitz.) While everything was going well in my personal life, my mom and I were having some growing pains. It was the original battle of the divas.

My early twenties were a hard time for my mom and me. I had a lot of friends and I was really trying to figure out who I was. All of this change sounds amazing, but it made my mom worried that I wasn't going to keep the same focus on my training. Skating had always been something that was our thing, and as I was getting older, I wanted to take more control over it, but it's hard to take control over something that you aren't paying for. My mom was putting a lot of money into my skating, and as any parent would, she didn't want me to fuck it up for myself. Going to the Olympics was always my dream, and my mom knew that. Sometimes it felt like all she wanted me to do was skate, eat, go home, and not do anything else. I felt like I wasn't allowed to be a normal human, but then going to the Olympics is not something normal humans do.

One of the people who helped me the most while I was living in Michigan was Cindy Silk, who, despite her name, was not one of James Bond's girlfriends but a judo champion and my personal trainer during that time. I've always loved going to the gym, especially when it's an empty gym. It's sort of my escape from the stress of the rink and competing, but it also makes me feel like I'm doing even more to help my skating. It's like a treat and one that doesn't make me feel guilty, but like I'm doing the right thing. It's my emotional Oreo McFlurry.

Cindy always made me feel not only like I was doing a bit extra, but like I was doing the most. I remember we had this one exercise where she wanted me to work on my focus. She would play my program music and I needed to do double-unders with the jump rope for the whole duration of the song. But while it was happening, she would take medicine balls, cones, chairs, and anything else that wasn't nailed down and throw them around me to try to distract me. The trick was to stay focused on what I was doing. It would just be her and me in the gym later in the evening (like I said, I love an empty gym), and she'd be just throwing shit, and even though it sounds insane, I loved those nights in the gym. When we were done, I would say thank you and she would smile at me and say, "Fuck you." It just made me love her more.

She was really tough on me but at the same time really took me under her wing, and I loved her. I think when it came to my mom, she felt like I was listening more to Cindy than I was to her. I would tell her something Cindy told me and she would say, "I've been telling you that for years. Why don't you listen to me instead of Cindy?" It was either that or, "Cindy doesn't even know what she's talking about." In reality, yeah, my mom was telling me exactly the things Cindy was, but sometimes when you hear it from someone else, it hits your ear differently and travels to your brain faster. If their words had to take the train, my mom's would have been on the local and Cindy's on the express. There was also less on the line with Cindy. She didn't drive me all around the country for training; she didn't need to pay for any of the lessons or costumes or choreography. She was just tough on me, and what we did in the gym was the only thing that mattered. Cindy and I were allowed to just have fun and work hard. When it came to my mom, she had my coaching bills and five other kids to take care of. I knew that I needed to do well because I wanted to prove to everyone that my mom's extra effort wasn't a waste.

My mom wanted to be heard. She wanted me to listen and I did, but sometimes I felt like I was being treated like a baby. I felt like I wasn't allowed to make my own decisions. If I tried to, my mom was still in charge of my finances so it was never my call. I was trying to break away a little and be my own person, be an adult. I was twenty-one years old at this point, and I wanted some independence. I felt like any time I tried to take a step in that direction, I made my mom upset, and it was always two steps forward and two steps back, as Paula Abdul sang in the classic "Opposites Attract."

Every year all of the athletes that receive funding from US Figure Skating have to submit a certain amount of paperwork. This particular year I told my mom, "I want to do my funding paperwork. I'll do it on my own."

"You don't have time to do that," she said. "I'll take care of it."

"I want to do it on my own."

"No, I'm going to do it. I've always done it. You need to focus. You're not focused."

"Mom, I'm twenty-one. Let me do my own paperwork."

"No," she said finally. Looking back, I can't believe I got that worked up trying to fight for *paperwork*. Now I would rather set myself on fire than do paperwork. I'm wiser now than I was then.

I didn't realize it at the time, but I think my mom felt like I was saying, "Thanks for all your hard work and sacrifices; now, get out." What I thought she would say was, "Oh wow, Adam is turning into a man and taking responsibility for himself. I'm so proud. He's my smartest and most handsome son." But my mom knew how expensive it was, and at that moment in time, there was no way I would have been able to handle what I was asking to take on. Money was really tight for us. My mom was scrambling financially and at times getting in way over her head and never letting me know. The last thing we needed was for me to fuck up my funding somehow and not get what limited money they gave us.

It wasn't all struggles between my mom and me though. We had lots of great times. She came to visit me a few months after I moved to Detroit. We went to the craft store and got plants, pillows, and curtains to decorate my apartment and make it feel like home. Because I lived with other families during the week when I was a teenager, I never got to do those things with my mom, so something as simple as going to the grocery store together was a great time.

She was always my biggest cheerleader. I'd call her every day (because if I didn't, she probably would have called 911 and put out an Amber Alert) and she'd say, "Tell me five things that were awesome about today." I thought it was cheesy, but I would do it. She conditioned me to be smart, thoughtful, grateful, deliberate, positive, respectful, and kind. I got that all from my mom.

Whenever I would feel down and get critical of myself—which shockingly happened more than you would think, considering I'm so perfect—my mom would always say, "Don't talk about yourself like that." She told me to remind myself every day that I was a champion, because that is the only way you will ever become one.

Still, there was a lot of pressure on me. If I tried to do anything outside of skating or anything that she didn't like, I'd get a call and she would say, "Can you just focus on your skating right now? You have your whole life to do all of that later." Also, to be fair, if I had a child that was doing a sport that was as expensive as skating, I would probably put them on a leash and give them the blinders racehorses use so they wouldn't get into trouble and would stay focused. I'm honestly blessed that my mom didn't go that far.

Regardless, I felt like I was in a box, and I had just come out of the closet so I didn't want to do anything with anyone's box, let alone be in one. I felt like I was stuck.

Instagram was a battle for us, because whenever I would post anything she deemed inappropriate, I would immediately get a call. Her favorite trick was to say, "I got a note from someone..." or even worse, "I got a note from one of the officials..." These notes were always criticizing my music choice or my hair or a costume I was wearing. I was convinced there were no notes, that this was just my mom expressing herself through a series of imaginary ghostwriters in an effort to have the criticism not be directly from her. She was taking a "don't shoot the messenger" kind of approach. Honestly, though, because of my mom being so intense, I don't have any regrettable tweets or Instagram posts, which now is the gift she didn't know she was giving. Another blessing.

Once, I posted a picture of myself on Instagram where I was shirtless by the pool. I was a fresh gay and I needed to spread my wings on social media and my shirt was in the way. Immediately I got an email saying, "I'm getting notes from people saying they really think that picture is inappropriate and that it looks like you're not taking your career seriously." I had to promise her I would take it down and then I ended up apologizing for three days about posting it in the first place.

I once asked her not to come to one of my competitions. They can always be so nerve-wracking that I thought not having my mom there would make it feel more like a practice at home than a huge event. My mom never got to watch me train, and the only time she would be able to see me skate was at my events. Whenever she was there, I always wanted to impress her and I would put way more stress on myself to be amazing. It sometimes made my already pressure-filled competitions feel like a sudden death lip sync for your life, only instead of staying in the competition and competing for the crown, you just lost and put your mom in debt.

"Can you not go to one of these competitions? Can I just go by myself?" I asked her. "I want to know that I can go there by myself and do everything on my own."

"That's ridiculous," she said over the phone. "Why don't you want me to come?"

"I just feel like there's a lot of pressure when you're there," I told her.

"If you can't do your program in front of me, how are you going to do it in front of a thousand people you don't know?"

"I just don't want the added pressure of trying to please you."

"That's what somebody weak says."

"No it's not."

"Yes it is. I don't care what you say—I'm going. Somebody is talking to you about trying to kick me out of your life."

She didn't want anyone else to have influence over me—not Cindy, not my coaches, and certainly not my friends, who she always told me were "a distraction." I was asking the woman who did everything in her power to help me succeed to not be a part of the most exciting part of the journey. I see that now, but what I was really asking for was a little freedom. Every mistake I made felt like a disappointment not only to me, but to my family. Every competition I entered I could hear "Please bring honor to us all" from the movie *Mulan* in my head, and just like Mulan, I didn't know the girl staring back at me when she looked at herself in the river in full drag.

My mom and I were thrown into this world that neither one of us knew how to negotiate, and the stakes were incredibly high. My mom grew up very poor with six siblings in a house that was condemned. Sometimes they didn't have running water, and the ceiling was falling down in their dining room. How was my mom supposed to know how to raise an Olympian? She did the absolute best she could and then some.

She watched movies about people becoming the best, she read books about people overcoming adversity, and she did everything she could to help me achieve my dream. When you're born in the rough part of town like she was, people can take advantage of you, and my mom never wanted that to happen to me. She didn't want me to make the mistakes she made, and she wanted me to have the opportunities she didn't. If I learned anything from my mom, it was "Fake it till you make it," because she never let on that she was in uncharted waters. When she didn't know what she was doing, no one was the wiser. She was a leader and she was a protector. And sometimes she was annoying, but more than anything, even if she was being crazy, I knew she was the best support system I had.

That year I went to the world championships in Nice with my mom and my coaches Jason and Yuka from Detroit. I placed a disastrous twelfth. When a skater is in the top ten at worlds, he or she is then placed in the highest category for funding from US Figure Skating and also gets invited to participate in touring ice shows in the summer, which can mean very lucrative contracts. I was out of the running for all of those after my bad skate.

I was just devastated, and as my mom and I sat in the lobby of the hotel where all the skaters were staying, different ones would walk by and she would say, "Oh, there's Jeremy. He made the top ten," or "There's your friend Ashley. She made the top ten." At the time, it wasn't making a bad situation any better and I thought my mom was taking a page out of Sofia's book and charging me for the shame of having a non-top-ten skater for a son. In hindsight I know it was my mom's honest and panicked reaction to not knowing how we were going to pay for my next season of skating. In the moment I wished her reaction were different, but I'm also sure in the moment she wished my placement were different.

My mom is someone who would do anything to help one of her kids. Looking back on it, she was freaking out about how she was going to keep raising six kids and paying for all of my skating without that extra money coming in. As it was, I never saw any of the prize money from my competitions. I remember when I was a junior, one of the other parents on the team asked what I was going to buy first with my prize money. I looked at my mom and we both knew exactly where that money would go. It would go right to my coach for past lessons and maybe, if I was lucky, to some future ones as well. When the money came in, it would disappear as quickly as it arrived. Making money disappear quickly is still something I'm really good at. Don't believe me? Give me some coin and watch me go.

My mom was never shy in letting me know money was tight, but I never had any idea how tight it really was. When I got older, I later learned that to make sure I could keep skating after her divorce, she took a mortgage out against her house. At this point, that money was almost all gone and she was worried.

This is how skating can make people crazy. The expense is astronomical, and it's not like it's a team sport where the best teams will recruit players and take care of their coaching and training. In skating, the parents are essentially the skaters' managers. My mom didn't have Kris Jenner's *How to Be a Momager: A Rule Book*. She was making it up as she went along and looking to other skaters' moms for how she should act. But they're very intense because we're all doing this very intense thing. Being an elite athlete is crazy, and they should put us all in some sort of insane asylum (one with a really great gym, of course) for even attempting it in the first place.

The summer after the world championships, I was thinking about what was keeping me in Detroit, and if I'm being honest, it was mostly my time with Cindy Silk. She made me feel like a warrior. Before competitions I felt like I was fragile, or the nerves would get the most of me. After working with Cindy, I felt like I was going out there and fighting.

Devotion to a trainer is not the best reason to stay in a place, as she wasn't even a skating coach, just a beautiful soul who would throw things at me while I was jumping rope and tell me to fuck myself. There was also something still in me that wanted to work with Rafael Arutyunyan, the coach Frank Carroll had suggested for me about a year prior.

I was talking about all this with my friend Bianca, who had retired from competition at this point. She told me I should go check things out with Rafael where he trains in Lake Arrowhead, California, about an hour from Los Angeles. She lived in Orange County at the time and told me she would even go up there with me. I booked a two-week trip, and my mom was going to come meet me out there the second week because she wanted to see me with Rafael.

At this point I had taken my earrings out a while ago, and my ears were totally healed. Bianca had an ear cuff that sort of clips onto your ear that was a little tiger. I put it on because wouldn't you, if you had the chance to wear an ear cuff? We took a picture and Bianca posted it to Instagram. I immediately got a pit in my stomach knowing that even with the low resolution of an iPhone 4 front camera, my mom was going to see it.

"I know that my mom is going to call as soon as she sees this picture," I told Bianca. And just like that, my phone rings and it says Kelly Rippon right there on the screen.

"What's going on? I'm getting messages from everyone telling me that you have something in your ear," my mom says.

"What are you talking about? I don't even know what you're talking about," I tell her. Of course I know exactly what she's talking about, and I'm playing both dumb and dumber.

"You're wearing an earring in that picture with Bianca, and I got a ton of messages about it."

"It's just an ear cuff. I can take it off. It's not a piercing."

"Bianca isn't looking out for you."

"OK, I'm sorry. I'll ask her to take it down." Bianca, of course, took it down, and neither of us had to say that my mom was acting crazy, because we both knew she was acting crazy.

The good thing about the trip is that I absolutely fell in love with Rafael. My mom did too. We both loved him because he was brutally honest. He was going to make sure that I wasn't cutting any corners, be really hard on me, and expect a lot. After a skate he would say, "That's awful. You need to work on this or it's unacceptable." But it didn't feel like he was treating me like garbage, even when he was yelling at me from the side of the rink while I did my spins and jumps, because when I would finish, he would say, "That was great." It was in those moments that I could tell he liked me too.

I had to get to California and start training so quickly that my mom packed up my apartment in Detroit and drove all my things home to store in her garage. If my mom was crazy intense with me, she was equally crazy in the things she did for other people. She has always done more for others than she ever does for herself. With a one-way ticket and two suitcases, I moved to Lake Arrowhead, a small resort town in the mountains. I told everyone I was moving to LA. They didn't need to know that the *L* stood for "Lake" and the *A* stood for "Arrowhead." Rafael had an apartment in the basement of his house that had its own separate entrance, so it was like I lived by myself, just under the watchful eye and very heavy steps of my coach.

When I first started training with Rafael, he called me "the bodybuilder" because with Cindy I was really working hard on developing my upper body, mostly because I thought it would make me look better in the shirtless pictures of me by a pool that my mom wouldn't even let me post on Instagram.

One day at lunch, in between sessions at the rink in Lake Arrowhead, Rafael called me over and said, "Look at this." He took a stick, like a wooden skewer, and spun it in between his hands and it spun wonderfully on its pointed end. "Now look at this," he said. He took a grape, put the skewer through the juicy center of it, and then tried to spin the stick the same way. It immediately fell over. "That is you," he said. I was just trying to be cute, but now I was a grape on a stick. (Also, this was the closest my homeschooled ass ever got to being in a physics class.)

I was by no means fat, but Rafael wanted me to be smaller and leaner so that I could rotate faster both on the ice and in the air. When I would greet him and give him a hug, he would grab a little part of the fat on my arm and say, "We need to work on this." Sometimes he would be grabbing the boniest part of my elbow and I would think, "How do you want me to make my elbows smaller? Does Atkins work on that?"

Since I needed to lose weight, I started doing the elliptical machine every day for an hour and riding the stationary bike for an hour. One day I told my mom what I was doing.

"That's too much training. You're going to hurt yourself," she said.

"Rafael said I needed to lose weight and I don't have much time. I'm just doing what he told me to do," I replied.

"He didn't tell you that."

"Yes he did!"

"No, you're trying to coach yourself."

The next time my mom saw Rafael was about two months after we started training together, when we went to Cup of China, one of the Grand Prix events for that year and my first event of the season. She asked him if he really told me I should be doing two hours of cardio every day. "Well, it would be great if he could do three or four hours, but there are only so many hours in the day," he told her, proving that I would never lie to my mom about any of this—mostly because if I got caught, I knew what she would do.

My mom also asked Rafael about how much money she owed him for the two months of training. He said, "I'll talk to Adam about it and he'll let you know." We left it at that.

That trip to China was my first competition with Rafael, and it was a total disaster. I skated all right and ended up getting fourth place, but during the six-minute warm-up, I headbutted another skater, a Chinese competitor named Song Nan, and totally knocked him out. Cold.

He was skating forward and I was skating backward, and I turned forward and he thought I was going to cut around him. He kept skating forward and our patterns just didn't match up. In the six-minute warm-up, things like that happen sometimes. But it kind of looked like I tackled him, because we both skated forward into each other, our heads collided, his neck snapped back, and I grabbed hold of him.

When anyone first learns to skate, they teach you if you collide with someone to grab on to them. That way either you'll both stabilize each other and stay standing or you'll fall over together. There's a lot less risk of injury falling together than ricocheting off each other and possibly running into the wall or another skater.

So I grabbed him based on reflex, but to those watching, it sort of looked like I charged this kid, headbutted him, and then wrestled him to the ground like we were on Maury Povich and it had just been announced that he was indeed the father. He was taken from the rink in a stretcher and neck brace and had to withdraw from the competition. I had to find a quiet place to myself to cry for a minute. I was thinking, "This is my first competition with Rafael, he thinks I'm a mess, I just headbutted somebody, and now I'm going to have to perform with blood running down my forehead." I wiped the bead of blood dripping down my face. I would be fine. It would be fine.

This all happened after I told Rafael he wouldn't need to apply for a Chinese visa before we left because he had a Russian passport. This is something I totally made up. I figured Russia used to be communist and China was still communist, so they had to have some kind of understanding. Sometimes things I say as facts are really just opinions. FYI, if you have a Russian passport, you still need to apply for a Chinese visa, and if you don't, you will get detained at the Shanghai airport for about eight hours. I know this now from experience.

When we got back from China, Rafael finally had that talk with me about money he had told my mom we would have. It did not go as I expected.

"I'm not taking money from your mother anymore," he told me. "I don't care how long it takes you to pay me, but you need to take care of it from now on."

"OK," I said, having no clue what I'm going to do for money.

"When it goes well, you need to have this undeniable sense of pride, not like 'I barely made it.' You need to say, 'I fucking did that!'" he said. "And when it doesn't go well, you might not know how you're going to eat, but you're going to figure it out. And if you don't perform well, you're going to do what it takes to get better. It's going to make you an animal, and it's going to make you hungry, and it's going to make you a champion. But you need to do it on your own."

I agreed with him, but he wasn't the one who was going to have to tell my mother. It was the light I had been looking for. I had a coach who was willing to wait for me to get my shit together, and he wanted me to do it by myself. I called her that night and said, "Rafael says he's not going to take your money, that he wants me to pay for everything myself."

"He didn't say that. You're lying," she said.

"No, he really said that. I wouldn't lie to you."

"Why are you trying to kick me out of your life?"

I needed my independence and Rafael was giving me this opportunity to take it. I understand how she felt. I think my mom thought she was an outsider sometimes, because I was always living away from her. Her way of staying connected was when we would make the choices about programs, music, and costumes together. My skating was always a team project for the two of us. Now I was trying to take control of the whole thing.

We had a few days of tense communication, emails back and

forth about certain logistics and sponsorships, me trying to get all the information I needed to become a solo act. These were conversations I didn't want to have but that I also didn't have the guts to have when I was within driving distance of my mom. If I had still been living in New Jersey or Detroit, my mom would have already been in the car, getting ready to let me have it.

Things got so bad that I called my dad to talk to him about what was going on. "I don't understand why this is happening—this isn't what I want," I told him, hoping he might be able to make some sense of the whole situation. "I just want Mom to have less pressure, and I don't understand why this has to go down this way."

"Your mom has just been fully invested in what you've been doing forever, and it's going to be a huge change for her to not be. You have to be patient with her," he said. It's not the answer that I wanted, but maybe it was exactly what I needed to hear.

At this point it was my mom's way or the highway, and the highway was my only option.

On my birthday, which you all know is November 11, I sent her an email telling her that I needed some time apart to figure out how I was going to start paying Rafael and my skating all on my own.

She emailed me back and said, "I can't believe, on your birthday, that you're cutting ties with your entire family." She still didn't get it. Then she started calling and I decided I wasn't going to pick up the phone. She called about every other minute. Soon I had twenty missed calls, then thirty missed calls, voicemails, emails, and texts wondering if I'm still alive. She might have even DMed me on Instagram.

I shut my phone off and walked from Rafael's to another skater's house where her mom made dinner for a few of the skaters that lived in Lake Arrowhead. When I turned my phone back on, there were eighty-five missed calls, all from my mom. She wouldn't listen to anything I said, and the last time we talked she hung up on me. She didn't even believe the things I was telling her. If she wouldn't listen to my words, I was going to let my silence speak for me.

After dinner, I emailed my mom and told her that, yes, I'm still alive and that everything was fine, that I just needed to do this on my own and I would call her when I was ready.

The next day I went down to the bank to see what little money I had left in my checking account. I put the card in the ATM and it said the account was invalid. My mom was in charge of my banking up to that point, so she had every right to cancel my account. As I stood with a giant INVALID sign on the ATM screen, it felt official. I was on my own. This is also exactly what I had asked for. I told her I wanted to do it on my own. I said I needed to do this without her help and it didn't matter to me if I needed to start from literally zero.

I wanted independence from my mom. It didn't go down the way I wanted it to, but now I got it. All of this started because I wanted to prove to myself that I was an adult and that I was strong. I never meant to hurt my mom, but it was hurting me more to feel like my skating was ruining my family's life. I had no idea how to move forward. Just like my mom was able to make it work when she didn't know how she was going to do it, I would do the same. I took a page out of the Kelly Rippon book of making the impossible happen. Luckily I had the world's best teacher.

Help Me—I'm Poor

I remember once I bought a pair of twenty-dollar sunglasses that were *on sale* at Armani Exchange, and my mom told me I should take them back because people were going to start thinking I had a lot more money than I really did, and twenty dollars was out of my budget.

Most of my friends got to buy themselves a little present when they won a big competition, but I never did. Three years before the "breakup" with my mom, after the second time I won junior worlds, I decided that I was going to buy myself a treat because I was worth it. I bought a pair of UGG slippers because my old coach Nikolai had a pair and I thought that meant he was rich. They were $59.95, and they were the most expensive thing I owned. With my $10,000 in prize money, $9,940.05 of that went to pay my coaches. I wore those slippers for ten years until they looked like something antique that I had stolen from the Smithsonian.

Still, after all that, I never had as little money as when I lived in Lake Arrowhead, because then I had absolutely no money at all.

I had no idea what to do, so I called my friend Douglas, who is both the most anal and the most practical person I know.

"You need to get a bank account," he said very matter-of-factly, as if I might have been homeschooled.

"Yeah, but I don't have any money."

"You need to go through your whole apartment. Check the couch, check the pocket of every jacket, find every penny you can and take that to the bank."

I did just what Douglas told me to, and I found eighty euros from a competition and some leftover Chinese yuan from when I was just at the Cup of China. I took that to downtown Lake Arrowhead and went to the Bank of America, the only bank on the mountain.

"Do you accept foreign currency?" I asked the teller.

"Yes, we do." I felt like the clouds had parted and God was finally looking down on me and said, "I got you, boo."

"Well then, I would like to open an account," I said, spilling my euros, yuan, and any spare coins from the couch onto the counter of the bank. That was everything I had in the world.

I knew I had $3,000 in prize money coming in shortly from the Cup of China. I still had to pay for my ice for the month and my gym membership, but those could wait a minute, even though they were necessities. I just had to live on spare change and foreign bills until that $3K hit my account.

The next day, I was at the rink and my phone rang from a strange number. "Hello, this is Verizon," the woman on the other end said. "This number has recently been taken off an account. Do you want to take the number over and open your own account at the end of the month?"

Great, a new expense I had forgotten about. I of course told them I would (does a Millennial even exist if he doesn't have a phone plan?), but now I had to figure out how I was going to pay that as well.

This might be the point in the story where someone else might call their mom and say that they need help, but at that point, I would have rather worn that stupid cardboard collar that I hated when I had to dress like a Pilgrim in preschool for eternity than admit that I thought I was in trouble. As stubborn as she was, I was going to be ten times more stubborn. I wasn't going to ask for help—I told her I wanted to do this on my own and now I was going to have to fucking do it!

Because Lake Arrowhead is a resort town, the gym where I worked out wasn't a Planet Fitness or a Curves (if only!) but was the gym at a fancy (by Lake Arrowhead standards) resort where I could buy a membership for fifty dollars a month. I needed to keep paying for that because I needed to keep training but also because that is where I was getting most of my meals.

The resort had free green apples and TAZO tea in the lobby, and I would stuff as many into my backpack as I possibly could, and that is what I ate for weeks because the only thing I could afford was anything free. Fun fact about me: I'm allergic to apples. I had an itchy throat for that entire time, but whenever I felt like I was going to be sick and die, I could just have the TAZO tea I had also shoved into my bag. Yin and yang. I looked at it as a blessing in disguise, to lose even more of that weight that Rafael was always bothering me about.

Eventually I realized I needed protein too, so I went and bought the biggest, cheapest container of trail mix I could possibly find, the kind with the fake M&M'S in it that don't have any *M*s on them at all. Between the nuts and the chocolate, it was like having protein and dessert all in one. Winner, winner, trail mix for dinner (and breakfast and lunch and snacks).

My Chinese check came and finally there was enough in my account to pay for my ice for the month, which was $500, pay my gym membership, and buy some groceries and maybe even some trail mix with real M&M'S. Then Rafael says to me, "Do you have some money in your bank account?"

"Yeah," I said, trying to act all casual though I'm worried that if he asks me to pay him, I don't know how I'm going to live for another month.

"You need to get a car," he said. When I left Detroit for California, my mom drove my Subaru Outback from Detroit back to Pennsylvania where it was handed down among the Rippon children. (It still runs, if you count needing to occasionally shut the engine off and turn it back on at a stoplight as "running.") My plan was to not have a car while in California. Instead, Rafael told me, "You need balance in your life and that means you can't live here on the mountain. You need to go visit your friends."

"I don't need them," I told him. "I can just stay focused here and walk everywhere."

"Adam, you're being crazy," he said—and he should know because crazy recognizes crazy. Rafael insisted. He said his wife, Vera, was going to drive me down the mountain and that I had to get a car.

At first I thought I'd just buy some junky $1,000 used car, but we were living on a mountain. Even Rafael's brand-new BMW didn't sound that great on that steady incline—there was no way some trashy car would make it up the mountain. I needed something new.

I found a "sign and drive" deal at the Riverside Volkswagen dealership where I could lease a brand-new Jetta for $129 a month. I figured between prize money for the season and teaching a few skating lessons between my own training sessions at the rink I could cover an extra $129 a month.

Vera drives me down the mountain, and I walked into the VW dealership and tell them I would like the $129-a-month sign and drive, please. In black. If you have it. It was my Julia Roberts in *Pretty Woman* "Big mistake... Huge" moment.

"Do you want power windows?" the salesperson asks me. "Air-conditioning? A radio?"

"Yes, yes, and yes," I said.

"Well, that's going to be extra."

"What?"

"Yeah, the $129 model has manual windows, no air-conditioning, and no radio."

I was wondering why they even make such a car. A hot box with a chair? I don't need much. No radio I could live with. No

AC felt a little extreme, and windows that you have to crank is where I drew the line.

I asked them how much it would be for all of those "luxury" upgrades. It would be $189 a month. I figure I can do a couple of extra coaching shifts and find the $60 a month. They run my credit, I fork over $2,000 to get the lease going and cover expenses, and I am the proud leaser of a brand-new Volkswagen Jetta. Yes, they had black. The whole way driving up the mountain I really did feel like an adult, like I was finally getting my shit together. But with only about $50 left in my account, I would have to come up with next month's payment all over again.

When it came to things like getting a car, I missed being able to ask my mom for advice. She's the smartest person I know. Nothing was ever too big of a challenge for her. Then I realized that she didn't always know what she was doing either, but there was nothing she couldn't figure out. She taught me well enough that there's nothing I can't figure out either—I just had to do it myself.

Three weeks after I signed for my car, I was headed to compete in the NHK Trophy in Japan. I was excited because that week all of my meals would be paid for by the Japanese skating federation, and because I would be away, I wouldn't have any ice time that needed to be paid for back in California. It was a dream not to worry about those things.

When we got back to California, I had a letter from the Volkswagen dealership. The first time they ran my credit, they saw my mom's credit score because we used to have a joint credit card. The second time they ran it, after my mom's cancellations had gone through, it looked like I had just walked out of debtors' prison dressed like Anne Hathaway in *Les Mis* and had never had a real job in my entire life. They were going to come and repossess my car.

I frantically called the dealership and asked what I needed to do to keep it. They told me I needed someone to cosign the lease. Rafael agreed to cosign for me.

"I will not let you down," I told him, grateful for his generosity. "I will never put you in a bad situation. I will get this paid for. I will never make it so that you need to worry about this." I was true to my word and I always paid for my car, even if I couldn't quite afford to pay Rafael yet.

By January I started to have things figured out where I'd consistently have at least $150 in my checking account and I could relax a bit. Then I came in fifth at nationals, which secured my funding for the next year. However, I sprained my ankle pretty badly in practice, which meant I had to pull out of the rest of my competitions for that season, which meant no more prize money. I got a contract to do one show in Germany where I would make 2,000 euros, or about $2,700 in cash but that was all the money I would have coming in until the next season started and I'd get my USFS stipend again. That meant I had to stretch the $2,700 I had until July. It also meant another trip to the bank to deposit euros, seemingly the only currency I was good at hoarding.

I had just enough to pay for my ice, my phone, my car, and my gym membership with an unlimited supply of green apples. If I went out to dinner once or had an unexpected expense, it was all over.

That spring, my best friend Ashley's coach told her he was going to retire. It was the year before the Olympics, and she didn't know what she was going to do about finding a new coach. She called me up one day sobbing and I said, "Why don't you just call Rafael and come up and take a lesson or two? He's pretty awesome and he's changed my life. I love him and I think you should just try and maybe skate with him a few times and see what you think." I mean, Ashley is a two-time national champion, and I knew if Rafael would take on a charity case like me, he would love to have Ashley.

She came up from Orange County, where she lived, to skate a

few times and said, "Yep. I'm gonna do it." It was just such an Ashley thing, where she met him twice and decided to move her entire life around for him.

While Ashley was moving her life around for Rafael, he was making me move my life around for him. I'm not sure what Rafael thought my financial situation was, but he told me, "This summer you should get your own place. You need some distance." I think he really meant that, but I think he also wanted to use my apartment for his friends and family to visit in the summer.

Because Lake Arrowhead is a resort town, there aren't a lot of small apartments for destitute figure skaters with an average of $150 or less in the bank at any given time. There are tons of luxury ski châteaux to rent, but I couldn't even afford a packet of Swiss Miss hot chocolate, so I certainly couldn't pay for the whole château. I never thought about moving in with Ashley, because she was still living down in Orange County, which seemed like too long of a commute for me.

Serendipity takes over, and there's a family that just moved to Lake Arrowhead, and they were from Sweden, and they were gonna be gone for three months that summer. They had a son and daughter who trained with Rafael at the rink, so that's how I knew them, their travel schedule, and that their one-bedroom condo was going to be free.

"Can we work something out?" I asked one day at the rink. "Now, I'm gonna pay what I absolutely can; I'll give you everything that I have."

They worked out a fee for the whole summer, and it was a few hundred dollars a month. I agreed but said internally, "GULP! How am I going to pay for this?" But it was good to have an apartment, and Ashley could stay with me there when she came up to train Mondays through Thursdays.

There was one condition of my tenancy in their apartment, however. The couple asked me to take care of these two songbirds they had; one was yellow and one was green. They had names but I certainly don't remember them, because they were annoying as fuck.

They would squeak and squawk all day. It was all I could hear whenever I was home. There was a blanket I could put over the cage to make them go to sleep, but I couldn't do that all the time or they would think it was permanent midnight and die. I would let them stay awake until dusk and then it was blanket-over-the-cage time for them, which would shut them up completely and give Daddy some peace and quiet.

The birds were especially loud in the morning, so one day I came up with an idea. There was a small balcony on the apartment, and I thought I would put the cage outside the sliding glass door to give them some fresh air. "They probably love it out there," I told myself. "If they can't fly free, at least they can feel the breeze on their feathers or something." I thought I was being a good parent even if I didn't care if my bird children lived or died. Really, I just wanted those damn birds to shut up.

I would do that every day, place them outside on the balcony until about dusk and then bring them inside while they went to sleep. Problem solved.

One morning I was doing something in the house and all of a sudden the birds got really loud—like, louder than usual, so it was almost deafening. I went to check it out, and I look out the window and there is a hawk standing on the cage. I had actually never seen a hawk before, so it was either that or an owl on crack. I don't know. I took out my phone and Googled "hawk." Yup, this thing is definitely a hawk. He was a beautiful and strong-looking bird but also, I assumed, hungry.

Then the hawk flew away, did a lap around the building, and came back and sat on the railing of the balcony. I couldn't go out there, because a hawk will seriously fuck you up and I wanted to protect the birds but not at the expense of my moneymaker.

From the railing, the bird lunged at the cage a few times and knocked it, but nothing happened, not even a dent. He must have gotten bored, because then he flew off. After about fifteen minutes, I rushed outside, picked up the birds, and brought them inside.

I was so glad that hawk hadn't eaten them. I had one job that whole summer to help these generous people who were letting me stay in their house—how could I say to them, "Sorry, but a hawk ate your birds because they were too annoying and I left them out on the balcony"? Would they even believe that?

At the end of the summer, the family came home and thanked me for doing such a good job looking after the condo and the birds (of course, I did not tell them about their near-death experience with the hawk). They decided they weren't going to charge me any rent for the summer, which was a huge relief and something I'll forever be grateful for.

Then the father said, "We're going to be honest with you: Thank you for taking care of the birds, but we were kind of hoping that they were going to die. We hate them. The kids got them, and we thought maybe you would kill them by accident, or maybe they wouldn't make it."

After that I finally told them about the hawk, and I think the father, the mother, and I all wished that hawk had had a delicious songbird meal that day.

That summer was really hard moneywise though. I wasn't really doing much other than training and working out. I couldn't even coach students, because coaching insurance was one hundred dollars for the year and I couldn't afford that. Instead of making money, I was just saving as much as I could by not driving anywhere and not having to buy gas.

One weekend Ashley convinced me to drive the hour down to Dana Point in Orange County where she lived. She told me we could just hang out at her place and she would make us dinner, because she knew that I was trying to be crowned Ms. Frugal Ice

Prince 2013. I agreed, but when we went to the grocery store, I told her I would buy the groceries for dinner.

We get to the checkout, and it came to about thirty dollars for the chicken-salad dinner ingredients. I go to use my debit card and it gets declined. "That's weird," I said. I checked the Bank of America app on my phone and it said I had negative five dollars in the bank. Not only did I have no money, I had *negative* money.

"Huh, that's so weird. I have money in here but my card won't work," I lied to Ashley, super embarrassed and my face getting redder by the second.

"Don't worry–I got it," she said and paid for the groceries. She probably knew exactly what was going on but never made me feel bad and never brought it up again. I was so embarrassed at that moment that I wished that fucking hawk would have flown to that checkout counter and eaten me to take me out of my misery.

Finally I made it to the start of the figure skating season in August and got my first check from USFS so I could breathe a little bit. To make it even better, I came in second at my first Grand Prix event, which got me $12,000 in prize money and a $5,000 bonus from USFS. Also, the amount of my stipend went up for that year because I medaled at a Grand Prix.

For the first time since I opened it, there are four figures in my checking account. Hell, there were even five. But it didn't last for long. Having money meant I could finally pay the choreographers–one was $4,000 and the other was $3,000. I could pay for my costumes, which were $1,500 each. I could pay for my ice time for a few months. I could pay Rafael, who had been giving me a break for a year, so I owed him $7,000. It was gone in a heartbeat, and I knew exactly what my mother was talking about when I asked her where my prize money went. It was spent before it was even won.

At least I knew I could enjoy my life a little bit. I could go out and get a salad with friends or go to Starbucks every morning if I wanted to. I at least had the freedom to afford Sun In from the grocery store to try and dye my hair in the sun. It paired beautifully with the at-home haircuts I was giving myself.

It's always nice to have some cash, but looking back, I don't think that if I had had tons of money during this whole period, I would've been better off. Along with the struggle, I also needed my independence and the confidence that comes along with shouldering my own burdens. I was all on my own, and just as Rafael had predicted, I was hungrier than ever. But no matter how hungry I ever get, there is no way I'm eating another fucking green apple.

I Can't Do This Anymore

Just by looking at me, you might think I'm perfect, but that mostly has to do with the number of Korean face masks I apply every week. No matter what my skin regimen is at the time (and it changes frequently), I never feel perfect, but I have always felt I needed to be, especially when it came to skating. Landing everything was perfect. Not making any mistakes in practice—that was perfect. Skating a clean program every single day was perfect and what I expected of myself. But that level of perfection isn't possible in any sort of job.

If I wouldn't be perfect—not just at competitions, but even in practice—I would think that I was, like, a complete failure. I would think I was a fraud who tricked everybody into believing I was good. I would think that I was a liar. I was just really hard on myself because I also felt like I was letting my mom and my coaches down. One little wobble on a landing and I thought I had tricked them into thinking I could do it, and I had tricked myself. I didn't know how I had gotten there.

I thought figure skating was a sport about being perfect—that is what the judges and my coaches were looking for, and that little Winnie Cooper inside me wanted to deliver perfect every single time. I didn't realize I was putting myself at such a disadvantage because I needed to be perfect.

Back when I was training and living in Toronto, I worked with a choreographer named David Wilson. He came to the rink to watch me skate a program he had made for me.

I skated a flawless program, and then when I did the last element I stepped out of it, which is just a minor error. After ending the program and holding my final position for a second, I rolled my eyes at myself. I went, like, "Uh," out of frustration and grunted.

I started skating around, and he yelled at me to come over. "How dare you disrespect my program that I made for you!" he screamed. He wasn't upset about my mistake, which he laughed off as an inevitability for a new program. He was pissed about my bad attitude. "How dare you have me sit here and watch the whole thing and you don't even end it properly! I don't know what kind of talk you're having with yourself, but it's so disrespectful the way that you just reacted, and I took time out of my day to watch you. You need to think about what you did. It's completely unacceptable. You have an awful attitude right now."

He did this in front of everyone at the rink, and it got so bad I had to skate to the other side of the ice and cry alone for a minute, because he was really going in on me.

I eventually learned what he meant. If I made a silly mistake, I could analyze it, see what I did wrong, and correct it. I could run my program again and learn from my mistake. However, at this point in my career, I would say to myself, "Fuck, I can't do anything right," and get really upset about the smallest obstacles. I thought my all-or-nothing attitude was helping my training, but really, it was hindering it. I don't believe I did anything that disrespectful, but he gave me the yelling I needed, not the one I deserved.

At that point in my life, up through when I was working with Rafael and scraping together change to buy trail mix, I thought if I took something 100 percent seriously, I needed to give it 100 percent intensity as well. I couldn't separate the two. At twenty-three, all I had was skating, and I took it very seriously, which meant I approached it with an intensity that burned brighter than me waiting for Britney Spears to post something to her Instagram story. Anything: a picture of corn, a runway walk, a picture of her in the gym where you can see some of her collection of tiny furniture—I live for it all.

But there were a lot of other things going on in my life at that time. In August 2013 the rink in Lake Arrowhead closed for good. Rafael moved himself and all of his students, including me, to Los Angeles. Finally when I told people I lived in LA, I wouldn't be lying.

My move to LA is when my friendship with Derrick Delmore really blossomed. Derrick is ten years older than me. I grew up watching him skate at competitions and he is someone I always looked up to. We started to hang out more and more once we were in the same city and had a lot of really long conversations about what was going on in my life during what was a difficult time. He became like a family member when my family was so far away and things weren't great with my mom.

Derrick works as a skating coach. I just needed to talk to someone who was older than me and who totally understood the intricacies of the skating world. It helped that he loved what he did and was also openly gay. I saw a lot of myself in Derrick. In addition to his amazing support, he set a great example of how someone could be successful after a competitive skating career.

I also felt like this was the time to be intense because it was going into the 2014 season, which is when the Olympic team going to Sochi, Russia, would be selected. I was twenty-four, which is prime age for Olympic skaters. I felt like I should be an experienced veteran at this point, but I hadn't made the Olympics yet, and I knew that in another Olympic cycle, I'd really be pushing it in terms of age.

The season started shortly after we all moved, and this is when I came in second at my first Grand Prix and fourth at my second one, so I started off the season strong. I felt like I was in a good place and I needed to find a life outside of skating. Yes, preparing for the Olympics was important, but I was miserable if I didn't have some kind of balance. All of my emotions and well-being revolved around how well I did at practice on any given day or how well I placed at competitions. I needed an outlet to take my mind off those things, even if just for a little bit. It's not like I was trying to take Molly at rave parties every weekend. I just wanted to, like, have a glass of chardonnay from a bottle with a twist top every once in a while.

One thing that I always admired about Ashley, who was training with me at the time, is how she managed to keep a healthy balance between skating and her personal life. I take everything out of my life and I focus on that one project, and everything else is a distraction. It kind of goes back to my mom always telling me I needed to focus. "It's great you want to hang out with your friends, go to the movies, go to dinner, and have, like, a life, but I'm sacrificing and putting my whole life and other kids at risk for you to go and enjoy yourself. You need to focus." She wasn't wrong, but who could have a life under that pressure? Ashley, that's who.

Ashley, who was the reigning national champion at this point, was someone who could always pull it out in competition. She was uber-confident in herself even if she wasn't the best in practice or didn't do the most training. She did just enough so that she would enter a competition and be like, "I've got this," and get first place. I'm not that person. I need to do it ten million times, perfect every time, and even then I would still think I barely had a chance to make the podium.

I started to look to Ashley to see how I could have a life and keep training. We decided that on Thursdays, after practicing, we would go to lunch and have a couple of drinks during happy hour, because you know Rippons love a good deal. Our favorite place was called Lazy Dog. I would order a cheeseburger and fries, and thanks to the drink specials, I would get a spiked hot chocolate. There we were, two athletes training for the Olympics, getting day drunk every Thursday.

Another way that Ashley and I are different is the way we eat. She'd say, "Oh, I'm dying for a hamburger and cheesecake," and we'd go and both order that, and she would have two bites of her hamburger and just sniff the cheesecake and say, "Oh, I'm so full." She has the willpower of ten men or five Octavia Spencers.

Meanwhile, I not only would eat my hamburger and cheesecake but I would finish Ashley's too. Maybe that's why she was doing better than me, because when we would go to Qdoba and get the cheesiest quesadilla possible, she would eat only a quarter of it and I would house the entire thing like I was training for Nathan's hot dog–eating contest instead of the Olympics.

This was my version of eating poor. If I were eating and drinking like that now, I would think I was trying to get a contract as a Jenny Craig "before" spokesmodel. When I moved to LA, I started to make a little bit of money so I could get groceries or go to Chipotle. That was a fun new thing for me to do, and I could do it without the pressure of feeling like I was spending my siblings' college tuition. Heading into 2014, I was too careless and I ate when I wanted and whatever I wanted. I didn't think about what I was eating, because I wasn't going to McDonald's every day. It was a little bit of me rebelling and trying to treat myself for the first time in my life.

During this period, I was also trying out what people generously call "dating" apps. My first experience being an out adult was when I was in Lake Arrowhead, a town of about twelve thousand residents. When I would open Grindr in my apartment, there wouldn't be any people, just a GIF of a tumbleweed that would never stop turning. When I got to Los Angeles, I thought it was time to start living my life a bit and downloaded both Grindr and Tinder. If we were going to do this, we were going to cover all the bases: no man, fuckboy, or potential boyfriend left behind.

My profile picture was one taken of me while I was on vacation in Hawaii with Ashley. I was by the pool in a bathing suit and looking quite nice. Of course, I cut my head out of the picture so that no one would know it was me (not that anyone other than the most ardent gay figure skating fan would have recognized me at that point anyway). It also felt appropriate to be a headless torso in a sea of other headless torsos looking for romance.

To further conceal my identity, I would tell everyone I met that my name was "Craig" or "John" or "Chad," and if they asked what I did for a living, I would say, "Advertising." It was the perfect job for Blake or whoever I was that day, both descriptive but also so boring and vague that no one would bother me with any follow-up questions.

It's not like I really had a slutty phase, but I did meet up with some guys every once in a while. I knew I wasn't trying to get into a relationship with anybody, because as a training athlete, I couldn't go anywhere—I couldn't go out to dinner, I couldn't meet at the club at midnight on a Thursday. I would chat with people for a little bit and we would meet and hang out for the day, and then I'd never talk to them again.

Don't get me wrong—there were a few times where we met online and I headed right over and headed right back home after an hour or so. An in-and-out job, so to speak. That's just good time management if you ask me. But there were also a couple of guys who I became a little friendlier with and would see more than once. Those few I finally told my real name and occupation. Then it all made sense to them. It's hard (but maybe not impossible) to get an ass like mine sitting in a chair at an advertising agency every day.

I didn't really love hooking up for its own sake, but I was a scientist and I needed to experiment. I think it was just making me feel more like a normal person. I was figuring out who I was and what I liked. I wanted to make sure when I did meet someone worth having a relationship with that I knew what to do in the bedroom. I didn't want to be just jerking off in the corner alone, because up until this point, that is pretty much all I had done. I wanted to make sure I had other tricks up my sleeve. I was just trying to put some miles on this brand-new car. If you asked Suze Orman, she would call this planning for your future.

Most important, I was figuring out what it was like to be an adult in the real world. I didn't have any of those high school experiences where you sneak around and make out with people or even go on dates. The most risqué thing I ever did was make out on the Toronto waterfront with Olympic champion Yuna Kim. I was very much making up for some lost time.

While I was doing all this to try to have a life, I wasn't even enjoying myself. Well, the sex stuff I enjoyed, except for the few times I got catfished. No one is safe. There was one time I matched with someone on Tinder, and his pictures showed that he was a hottie in his early twenties. There was even an Instagram attached to the profile to corroborate. When I arrived at his front door, the man who answered looked like an older, heavier relative of the guy I matched with. I wanted to give him the benefit of the doubt, so I stayed. Maybe his life was just too hectic to update his pictures? To make it worse, once we started chatting, he was boring too. You can be a catfish or you can be boring, but you can't be both.

Even after the catfishing I returned to the dating apps, but still I would be nervous that I wasn't giving skating my full attention. I don't think I was trying to be social because I particularly enjoyed it; I felt like it was something I was supposed to be doing. I was checking another thing off the list in some vain attempt at being perfect.

Because I was performing well, I was getting away with all this, so I just kept doing it. I was trying to find this perfect balance between my social and professional lives. What I was building was a house of cards: beautiful on the outside but able to be toppled over with the slightest breeze. There wasn't just a breeze coming—an entire hurricane was headed my way.

My performance early in the season was good enough that I still had some of that Olympic buzz, which is sort of like Oscar buzz but not nearly as loud. I thought if I was going to the Olympics, I wanted to have my mom back in my life because I didn't want her to miss out on that milestone, especially since she was so instrumental in getting me so far in my career, as well as, you know, giving birth to me and stuff. After I reached out initially we started to talk more and more, and while things were awkward at first, after about a year we got to a place where we reached a sort of understanding.

Right around the same time, NBC came out to California to make a package about Ashley, who was a shoo-in for the Olympics that year. It was going to be one of those inspirational videos they show in between events or while the audience is waiting for the ice skaters to finish their six-minute warm-ups. While NBC was getting some footage of Ashley hanging around with her friends, I met the whole crew.

NBC got back in touch with me and said they wanted to do a profile of me as well. They flew my mom out so she could be part of the whole experience. We thought it was so great that they believed I had a good enough shot to go that they'd spare the expense to send a whole crew to my apartment.

After spending the day together, during the last part of the interview, the producer in charge pulled me aside and took me into my bedroom and closed the door. "I'm going to ask you about being a gay athlete going to Sochi if you're OK with that." I hadn't come out publicly or professionally yet, but after spending time with Ashley and me, they all figured out that I was "a gay." I probably gave it away when I was chatting with one of the other producers at Ashley's shoot about some of the other hot Olympians and also probably by being gay. Two solid giveaways.

I was a little deflated because then I thought they were only there because they knew I was gay and that I might be going to Russia, which has a horrible record on gay rights and had just instituted an anti-gay propaganda law. This producer wasn't looking for me—she was looking for her Pulitzer for Best Olympic Inspirational Tearjerker.

I said to her that I didn't really feel comfortable saying anything before the Olympics, because nobody really knew if I was even going to go at that point. I also didn't know if I would be putting myself or any potential teammates in danger by being out. But I said if I do go to Russia, I am 100 percent available after I'm done competing to say something. That seemed to satisfy her as long as she got her Pulitzer one way or another.

I stayed in my room for a minute to collect myself, and my mom came in and asked what happened. "She wanted me to talk about being gay and going to Russia, but I told her I wasn't comfortable. I told her maybe after I'm done competing I would say something," I said.

"No!" she replied very quickly. "You're not going to say it. That is not a good idea. That is just going to distract from what you're doing and why you're even there." I know you're probably sick of readi[illegible]talking about "distractions," but if you're tire[illegible]ech every time, you can just imagine ho[illegible].

"Mom, I [illegible]ything right now—it's fine. Maybe afte[illegible]t not right now."

"You're [illegible]g a statement than going to the Olym[illegible]hat you should be thinking about right now. [illegible] your skating. You have your whole life to do whatever you want, but just worry about your skating right now."

That really stung because it was the first time I ever felt any sort of embarrassment or shame from my mom about being gay. The first time I came out to my mom, she was very supportive and playful, telling me all about the boys she thought were cute. Now I saw her saying no, it's not OK to be gay.

It felt so weird. My mom was a dancer in the earlier part of her life, and I remember finding pictures in her closet of old times in her studio and pulling out a few pictures of her laughing and hugging this handsome boy. They were smiling and I could feel my mom's heart warm up just looking at the picture. I asked her who he was and her mood changed. "He was one of my best friends, but he passed away. I lost a lot of friends I used to dance with." It was during the AIDS crisis, and the gay friends my mom had while she was dancing had all lost their lives to the disease.

We've had a conversation about it since, and my mom told me she felt that getting to the Olympics is such a rare thing. It takes being born at the right time so that you're the right age to go. It takes having the right skating routines at the right time. It happens only once every four years, and there are only three people maximum in the entire country who get assigned in the men's category. I think my mom thought that if I was an out athlete, it might be the one thing that kept me from being on the team.

In the moment though, a huge and whispered shouting match ensued, and I'm sure the NBC crew, just on the other side of my flimsy bedroom door, heard every single word of it. I was waiting for the producer to knock on the door and say, "Is everything all right in there?" She was smart enough not to come between two warring Rippons in the heat of battle. My relationship with my mom was still rocky, and we weren't ready to talk about something like this and have an open and honest discussion about it.

This all went down in December, and nationals were right after the new year, and that is the final event in determining who goes to the Olympics. This was in 2014. It was my fifth time at nationals and my second Olympic cycle, after not placing high enough to make the Olympics in 2010. That December the rink cancelled most of the ice time dedicated to figure skaters. They wanted to use it for more public skating because around the holidays people want to live their popcorn-tin fantasies and ice skate with a muff on. The rink was more focused on revenue than it was on producing an Olympic team, which is weird because the rink was owned by Michelle Kwan's father. I thought he would be more sensitive to us having our ice time, but he wasn't. Michelle wasn't competing anymore, and if we wanted good ice time, it wasn't really his problem. He already put in his hard time and he wasn't trying to take care of me.

We only had a few hours to skate in the morning, which meant that it was me and twenty other people in the rink at one time. It would take me an hour to achieve what I usually do in fifteen minutes.

Then I got the worst flu of my life. I was in bed for a week, shivering, sweating, and hallucinating that I was a figure skater training for the Olympics who had just gotten sick and would never make it. No wait. That last part was true.

This is when I learned that the house of cards I was building had no foundation at all. I had been doing just enough to (literally) skate by, but I didn't have any reserves in the tank for an emergency. When I took that week off with the flu, it erased everything I had been working toward because I had nothing to fall back on.

Even worse than what it did to my body, the illness really messed with my head. To anyone else it wouldn't seem like I was slacking, but when I got sick, I thought I hadn't done enough work. I got into this headspace where I thought I wouldn't be ready. I hadn't been doing any of the extra workouts that fed my sense of preparedness. When I got sick and was lying in bed, I couldn't say to myself, "But you did all of those extra workouts and program run-throughs, so you'll be fine." I had been doing what everyone told me to do, but in my warped athlete brain, that wasn't enough.

Right before we left for nationals, Rafael said to me, "We need more time. You're not ready. I have no idea how this is going to go," which is exactly what I wanted to hear going into the biggest competition of my career. He also said that my skating at nationals that year would be like going to Vegas because anything could happen, which was also a real confidence booster for me.

We got to the competition and I took the ice for my short program. I landed my first jump a little shakily but nothing major. As I skated around the rink and approached my second jump, I thought to myself, "If I land this, then I'm going to the Olympics." Of course, I fell. Then I go into the next jump and made a mistake on that one too. All I could think to myself was, "Fuck!" After that, the whole routine was a disaster.

When I got off the ice and sat down in the "kiss and cry" where skaters get their scores, Rafael says to me, "I knew that was going to happen. You weren't ready." Yeah, thanks again. And by the way, I still have to skate another program tomorrow, so this pep talk isn't doing much for morale.

I wasn't just physically depleted; my whole mind-set was ruined. I was down on myself, and I really felt I needed two extra weeks. Normally, after a bad skate, I would focus on how hard I've worked and psych myself out of it. Now all I was thinking was, "Why did this have to happen to me? Why did all of this happen right now?"

The next day my free skate was just as bad. I ended up eighth, which is the worst I've ever done at nationals. There was no way that I was going to the Olympics now; I just didn't have the criteria.

When I got out of the locker room, Rafael was waiting for me. "I don't think I want to do this anymore," I told him. "Maybe going to the Olympics isn't for me. Maybe it was never meant to be."

"Let's not make any decisions right now," he said. "It's still fresh. Let's talk again in a few days."

The immediate challenge I had to face was at the bar of the host hotel. Every year when nationals was over, everyone would go and hang out in the hotel bar like a family reunion. I was really sad about my performance and knowing I wouldn't go to the Olympics, but I also knew that I had to go down and see everybody. I didn't want anyone to say, "Oh, he was so sad he couldn't even say hi."

In the small hotel bar in Boston, my friends just came up and hugged me. No one said anything. We were all aware of the realities of the sport and that I probably missed my last shot at going to the Olympics.

One of the other coaches who trains people at our rink, Karen Kwan, Michelle's sister, came up to me a little teary and gave me the biggest hug of all. "You're not done," she told me.

"I don't know," I told her, starting to well up but not wanting to ruin my metaphorical mascara.

"You're not done," she told me again, with even more confidence. "It can't end like this."

I think about this moment a lot because I'm someone who looks for signs, and I was really looking for a sign. It was a good time for her to say it, when I was super down on myself. When one Kwan closes a door and cancels your ice, another Kwan opens a window and lifts your spirits. I wasn't sure I totally agreed with her, but she was right—there was no way it could end like this, which you obviously know because you're still only, like, halfway done with this book.

Choreographing My Own Disaster

Instead of spending February 2014 competing at the Olympics, I spent it drinking on the roof of my friend Mirai Nagasu's house in Arcadia, California. Mirai had gone to the Olympics in 2010 and came in fourth. In 2014 she was the first alternate and would also be sitting out these Olympic Games with me.

Mirai and I had been friends for a while. When I first moved to California, she lived the closest to Lake Arrowhead and always offered to have me over, so we spent a ton of time together my first year there. We got especially close when all our friends were off competing on the world stage while we were at home pretending like everything was all right, even though our worlds felt like they were falling to pieces.

That night on the roof, figure skating was airing on television. Mirai and I went to In-N-Out Burger, got dinner, and took it back to her house. We made screwdrivers in plastic Dave & Buster's cups and climbed up on the roof of her house to eat our gourmet dinner and drink. We didn't even get drunk, because we were spending too much time crying and it was keeping us from getting wasted.

Through my tears and over the grease-stained In-N-Out wrappers, I finally asked Mirai the question that both of us were trying to figure out: "What the fuck are we going to do now?"

"I'm going to keep skating," Mirai said without any hesitation whatsoever while the *Les Misérables* soundtrack was blaring through her iPhone speakers because it made her feel better.

"I don't know if I can," I said, completely unsure of what I was going to do next while Hugh Jackman sang "24601," the same number of shots I wanted to take that night but didn't.

Doing poorly at that one nationals was more than just having an off competition, which I had plenty of before. It really knocked something loose in my brain in a way that had never happened before. That was the one competition that mattered, and I screwed up when it really counted. Training for the Olympics is so weird because it always feels so far away, like a magical kingdom. It's only close for a few months every four years, and you either make it or you don't. Now it would be another four years before it would be close again. I would be twenty-eight, and it felt unrealistic to think that I could keep training and improving for another four years when there were younger competitors coming up behind me.

I felt like skating was the only thing I had in my life and that I needed to make the Olympics in order for it to count. Being on that world stage would validate everything that had happened to me up until that point—all the sacrifices I'd made, all the time I'd spent, everything I'd gone through with my mom. Now it seemed like this thing I always thought would happen wasn't going to happen, and it made me think that everything I had done was in vain. I felt like a fraud, and even worse, I felt like I had wasted my life chasing a kingdom that doesn't even exist.

That night on the roof, the one thing we did know was that Mirai was going to do the Stars on Ice tour. She didn't have a new program for it and didn't want to spend any money on a choreographer to make one for her. Like Katniss Everdeen, I volunteered as tribute to take on the job.

I had a little experience choreographing for myself, but I certainly had never done a program for a former Olympian and national champion that was going to be seen by arenas of screaming fans. We both decided it would be fun to work together, and if the routine totally sucked, well, Mirai got exactly what she paid for.

Putting together a program meant going back to the rink, so I was still keeping my foot in the door. I was doing a bit of teaching, skating regularly, and helping Mirai with some choreography. I figured eventually the answer for what to do with my life would suddenly fall out of the sky like a sign from God and hit me on the head while hopefully not messing up my spray tan.

Mirai was a great student, and by that I mean she did everything I told her to and didn't really ask questions. The program turned out brilliantly and it got a lot of compliments from the Stars on Ice audience, but more than anything, we both used it as a chance to get our feet back out onto this ice. When you're an athlete who competes in an individual sport, you do everything alone, and in this moment in my career I didn't need to be "On My Own," as Éponine had reminded me over a thousand times at this point because *Les Mis* was still constantly on repeat. We got to take those first few rough steps back out onto the ice together.

Mirai liked her program so much that she asked me to choreograph both her short and long programs for the next competition season. I also started to choreograph for some younger skaters who were definitely not as good as Mirai but who brought their own flair. One girl I worked with had two jumps in her program that she had never landed. I asked her if she thought that maybe in competition she could pull it off. She laughed. I did what any choreographer would have done and planned on her falling, and we choreographed the way she would get up from every single fall. If you're going to be a mess, at least choreograph your own disaster.

There was no way I could charge Mirai, because I didn't want to put her in a position where I gave her such a bad routine she had to go out and pay someone a second time to correct my less-than-award-winning choreography. I know firsthand how expensive everything is, and I was just really grateful for the opportunity. Her programs were the best advertising that

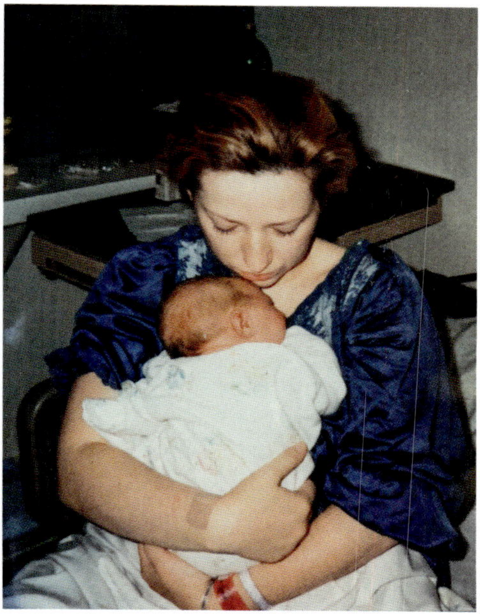

Day 1 and already a momma's boy.

I never liked the winter.

Hello, God. It's me again.

My first romper and my always limp wrists.

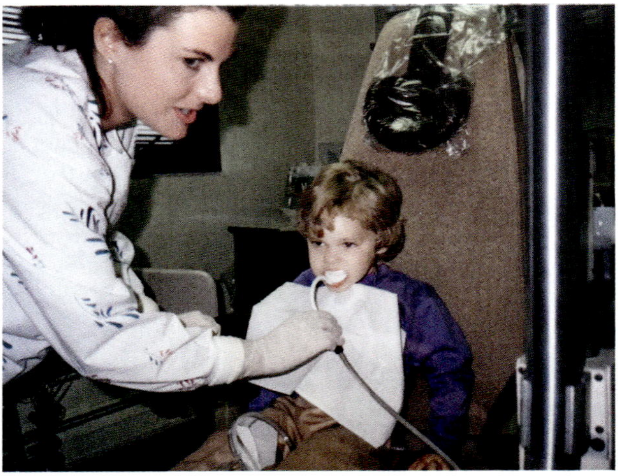

My long journey with dental beauty begins.

I'm on the right track, baby, I was born this way.

My fourth birthday party at the McDonald's in Scranton. I can still taste the cake.

I've always loved an accessory and a split.

Here I am crying, being dragged into preschool.

Looking dusty in my school photo.

My fifth birthday at Wegmans. I went from McDonald's to a supermarket. We were moving up in the world.

Thank God I grew into those ears.

Future influencer.

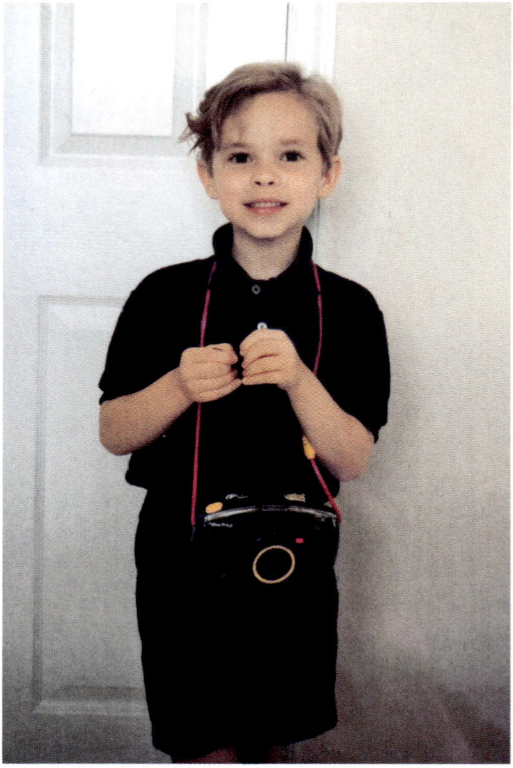

Me sitting with my newborn brother Brady. (I think it's Brady. There's so many of them.)

Winning a gold medal at the Keystone State Games in 2000. I came in first, but there were only two people competing.

Singing "Ironic" in the Olympic Training Center cafeteria.

My brother Brady and me braving the Scranton elements, circa 2007.

Going to buy cases of water in Toronto and I was threatening to wear this comforter on my head.

Yuna Kim and me in Korea at her show. I was trying to convince her to be my girlfriend before she didn't want to be and before I was gay.

Celebrating my junior national title with my mom in 2008.

Ashley and me right after we first met each other. We had a long way to go.

Bianca and me. I have a popped collar and she looks like a Romanichal gypsy. She is my obsession.

Me and Bianca my first day in California. This is what a grape on a stick looks like.

Mirai and me in her family's restaurant in Arcadia, California.

Me curled up in Mirai's bed avoiding watching the 2014 Olympics, which we didn't qualify for.

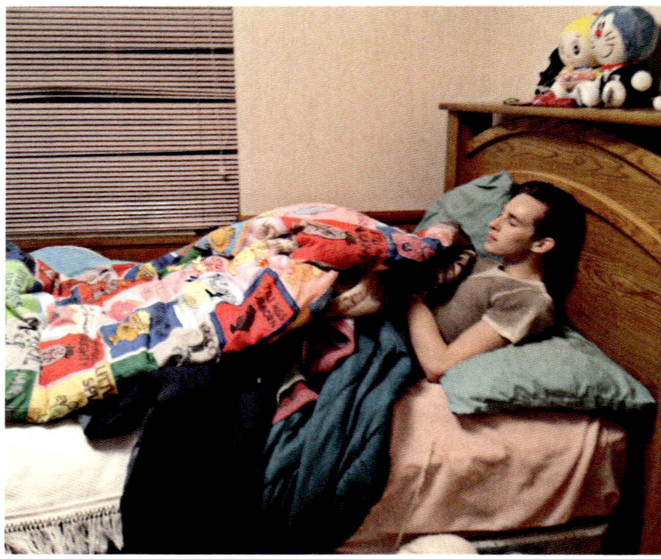

On vacation with Douglas and Bianca in Arizona, dressed up for a "fancy" dinner.

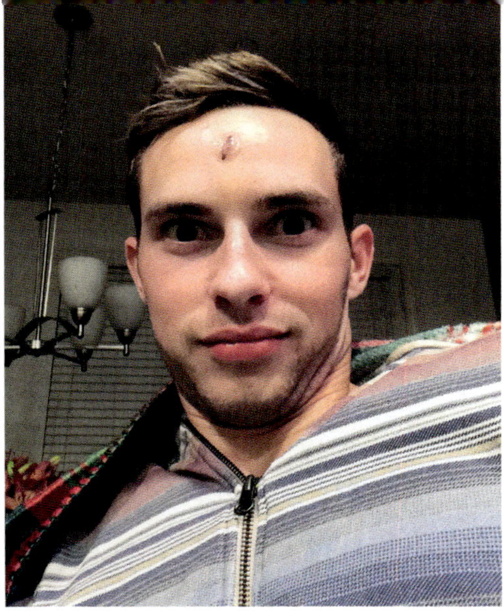

The notorious gash I got from Ashley's teeth right after I came back from the emergency room.

Ashley and me pre-nationals 2015 when I was fully dried out and the thinnest I ever was.

This is the costume I stole from Derrick when I was poor. This is a bad picture, but my abs look great.

My purple hair and Bianca pregnant. I hope it didn't scare the baby.

My sister Dagny and me in New York the week after I won nationals.

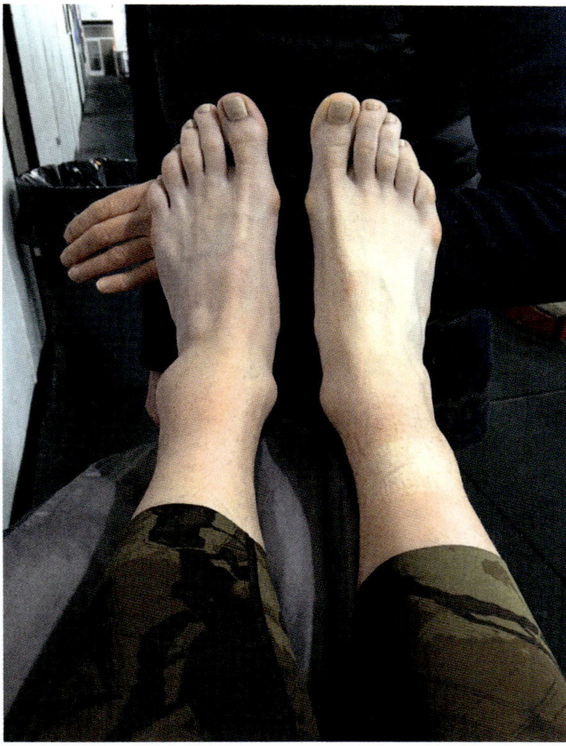

A broken foot and a fresh pedicure.

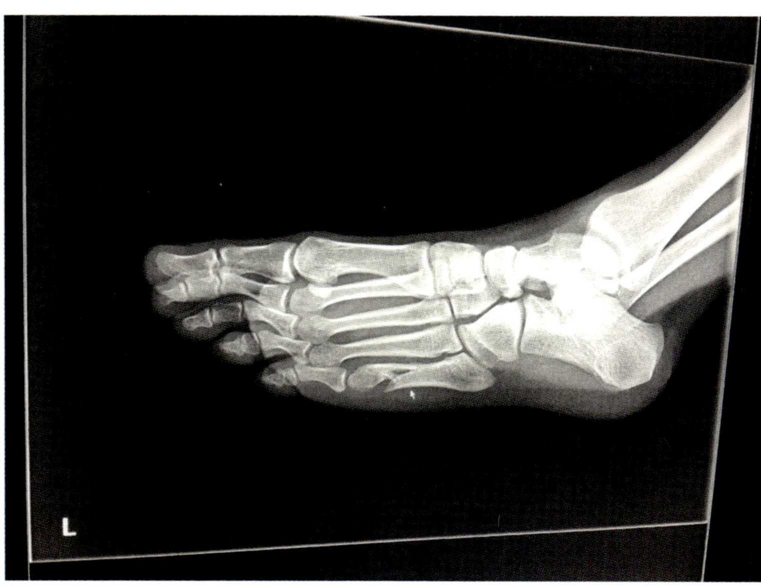

The X-ray to prove my foot was really broken.

Molly and me. She's an angel in my life.

Ashley, me, Sarah, Stephen, and Brett dressed in white at the Paul Smith pink wall in LA. An iconic moment.

My mom and me in a church in Helsinki while I was simultaneously swiping on Tinder. Was not struck by lightning.

Derrick and me when we arrived in Korea for the Olympics.

This is literally the only picture I have of Rafael. Believe it or not, he's smiling.

Me in my famous slutty tank top in an Olympic promo shot.

Signing the paperwork to donate my Olympic costume to the Smithsonian.

Me and my Olympic team leader Tina Lundgren before the opening ceremonies.

Jenna Chmerkovskiy and me during our first rehearsal for *Dancing with the Stars*.

Looking good is the best revenge.

Courtesy of Roxie Full

I didn't pay for anyway, so we were both getting something out of the deal.

Ashley liked what I was doing with Mirai and asked me to do a program for her as well. I'm twenty-four, a brand-new skating choreographer, and I already have two national champions and an Olympic medalist on my roster. Rippons don't do anything half-assed.

Ashley was much different as a collaborator than Mirai. She's incredibly headstrong, which is one of the things I admire most about her, but if she didn't like something I wanted her to try, she let me know right away. Who was I to argue? It was also hard because we were like brother and sister. In this situation, she was both Ashley and Mary-Kate, and right now I just felt like the bowl of cigarettes at the wedding. She knew exactly what she wanted, but I didn't know exactly how I was going to deliver.

Finally I called in another choreographer I used to work with, Cindy Stuart. She came to a session one day, and when I would make a suggestion, Ashley would say, "No, no, no. I don't like that."

I would just give Cindy a look and say, "Cindy, what do you think?" Cindy would suggest a move that was very similar to the one I had just suggested (and sometimes completely different), and Ashley would do it and love it. Cindy was like our Seeing Eye dog and in those moments became something of a mentor to me. I was totally new and had no experience, so I needed Cindy there to back me up and help me work through different problems that come when putting together a program, because I wanted Ashley to walk away and not feel like she messed up by asking me for help.

Ashley paid Cindy for her time, of course, and she helped us create something that made Ashley feel really good, which, as a choreographer and friend, is all you want. Ashley would eventually win another national championship, so whatever the three of us did together, it worked. (I just breathed on my nails and pretended to buff them on my shirt, but you can't see that because this is a book.) It also had nothing to do with my help, because Ashley skated great on her own.

This was all going down the summer after the Olympics, and being in the rink choreographing reminded me I still loved skating. I wasn't sure I was that excited for the competitive aspect of it as I used to be, but I knew my future was going to be on the ice.

I was still practicing and working with Rafael, but he was sort of checked out. Because I was being half-hearted, he was being half-hearted. He was still giving me the usual technical help so I could improve, but when I would ask him what to do about my skating career in general, he would just say, "You need to figure it out on your own." He was absolutely right about that—it was a choice I needed to make. I'm not one to listen to advice much anyway.

I was split between going back to being a competitive athlete working full-time and focusing on my career as a businesswoman being a coach and choreographer. I still hadn't achieved all my goals competing, but I never wanted to be that skater where people say, "Oh, he should really hang it up before he embarrasses himself."

Maybe if I was going to the Olympics, it wouldn't be as an athlete but as a coach and choreographer. I was already making some money doing that, so I knew it was possible. Should I just dive into that and become the best coach I can be and maybe have skaters in the 2018 Olympics or the 2022 Olympics? Should I take all the focus I've put into being a competitive athlete and dedicate that focus to helping others? I was split right down the middle.

While I was trying to figure out my professional life, my personal life was—how do you say this in English?—a raging dumpster fire.

When Ashley came back from the Olympics, she was a star

and took me as her plus-one all over the place, including the Oscars. We were still so young, so I naturally rented my tuxedo from a place at the mall, and she got tricked into buying her Oscars gown. You live and you learn. The two of us walked into the Governors Ball while John Legend was playing. We did what anyone else would have done: We ran to the cheese table and enjoyed the musical stylings of John Legend while we ate our cheese with chicken tenders. I also had poked myself in the eye earlier that day and it looked like I had pink eye, which pretty much summed up my life during that period of time: in a corner with potential pink eye eating cheese, but still with celebrities.

One night we went out to Eleven, which was a trashy gay bar in West Hollywood that is now closed. Of course, the bartenders were enamored with beautiful Ashley who they had just watched in the Olympics, and they gave us all these free drinks. Well, they gave Ashley free drinks and she fed them to me, like a true friend. We were having a great time, celebrating her being back and me not actually having pink eye.

We sashayed into the VIP section at the club, which was full of people, none of whom we knew. Ashley just plopped down on the couch and took a seat next to a pair of crutches that at the time we never questioned why they were in the club in the first place. I went on the dance floor and started dancing with this random girl. We're both drunk, so we're doing this move where we grind on each other all the way down to the floor, like a dirty version of when it gets "a little bit softer now" during "Shout."

We both fell onto the floor, which, at Eleven, is disgusting and probably looks like a Petri dish from Area 51. I know where that floor has been, but in this exact moment it made perfect sense that I ended up on it. While on the floor I looked up and Ashley was looking down from in the VIP section. All the people had gone and she was still sitting next to that pair of abandoned crutches. We had no idea whose they were—maybe the drinks at Eleven cured someone's broken foot and they left without them?

Ashley shouted over some Beyoncé remix, and even though I had heard "Single Ladies" at least twenty times that night, lying on the floor of this club made it feel like the first time. "Don't dance with her; come dance with me!"

I picked the girl up who is also on the floor with me and said, "It was a pleasure."

I joined Ashley but I'm not quite in the VIP section, which is raised up a little bit from the dance floor. She's up there and I'm below dancing. I did a head roll to one side, and my forehead connected with Ashley's two front teeth. Immediately my head was killing me, and I put my hand on my forehead. "Ashley, are you OK?" I ask.

"Yeah, I'm fine. Are you?"

"I think so," I said, but then I took my hand off my forehead and it was covered in blood.

Ashley was clearly alarmed that my forehead was gushing blood, but I said, "No, it's fine. It's fine. Look." I brush my hair over it and just pretended like nothing was happening. There's nothing a bang can't hide.

Right then a friend we had made in the club came from the bathroom and saw my forehead covered in blood and brain goop with my hair congealing in the whole mass. The first thing he said is, "I think you need to leave."

"No, it's fine," I told him. "I covered it up."

"I think you need to leave," he repeated. "If only for your dignity." I had already lost that while rolling around on the floor, so I still need convincing. I kept seeing people looking at me and saying, "Oh my God," when they spotted my injury. It was the shock of the gore that made me realize maybe it wasn't everyone else being dramatic—maybe it was me.

We went home and I decided to do the responsible thing, which was clean and dress my wound. I made a mess washing it out in the sink and then globbed Neosporin on it, put a piece of gauze over that, and secured it to my head with a piece of Scotch tape, like I was Dr. Quinn, Medicine Woman. Ashley and I then passed out in the bed together.

When I woke up in the morning, I had bled through the gauze and the cut hadn't closed at all. I went to the hospital, where I told the doctor, "Yeah, the craziest thing happened this morning. I hit my head on the counter, and I'm really worried about it." I might have been more believable if I had told her I had walked into a door.

"Well, there is a bunch of dried blood around this wound, and it looks like it happened about ten hours ago," the doctor said skeptically.

"That's weird," I said, keeping up the lie for a second. "OK, fine. I did it last night." Kids, never lie to the doctor. If you have a LEGO stuck up your butt or something crazy, just come clean. They always know.

I told the doctor the whole story about what happened and she says, "Are her teeth all right?"

"Um, excuse me," I say. "Can we focus on me?" And yes, her teeth were completely unharmed. I think maybe they are even stronger now.

The doctor thought the whole story was hilarious. The only thing she could do was put a giant glob of glue on it to keep it closed, so I had to walk around with this giant glue ball on my face until it fell off, which took about two weeks. The grossest part was when I would skate or exercise, I would sweat and it would come unglued, and a little stream of blood would trickle down my face. It was just a metaphor for my life at the time—a sloppy, somewhat-self-inflicted wound that wouldn't heal.

In the wake of my post-Olympic blues, I decided that I wanted a boyfriend. Why not add flames to the fire? Of course, I had my liaison with Scotty, and then I dated two guys after that. It's always challenging dating new people, but imagine doing it now with glue from the hospital on your forehead.

Right before the 2014 Olympics, I started dating this guy

named John that I met "at the gym." (For all you straight people out there, let me translate. "At the gym" means we met on Grindr.) John was cute and sweet, but he was incredibly passive. If I wanted to see him, I would have to text him. I'd always have to come up with the plan, pick the place to eat, and decide what time we were going to meet. It felt a little like babysitting more than dating. I finally decided to give him a test. I wasn't going to text him, so I could see how long it would take him to reach out to me. He failed this test, and I actually still haven't heard back from him. That was the end of John.

I wanted a real, actual boyfriend who thought I was cute and wanted to be around me all the time and would hold my hand in the movies. I was searching Facebook, looking at cute friends of friends, and that is where I found Pete. He was tall, handsome, and had a few random modeling shots on his profile. A part-time model seemed nice! It said his location was LA. Perfect.

We started messaging and hit it off, but it turns out he wasn't in LA yet—he was still living in Boston. I thought I was catfished once again. But he moved to LA a few months later, and we started dating.

The problem was that Pete was a dick. I was so blinded by love I didn't see the early red flags. When he moved to town, he lived in Hollywood, which was about forty-five minutes' driving distance from my house. Well, forty-five minutes on a good day or if every car in Los Angeles were vaporized by nuclear Armageddon. It was far, but if my ancestors could travel to America from Ireland for a better life, I was going to travel to Hollywood for the same.

Pete had a really nice car but insisted we always take mine whenever we went anywhere, and I never got to drive. I thought it was weird, but I didn't really question anything, because I was just like, "I never had a boyfriend before; maybe this is the way it goes and now I'm only allowed to drive when I'm alone?"

Once, I drove up to Hollywood and parked on the street. When we went back to my car a little bit later, I noticed something was different. It was familiar yet somehow strange, like a face without the eyebrows. Someone had stolen all four hubcaps—which are basically a car's eyebrows—off my sign-and-drive Volkswagen Jetta. I was devastated and felt totally violated that something like this had happened.

"We're so lucky," Pete said, as a way to console me.

"Lucky? How is this lucky?" I asked.

"It could have been my car. We're just lucky it wasn't."

Yeah, *we* weren't lucky. He was lucky. That I didn't murder him.

About two months after we started dating, I was performing in an exhibition skating show in LA. I invited my mom out to watch me skate, and I was so proud to have this hot boyfriend that I wanted to show him off to my mom.

We all went to the show, and afterward my mom went back to my house to go to sleep, and Pete and I went out to the cast party. Pete came home with me and spent the night. The next day the three of us hung out in the afternoon, and the plan was that I was going to drive Pete home to Hollywood in my eyebrowless car and then spend some alone time with my mom before she went back to Pennsylvania in a couple of days.

That day everything was going great, and my mom and Pete were really getting along well. Then Pete pulled me aside and said frantically, "Please don't drive me home tonight."

"Why not?" I asked, concerned. "Is everything OK?"

"I just don't think I can be alone tonight. Please don't leave me alone."

Looking back on it, I should have yelled at him. "What is wrong with you? You're a twenty-seven-year-old man. There is no crisis; get over it." But twenty-four-year-old lovesick Adam said, "OK. That's fine. I'll take care of it." I thought I was supposed to support my boyfriend no matter what happened—my Stockholm syndrome was flaring up.

Finally, my mom starts to get a little annoyed that there

is this third wheel around. "When is Pete going home?" she finally asked.

"Oh, he's not," I told her. "He's going to spend the night, and I'll drive him home in the morning."

"I came out here to see you. I want to spend time with you. I thought we were going to be able to spend some time together," my mom said.

The two of us started fighting, and I finally yelled for Pete, who was sitting in my bedroom. "Pete, get your things. I'm going to drive you home, and then come back here."

Pete gets his things together and I pack a quick bag, and we're getting ready to head to the garage and get in the car. By this point it's getting kind of late. Just as we're about to leave, Pete turns to my mom and says, "You know, if Adam leaves now, he's not going to get home until, like, two a.m."

"Oh," my mom said completely emotionlessly but with power.

I told Pete to get in the car, because I knew from experience that fighting with my mom was not going to end well for him. He was a rat, and my mom was a hungry Komodo dragon.

As we walked to the garage, my mom looked at Pete and then looked back at me and said, "He's weak." This "mom meets your boyfriend for the first time" scenario wasn't going the way I had planned. Or maybe everyone's mom calls their boyfriend weak to their face at first. I was still a beginner.

I drove Pete back to Hollywood and, since all that fighting erupted, decided to spend the night at his place. The next morning I went back to my place, got my skates and my mom, and headed to the rink to practice a bit. The whole drive there was completely silent. I spent the day skating while my mom sat on the side of the rink just watching. It was a Rippon vs. Rippon stubborn-off, and there is never a victor in one of these contests of wills.

In the car on the way home, my mom finally says, "So we're just not going to say anything all day?"

"What were you trying to pull yesterday?" I said. "You can't do that. I'm an adult. If I want to have people stay over, I can have them stay over."

"Pull the car over right now," she yelled. "I'm getting out." My mother is opening her car door on the 405, and I think she's going to get us killed, and if she doesn't get us killed, my car will be missing four hubcaps and one passenger-side door.

I pulled off the freeway and into the nearest parking lot I could find so that we could fight in a parked car like civilized people.

"Why do you need a boyfriend right now?" she asked me.

"I don't need a boyfriend," I said. "I want a boyfriend. I like Pete."

"He's not what you need right now. I'm not going to leave LA until you tell me that you're not going to date Pete anymore."

"You can't do that."

"Yes I can. I can tell you're really depressed right now."

"Of course I'm depressed. I don't know what's going on in my career, there are so many things up in the air right now, and now you hate Pete."

"I'm going to change my ticket and stay another week."

"No, you are not going to do that!"

Now I was stuck in this impossible position. Pete was so insecure he wanted me to pick him over my mother. My mom was so worried about me that she was certain I was wasting my time with someone who might get in the way of my being something more than I was. I had no idea what I wanted other than really wanting my mom to take her flight home later that day so I wouldn't have to deal with this anymore and I could have some time to think by myself.

I don't remember what I said, but I finally convinced her that Pete and I would just be friends and I would go back to being like a Ken doll with just a flat plastic front who did nothing except eat, sleep, and skate. I would have gotten a flat plastic front installed in that moment if it would have gotten my mom on that plane and helped end this nightmare trip.

I didn't break up with Pete, but I probably should have. We started to fight all the time because he was so insecure. He wanted to know where I was at every moment and wanted me to pay attention only to him. He didn't like my friends, because he said they weren't "cute" enough. It was really important to Pete to have cute friends. I don't know who is cuter than a bunch of professional figure skaters in their twenties, but to Pete it was cuter to be friends with other part-time models from Facebook who all went to Equinox at the same time and meal prepped together every Sunday than with us.

He also wanted to go out to bars and clubs all the time, which I couldn't do because of my training schedule. I told him, "If you have friends, you can go out with them—I've never stopped you. If you wanna go out to dinner with somebody and I can't, you can do that."

"We need to be doing everything together," he said. Even when I was in the middle of it, that neediness was exasperating, but I thought it meant that he just really liked me.

When we would fight, Pete would have an awful temper and he would throw things, and I would get really worried that he'd soon start throwing things at me. But when things were good, they were really good, and I thought that this is just what relationships were like—sometimes your hubcaps get stolen, and sometimes "we" are really lucky. I had never had one before, so I didn't know better.

While this was going on, the competitive figure skating season started again, and I had a few international events that I was invited to. More out of inertia than interest, I accepted. It's what I had done every year—why wouldn't I do it again this year?

I went to my first Grand Prix event in Canada, and it was awful. During the short program, I landed my first jump fine but fell on my second jump and popped my final combination. (A "pop" is when a skater takes off wrong and the body knows that if he pulls up and starts rotating, he will land badly and hurt himself, so the body involuntarily aborts the jump.) I only did a single and got no points for either jump. I could have gone out on the ice and picked my nose and farted at the judges and gotten as good of a score. Only twelve skaters are invited to each Grand Prix event, and after that skate I was in eleventh place. That's only because one skater withdrew. I was dead last.

After my skate Rafael asked, "Adam, do you want to skate or not? You really need to figure it out, and you need to pull it together for tomorrow for the long program. If you don't want to skate, that's fine, but if you keep skating like this, you're going to ruin your reputation, and it will be hard to start coaching."

I was embarrassed. I had just placed the lowest I ever had at nationals, and now I was last in my Grand Prix. The next day I was warming up for the free skate when the team leader approached me. At every international event there is a team leader who is basically the nanny for the entire delegation from each country. The leader makes sure you're on time, has the schedule of events, and will get you emergency supplies and everything and anything a skater could need. When I was skating, the team leader was a judge or technical specialist who was not judging at that particular event. Now the rules have changed, and the team leaders are all former skaters who no longer compete.

At this event the leader was Lori Johnson. She approached me while I was warming up, and she's crying. "I know you're better than this," she told me through her tears.

Then I started crying, and we're standing at the edge of the ice, a blubbery mess.

"I know; this is awful," she said.

"Yeah, this is awful," I agree. "I don't know what I'm doing here. I don't feel like I belong anymore."

"You're going to find your way," she said. I wasn't sure if I believed her. "It's going to be fine, but you've got to keep going."

I skated a bit better in the free skate and ended up tenth in the competition overall. The year before I had been second and fourth in my Grand Prix events.

Thanksgiving was right after that Grand Prix, and my friend Bianca—the same Bianca who drove me to Lake Arrowhead for the first time—invited me and Pete over to her parents' house in Orange County for dinner. I was so close with Bianca for so long that her mother and father were like an aunt and uncle to me.

At dinner Bianca's mother, Angie, asked me what I was going to do. I gave her the usual answer about how I didn't know if I wanted to keep skating and compete that year or if I wanted to start coaching or choreographing. I must have just sounded lost.

"You need to pull your shit together," Angie told me point-blank. "You either need to do it now and get to the Olympics or you need to stop skating. If you keep doing this half-assed, it's going to be really sad." She said it so matter-of-factly between bites of her tri-tip steak.

That is exactly what I needed to hear. I thought that sadness would probably start creeping if I did badly at nationals, but Angie made me aware that it was already happening. Rafael was still waiting for me to figure out what I wanted to do with my life and wasn't giving me much guidance. My mom wasn't offering any advice, because she had no idea what to say and she knew this was something I needed to figure out on my own. Pete, well, he just wanted to hang out with cute people at the Abbey and didn't care much about anything else. Angie had nothing to lose and was very black-and-white with me. She also told me she thought Pete was really hot, which was what I wanted to hear.

With all this still rattling around in my head, Pete and I had a ninety-minute drive back to my place, where we were staying that night. Pete insisted on driving even though we took my car so that nothing would happen to his. We were having just a boring conversation about something, and Pete brought up how we should invest money together and start a business one day. He didn't even have a business idea; it was just a vague notion that that is something we should do together. I, who wasn't being allowed to drive my own car, had some questions for my future business partner, the first one being, "LOL WUT?"

What inspired him to bring up me investing my money with him? Baby, I'll never know, but when I told him that I thought maybe this wasn't a good idea, he got very upset. "You don't believe in what I'm saying. You're not listening to me," he said.

"No, I listened to you," I told him. "I just think that maybe when the time comes, it might be best if we weren't business partners. Don't they always say not to mix business with pleasure?" None of this was pleasure, to be honest. I was dumb, but I wasn't dumb enough to think that getting into business with someone who threw things without warning was a good idea.

As we continued to argue this mysterious point, Pete started driving faster and faster down the freeway. Finally I realized how fast we were going. I looked over and the speedometer read 105 miles an hour. I didn't even know that the speedometer on the Jetta could go into the three digits. I thought to myself, *Holy shit, is he going to crash this car on purpose and kill both of us just to make a point?*

Finally I relented and told him he was right. I was wrong all along. Gosh, how stupid of me. Pete, you are the smartest and everything you say is right and I will love you forever and never leave you. Whatever I had to say to get him to slow down.

He got back to a respectable seventy-five miles an hour and I relaxed, but I didn't want to talk much more. I was thinking about what would have happened if I really had died in that moment. My obituary would have been about a skater who never quite made the Olympics with a shitty boyfriend and an excellent head of hair above a small scar on his forehead he got from drunk dancing into his best friend's front teeth. I wasn't going to have that. I wanted something better for myself. I still wouldn't break up with Pete for another few months, but I finally felt like I deserved better, and to do that I was going to have to grab on to the steering wheel myself.

Adventures of a Skating Raisin

At that same Thanksgiving dinner, another fortuitous thing happened—I met Bianca's new boyfriend, Denis. He was a professional ice skater and her co-star in Disney On Ice. I was excited to meet him because she had been talking him up for months about how nice he was to her. And I had seen the Instagram pictures, and this guy was like a Ukrainian Adonis with 0 percent body fat. I needed to see this in real life.

After Thanksgiving dinner, as we were talking about what the hell was going on with my life, Bianca had an idea.

"You should train with Denis," she said. "He will whip your butt right into shape."

"I don't know," I told her.

"What is the worst that can happen?" she said. "You have about two months until nationals. What have you got to lose?" I had already been on the floor of Eleven, so she was right.

I agreed to let Denis train me, and for a cold Ukrainian, he was pumped. "Let's do this!" he said like someone who knew they were about to introduce me to a world of hurt. We high-fived, and my fate was sealed.

We met down the street from my house—there is a track there that is attached to a school, which means we didn't have to pay to be there. (A bargain!) Denis showed up with a bunch of hurdles he had made himself out of pipes. Was I about to become a track star? Was I about to become the next Allyson

Felix, except not as pretty and slower? But these weren't like full-size track-and-field hurdles—some were shorter and some were taller. They were maybe about two to four feet off the ground and looked like half-finished contraptions he stole from Home Depot. Still, I had no clue what was going to happen.

Denis had me jumping over the hurdles in all sorts of drills. I'd face the hurdles and jump over them with both feet, then I would jump over them all with just one foot and then on the other foot, then I would jump over the hurdles sideways to the left, and then I would jump over the hurdles sideways to the right. It was the hardest I had ever worked out in my life. At the end of the first session, I thought Denis was going to see me either die or puke, or die and then puke right there next to one of his homemade Frankenstein hurdles.

As he was loading up everything into the car (I did not die or puke), he said to me, "You just need to dry out."

"Dry out?" I asked him. I was confused. Did he think I was wet?

"No, no," he said, in his thick Ukrainian accent. "Like a grape. You're too juicy. We are going to dry you out. You need to be like a raisin."

I still wasn't entirely sure what he meant, but I was pretty sure that he was about the hundredth former Soviet to call me fat in my lifetime. I felt like I was home.

Denis and I would work out at the track four times a week for about two or three hours each time. This was on top of starting to skate again full-time, which meant four hours of skating each day. My skating was getting worse at first because I would show up to the rink so sore from Denis and those goddamned hurdles. Still, I had this feeling it was working.

The best thing about working with Denis, though, was that it was like I was in the movie *300*. I felt like I was doing absolutely the most that I could possibly do. We were getting ready for battle, and I was becoming a badass. It also helped that our free "gym" at the track was no-frills. Denis would bring weights with duct tape on the plastic plates because the sand was falling out of them. We made do with what we had. It was the opposite of Equinox, but in the best possible way because I was getting down and dirty. There was even one time when the track was closed, so Denis and I made our way to a public park to work out. When we were at the park, a police officer came over to us and told us that we weren't allowed to train on city property. Now even the police were getting involved in our workouts.

I also loved Denis's cold, detached demeanor, because what we were doing had no emotion to it. At this point, skating was so fraught with emotion for me and had been so up and down over the past couple of years that I needed to be in an environment where everything wasn't on the line all the time. I would just jump the hurdles, and once I got good, Denis would give me a weighted vest and make me do them some more. It was matter-of-fact, and I loved it.

When I was training at the rink, I would maybe get about fifteen to twenty minutes of face time with Rafael where he was focused entirely on me, which is customary. The rest of the time he'd just be watching what I was doing out of the corner of his eye and pull me aside and give me notes.

Around Christmas the same thing happened as the year before, and they cancelled most of our ice. The difference is this year I said, "Not again, bitch. You guys can sit around and complain about how bad the ice is, but I'm going to do something else." I found another rink nearby that was mostly empty, and I would skate there on my own during the morning without a coach, and then I would go in the afternoon and skate with Rafael and the rest of his students.

The first day I showed up at the new rink and ran into some people I knew. They were like, "What happened to you? Something is different."

I had clearly lost weight after exercising so much with Denis, and you could see my sharp cheekbones and the cut of my jawline. But I wasn't just thin—I also looked powerful. I had officially dried out. I was a skating raisin.

That wasn't due just to all that hurdling and working out with Denis; it also had to do with my diet, which, frankly, wasn't a whole lot. I would have about six pieces of Dave's Killer Bread with I Can't Believe It's Not Butter every day. If I needed extra carbs, I would have a bowl of Honey Nut Cheerios with milk in the morning. And iced coffee, of course. There was always iced coffee, sometimes with six SPLENDA because you need to treat yourself every now and then.

I knew what I was doing was bad, but I found my funny way around it. I told myself that I didn't have an eating disorder. At least I didn't have the kind of eating disorder where I look in the mirror and think I'm fat even though I'm not. I was trying to be thin because, for my sport, the thinner an athlete is, the better he will perform.

I saw myself as a robot, and how would that robot perform better? He would perform better if he were thin. It didn't help that I was 148 pounds when I started my fitness journey. (Not that I'm fixated on weighing myself or anything, because I don't have an eating disorder.) Most of the guys I was up against were in the 130s and were starting to do quads—jumps with four complete rotations in the air. I know that 18 pounds of muscle is going to react differently, but that is 18 more pounds that I have to hoist up into the air and rotate four times in order to land a quad. That only makes my job harder.

As I was drying out, I got down to 142, and that was if I just had a haircut, didn't eat anything that day, and had just taken a massive poop. Still, I wanted to be thinner, always thinner, so that I could be competitive. Like I said, I knew it was bad, but I figured it was something I could deal with later.

I wasn't hungry all the time, because I got used to not eating that much food. The worst part is I started to associate that feeling of hunger and being tired with something good. I associated it with working hard. I associated it with being healthy, but it's not. My body was saying, "I'm hungry. I'm shutting down. I'm dying." And my brain is thinking, "Perfect. You go, girl. We're on the right track."

The hard part was that I had no incentive to stop. Before this, Rafael would make comments about my weight. I remember once at a competition he said, "You're the biggest one here, but you're not the worst skater," which is a compliment so back-handed it could slap me twice. He wasn't calling me fat though. He was telling me that I was out of shape, which I was, and I think something got lost in translation. He was trying to fine-tune the robot. I wasn't eating a lot, but I was doing really well and everybody's saying, "You look so skinny. You look good," and I'm thinking on the inside, "Fuck yeah!" As I started to perform better, there was no way I was going to change my diet. I was a skating raisin powered by nut-filled bread, and I couldn't believe it was working so well.

Denis was also really helping with my motivation. "Do you have all the hardest jumps in your program?" he would ask me.

"No," I said. "I've been playing it safe because I don't feel confident."

"If you're going to do this, you really need to do this," he told me. "You need to try quads again. You've got to keep pushing things."

Then I did push things. Then I did try quads again. Then I started to land them. Then I got some of my confidence back.

Then I started to change everything. I decided I wanted a new short program, so I choreographed one for myself. As hard as it was choreographing for others, the hardest client I ever had was myself. I couldn't step back and look at it. In the moment I would think, "Oh, I look beautiful. I look stunning." Then I would watch a video of it later and think, "Why do I look like an off-brand Janet Jackson background dancer?"

Speaking of which, I have the same reaction now when I see the highlights I got in my hair that year. Yes, much like coming out of the closet and going to your first Robyn concert, getting highlights is a rite of passage that every gay goes through. Pictures still survive, but if you love me, you won't try to find them.

I also decided to change up the choreography for my long program. It was about being in a dark place, because when I made it with my choreographer, Tom Dickson, at the beginning of the season, I was in a dark place. I didn't want to be in a dark place anymore. Mostly I just started smiling through the whole program and figured that was light enough.

At earlier competitions doing that dark program, I was wearing an old black mesh skating costume I had borrowed from my friend Derrick from when he was competing about ten years earlier. Now that my program was light, I needed a different costume. Sadly, I didn't have the cash for whole new costumes.

I ordered a shirt from a dance website. The shirt was white with a huge collar and a slit all the way down the middle of my chest. I asked my friend Braden Overett to add rhinestones along the collar and slit to give it a bit more flash. I had officially gone toward the light, Carol Anne.

I had new costumes, a new routine I choreographed, a new smile to add to an old routine, a new training program, and a new outlook on life. I finished my Grand Prix events before Thanksgiving and ended up tenth and fifth in the Grand Prix when I had been second and fourth the year before. To everyone on the outside, it looked like my stock was dropping, but I was saying to myself, "You can do this; you're on the right track." And now with Denis helping me out, I really thought I could.

When I was away at a competition in France, I got in a huge fight with Pete. I was at dinner with Ashley and all my other friends who were competing in the event, and Pete kept calling and texting me. We were in France, so it was nine hours ahead of the West Coast, so I figured I'd just call him when I got back to the room.

I should have known better because Pete hated when I was away at competitions. Every time he would drop me off at the airport to go, he would sob uncontrollably. Once before, when I was away, I was sharing a room with my friend Colin, who was always my roommate when we were traveling together. Pete called and I told him that Colin and I were hanging out and were probably going to go to dinner and that was it.

"That's great," Pete said sarcastically. "You're just going to go out and have fun while I have to sit here by myself?"

I apologized to him and told him I was sorry we couldn't be together, but I was thinking, "What do you want me to do—just sit in this hotel room and talk to you on the phone?" After that, whenever I was away and he would call, I would just tell him that I was going to bed instead of going to hang out with my friends, because I didn't want to deal with the fight.

That night in France I finished dinner with my friends, and we all went back to my room. Pete tried to FaceTime and it rang on my iPad, which was next to Ashley. She decided to answer it because she and Pete knew each other. "Hi, Pete," Ashley said, being nice.

"Hey, Ashley," he said. "Is my *boyfriend* there?" I knew the moment I heard the word "boyfriend" spoken like it was an insult that I was in big trouble.

"Hi, Pete," I said. "I was just at dinner with everyone and now we're back in my room."

"Don't you know I've been trying to get a hold of you for an hour?"

"Yeah, my phone died when we were at dinner, and I just saw when I plugged it back in." That was true. Pete had been buzzing me so often it pushed my 2 percent battery all the way down to 0.

"I don't appreciate you ignoring my calls and not calling me back. I have no idea what you're doing or who you've been doing it with."

He was screaming this on FaceTime in a room full of my friends. He should have known exactly what I was doing and who I was doing it with: I was competing and was with a bunch of other figure skaters. I mean, it's not rocket science. It's not even a word find on a diner place mat.

"I'm sorry, Pete," I said. "It was an accident. I'm so sorry. It won't happen again. Let me call you back in a little bit after everyone has left."

"Why do you have to go? Where are you going?"

"Nowhere, I'm just going to go hang out with my friends."

This went on and on until I left the room and Pete and I were having a yelling match over FaceTime in the hotel hallway. I finally calmed him down enough to get off the phone, and I went back into the room.

Ashley said to me, "I've never seen you back down from someone like that. Are you OK? That's really not like you."

That was the first time I felt kind of like an abused puppy who knows that a punishment is coming and there's nothing he can do at all to prevent it. As I started to settle back into my career, I had less and less time for Pete, which made things worse and worse.

After a year of being together, it all came to a head when I had to book some time to work with a choreographer out of town over his birthday.

I called him from the car on the way home from the rink and said, "I booked some time with Tom Dickson, the choreographer in Colorado Springs, but it's in two weeks."

"That's over my birthday," he said.

"Yeah, I know, but that was the only time that he was available that I could go out there."

"God, everything revolves around your schedule. You can never do anything. You can never go clubbing." Pete starts making it into this huge deal.

I said to him, “I don’t know if I can do this anymore. This is absolutely crazy.”

“You’re really talking like someone who doesn’t want to have a boyfriend.”

This was my window. He was giving me the chance to get out, and I was taking it.

“I don’t think I want a boyfriend,” I said.

“What?!”

“I don’t think I want a boyfriend anymore. This is nuts.”

“You’re kidding, right?”

“I’m not kidding.”

“You have to come over here right now.”

“I was already on my way over. I’ll be there in twenty minutes.”

“Promise me you’ll stay on the phone with me until you get here. I’m afraid that you’re serious.”

“I am serious, but let’s talk about this when I get there. This isn’t something we should talk about on the phone.”

“You’re joking, right?” he said, his voice starting to shake frantically. “Tell me you’re joking.”

“I’m not joking. I’ll be there soon.”

When I got to Pete’s house, he answered the door laughing. I didn’t laugh back.

“You’re so serious,” he said.

“Yes, I was serious about everything I said on the phone.”

“Well, I just want you to know that if you leave me, I don’t know anybody here and I’m going to be all by myself. I don’t know what I might do to myself.”

“I still care about you and I don’t want anything to happen to you, and I want you to know if you ever need anything, I’ll be here for you. But I can’t do this anymore. It’s too much.”

“I understand that, but you have to stay the night. You can’t leave.”

“No, I can’t stay here; I’m going to leave.”

I walked toward the front door, and Pete rushed past me to block the door. He turned the dead bolt and said, "You're not going anywhere." I've seen horror movies that start like this, and they never end well.

I said, "Pete, you need to move. I'm not staying." I went to reach around him, and he grabbed me by the shoulders and pushed me. In that moment I thought, "He pushed me; now he's going to hit me."

Again, I said, "I'm not staying here. You need to get out of the way and let me leave."

Pete started crying and said, "You think I'm going to hit you, don't you?"

"Yeah, I think you're going to hit me."

"This always happens."

"This has happened before?"

"Yes, with my last boyfriend. He thought I was going to hit him too."

Well, Pete, if this keeps happening, maybe you should change something about the way you treat your boyfriends. I never said that, but I probably should have.

I told him I was going to leave, and he didn't try to stop me this time when I left. I was still afraid he was going to chase after me, so I ran out of the building, walked a circuitous route to get back to my car to make sure he couldn't follow me or find me, and then I raced all the way home.

I didn't hear from Pete for several days after that, and then on Saturday morning there was a knock on my door. I figured it was the UPS guy with some crazy skin-care product I ordered on Amazon after two glasses of wine one night, as one does. I answered the door and Pete was standing there.

"Can we talk?" he asked, quiet and calm.

"Yeah, we can talk," I said and let him in.

"I don't know anyone here and I'm lonely. I'm not trying to get back together, but can we have a day where we're just friends?"

I'm thinking that this is the most adult thing he's ever said, so I agree. Yes, I'm that dumb, but I also wanted him to know that if he really needed someone, I would be there for him.

We hang out for a bit and then it's time for me to go to the track to work with Denis, so Pete comes to watch us. When I get there, Denis says, "What is Pete doing here?"

"I don't even know. Please train me really hard so I can just say I'm tired and this can end quickly," I said. The whole thing was crazy.

After that Pete and I had lunch and hung out for a little bit, and it was actually really nice. After lunch he told me that he had forgotten something at my house and asked if we could go back to pick it up.

We go inside, he gets what he had left, and he said, "We had a great day, didn't we?"

"Yes, we did."

"We can have more of these days."

"Actually, I don't think we can."

"Please let me stay the night. Just let me stay the night."

"I don't think that's a good idea. I think you should leave."

"You never cared about me."

"That's not true. I did care about you."

"Well, I'm not going to leave."

"Pete, you really need to leave now."

This conversation continued and repeated for the next three hours—I wish I were lying to you. I wish you didn't just have to read that I spent three hours of my life fighting with an ex-boyfriend who tricked himself back into my house like a clever gremlin.

"Fine," he said, finally tired of our back-and-forth. "But if I walk through that door, I'm never going to reach out to you ever again."

"I think you should leave," I said, really underlining it.

Pete walked out the door and I locked it as soon as he left. I locked all the doors in the house and all the windows. He was calm when he left, but I was still afraid he was going to break in and try to stab me like it was the opening scene of *Scream* and I was Drew Barrymore in a bad wig.

He was true to his word—after he left that day, I never really heard from him again. When he wanted back his fake Christmas tree that he had left in my storage space, he even had a friend of his call a friend of mine to set up a time to pick it up. I did what anyone would have done. I brought it to the Salvation Army and texted his friend the address of the drop-off and told him that if Pete still wanted it he could get it himself. If he had asked for it, I honestly would have driven it to him, but he couldn't even do that. My mom was right all along: He was weak.

Pete came along at a time when I was really feeling bad for myself, and I think I needed someone to make me feel better. I needed someone who was going to make me feel attractive and wanted. I needed to have a boyfriend to prove to the world that I had my life in order enough to at least carry on a relationship. I also felt so bad about myself that I thought I deserved to be treated the way Pete was treating me. I felt like I was someone who was always letting people down and upsetting them, just like I always let Pete down and upset him.

As my life got back on track, and especially after my skating got back on track, I knew that wasn't true. I deserved someone better, someone who appreciated all the hard work I was putting in and would love me for it, not think that it was getting in the way of their picture-perfect Instagram life.

With Pete out the door, it was time for nationals, which is essentially the culmination of the season, because after that the only competition is worlds, and only the top two skaters in the country go to worlds. I was skating very consistently and I had more confidence than ever, thanks to all the work I was putting in. Going into it, I had nothing to lose. It's not like the year before when I was slacking off but still pressuring myself to be perfect all the time. This year I showed up thinking, "If this is my last competition, I will walk away knowing I gave it everything I had."

I knew that everything would be fine, even if I was awful. I also knew I wasn't going to be awful, but just in case, I was prepared to be awful and walk away proud of myself.

I asked Rafael if Denis could come with us to nationals. I knew Rafael's attention would be split between Nathan Chen and me. Nathan had been skating with Team Rafael since he was eleven, but at fifteen he was turning into something of a phenom. I wanted someone who would be giving me 100 percent of their focus. Also, I owed so much of what had happened in the last few months to Denis, so if I was going to be celebrating, I wanted it to be with him and his freaking hurdles.

When I got to nationals, I had the white shirt I had bought on the internet that Braden stoned, which looked great but was still a little loose. I couldn't afford to get it tailored, but I knew that at nationals they always have an emergency seamstress on call in case you tear something or lose a button. I called her up and said I had a pull in my costume and then I said, "Do you think you can also take in my shirts if you have a chance?"

"I'd be happy to," the seamstress told me. "No one ever really uses me, so this will be great."

She made both of my costumes look like they were custom-made but on a T.J. Maxx budget. You know I love a deal.

Before I went out to skate, Denis was surprisingly pumped. "We're gonna do this!" he said. "Fuck everybody!" I've never been much of a hussy, but in that moment the idea of fucking everybody was pretty appealing.

I skated the short program I had choreographed for myself, and it is still one of the best performances I've ever skated in my whole career. I lightly stepped out of my one quad lutz, and I hit all my jumps and start to think, "I did it; I'm going to win nationals."

But I quickly remind myself that was the mind-set that had

been so detrimental—always chasing perfection, always chasing the top spot. Instead I tell myself, "Focus on what you need to do. Focus on enjoying this moment." That's what I did and I skated really well.

When I got off the ice, I was really proud of what I had done. I just felt like I was owning myself. I was confident in my own ability to be a competitor. But when the scores came in, they weren't great. I was one of two people in the top five to try a quad, and I still ended up in fifth. Even Johnny Weir and Tara Lipinski said on NBC that they thought my scores were lower than they should be, and those judges should know better than to cross two people who always look like they're dressed for the Hunger Games.

I did not think I should have been fifth. That's not to take away at all from the other skaters, because they were also very good, but I could tell the judges weren't doing me any favors. Why should they? I hadn't been consistent. Do they really want someone who has been so unreliable for the past year going to the world championships?

The judges and US Figure Skating were essentially saying to me, "You get to be on NBC tomorrow, but that's it. You should leave."

At first I was upset and a little bit sad, but then I thought, "You know what? I didn't come here to do anything else. I came here to give this my best shot. So if I skate even better in the free skate and I'm still fifth, I'm going to be the best fifth-place skater that ever skated at nationals."

I went out there and I skated so hard, jumped so high, and spun so fast that I nearly flung the highlights right off my head. Forget yesterday—*this* was one of the best programs I've still ever skated in competition. When I finished, I knew I had crushed it and everything I had been through up to that moment had been worth it. I screamed loudly from center ice, and it was like everything—ups and downs with my mom, eating green apples for months, being totally poor, not knowing what I was going to do with my life, stupid Pete—was all coming out. I had finally put it all behind me by giving up that endless quest for perfection and just focused on doing the thing I loved most in the world.

As I skated to the kiss and cry, I realized my score didn't matter. Nothing that anyone could tell me about that performance could make me feel better than the accomplishment I felt in myself. Rafael was right: I needed to figure it out on my own so that when success finally happened, the sense of pride would be overwhelming—not unlike gay pride, which is overwhelming in its own rainbow-colored way.

The score came in and it was not only a high score; it's the highest score in the record of the US championships. When I didn't care about the numbers at all is when they finally came in. Thank God that kiss and cry was sponsored by Puffs, because I needed all the tissues I could get my hands on.

Then the old Adam snapped back and thought, "Holy shit, I could win!" I was at the top of the leaderboard until Jason Brown skated and went right above me, but only by a few tenths of a point. If I had scored a little bit better in the short program, I could have been champion.

I had to stop myself from thinking like that though. I had said the day before if I had been fifth, I would have been happy. If I had gotten second the year before—hell, if I had gotten *fifth* the year before—I would have been overjoyed. I told myself I was still a winner and it had nothing to do with the points or the rankings or any of that. I realized that what every mom tells every junior athlete, which none of them really believe, is actually true: Winning doesn't matter.

For me to skate the best I absolutely could, come up short, and still feel like a winner was the best lesson I ever learned. Not only did I feel like a winner, but I was also genuinely happy for Jason Brown, who came in first. I was put into this place where I needed to just push as hard as I could and do anything I could. I came out of that place, and all the sacrifices and hard work paid off.

That feeling of personal fulfillment was worth so much more to me than any result. That mattered so little to me. The medal mattered so little to me. I still took it, but you know what I mean.

I can't take all the credit. I completely owe the turnaround in my attitude and training to Denis, and I don't know that I can ever repay him. I also owe it to Rafael, who gave me the space to either succeed or fail on my own but was always there when I needed him. And to my mom, who taught me to be strong and to fight for myself, and to Bianca for introducing me to Denis, and to her mother, who whipped my ass into shape. I owe it to everyone who showed me a little bit of kindness and support while I struggled and to everyone who saw the bleeding forehead wound I sported for weeks and was wonderful enough not to say anything.

After those nationals, I was more grateful than I had ever been, and I didn't even have to come in first place to get there.

Last Night a Tank Top Saved My Life

I'm not going to say that coming in second at nationals in 2015 solved all my problems, but it sure did help. Because of my place at nationals, I went to the world competition that year and came in eighth. Now I was in the highest echelon of funding, which meant my financial situation wasn't nearly as dire as it was a few years ago. I never got any corporate sponsors, but I always dreamed that one of the brands that advertised on *RuPaul's Drag Race*, like Fierce Drag Jewels or Anastasia Beverly Hills, would show up at my house with one of those giant checks that you only see with lottery winners or viral-video stars on *Ellen*.

My mom came to nationals that year, and it was the first time in my life she could just sit back and watch me skate. Once I started working with Denis, I asked her to come. I just had a feeling I would be OK and it would be a moment we could share. She came not expecting anything but just to be supportive, and I think it made my surprise silver medal that much more emotional.

She came to almost all of my competitions, but I never liked to know where she was sitting. It was so much easier to perform when the entire audience was anonymous rather than being aware that anyone I knew was watching. But after I crushed it on the ice, I wanted to know where she was in the stands. I saw her sobbing and cheering, maybe even more emotional than I was myself. It was the happiest I had ever seen her because I think she arrived with no expectations of me doing well. She was just there to enjoy my skating, and it ended up paying off for both of us. That pressure I had felt was finally gone.

After that, something in our relationship shifted for the better. I think she saw that I had reinvented myself as an athlete and for the first time in my adult life I really had my feet underneath me. She could support my decisions, and when she didn't like something I did, I told her I was going to do it my way anyway, and she was fine with that.

What I realized was we weren't in a position to get to that place before, because she was my mom as well as my manager, my therapist, my sponsor, and my accountant. How was she supposed to know which hat I needed her to wear at any given time? When I was able to grow up and navigate my own career and manage my own money, that wasn't a struggle between us anymore. My mom didn't have to be other things; she was allowed to be the one thing I always wanted her to be: just my mom.

Things were going well between the two of us when the season wrapped up after my eighth-place finish at worlds. During the summer break, I decided it was time to come out publicly. It was the perfect opportunity because I didn't want to come out before, when I had just missed the Olympic team and was kind of out of shape. There was all this momentum around me after my surprise second-place finish, and I felt like that was the best representation not only of me as a skater but also of me as a gay athlete. When I came out, I wanted it to be from a place of strength. I remember when I first started coming out to my friends and family, I would watch Tyler Oakley's YouTube videos and read lots of articles about gay athletes and gay actors. I would find any coming-out story I could, and it always made me feel that if they could do it and be fine, then I would too. Now it was time for me to add my own voice to the mix, because I thought I could be a good representative for the gay community.

I already had the highlights and just started using Invisalign, so I felt ready. What more did I need?

My mom was scared for me to come out for the same reasons she was before. She didn't want this to be the one thing that kept me from making the Olympics. I decided that if this was the thing that would keep me off an Olympic team, then so be it. Coming out was more important to me. It was bigger than me. It was for that insecure little boy in Scranton I had been so many years earlier and all the other insecure little boys out there who I could help.

I found the perfect opportunity because *SKATING* magazine, which is produced by US Figure Skating, wanted to do an article about Ashley and me. She had just won her third national title, I was back on the world team, we had the same coach, we trained together, and we were best friends. Who didn't want to read that story?

I told Renee Felton, who was in charge of media relations for USFS, that I wanted to come out in the article. It was important to me that I come out through US Figure Skating so it could be a subliminal sign to young people that the organization is behind this and they support their out athletes. I made my intentions clear to Renee before we had even met the journalist doing the story, and she told both the president and director of USFS. They both got in touch with me and said that they were behind me 100 percent. It's not like anyone in the sport didn't know. I always had too much charisma, uniqueness, nerve, and talent to ever present as straight, but now the world would know.

Renee told the journalist she assigned to the story, Amy Rosewater, I wanted to come out and that she should find a good, appropriate way to bring it up in our conversation. Since that NBC producer never got her Pulitzer for my coming-out story, maybe Amy would.

I told Ashley what I wanted to do, and of course she was on board, especially because when I came out to her and shared such a huge life moment with her, it only made our friendship stronger. One of the questions the reporter asked me was what my coming-out experience was like. We talked a little bit about that, but it was just neatly folded and tucked into the article, very inconspicuous. It was just there.

Once I took that leap, my mom couldn't have been more supportive and happy for me. She was the first one to post the article on Facebook and tell all her friends about it. For a minute, it seemed like she was the only one who noticed. It wasn't like I was on the cover of *People* saying, "I'm gay," like Lance Bass or Ross Mathews on any given day. This was a few sentences in a magazine that only ice skaters get. After about three weeks, it finally got picked up on ESPN and in the sporting press, but the main reaction was support from everyone, along with the feigned shock that a male figure skater came out.

Everyone believes that figure skating is gayer than your aunt who brings her "roommate," both of whom are avid bird watchers with matching haircuts, to Christmas dinner every year. In reality not everyone who skates is gay. I grew up in a skating world where Johnny Weir, who wears women's clothing, does Victorian women hairstyles, and wears high heels, didn't feel comfortable enough to come out of the closet until he was done competing. Now he's on NBC and everyone hangs all over his every outfit. It's a different world.

Part of what had changed was just something in the culture. Gay marriage was legal, there were gay athletes in other sports, and certain parts of the LGBT rainbow were gaining more acceptance by and large. (Trans people still have to fight to be in the military and use whatever bathroom they want, so there's still a ways to go.) But also, the difference between Johnny and me was one of expectation. I was a national champion, but he was a three-time national champion. There was an expectation during his career that he could win a world championship. I never had that kind of scrutiny, so maybe it was easier for me to come out because I had less to lose. But just like I refused to, Johnny never compromised himself. He just told people it wasn't any of their business.

People like Johnny are what allowed me to be me. Even before he was a broadcast superstar, he really pushed this idea that someone could be a successful skater and also maybe an alien from a different planet.

Rudy Galindo, the first openly gay ice skater who came out in 1996, was also a big inspiration for me, especially later in my career. He was a national champion in 1996, came in third at the world championships that year, and then retired before the 1998 Olympics. He was always an underdog, and it made me feel like I could be who I wanted to be, and if I delivered, like Rudy did, I could still get the scores needed to win.

When the magazine came out, it was around the same time that I met a boy named Shawn, who was the videographer for USFS. Every year there is a governing council meeting for the organization where everyone gets together to talk about the rules. My friend Douglas, who loves a deal as much as I do but is way more practical, told me to sign up for the governing council and volunteer for a committee. Everyone who is on a committee gets flown to wherever the annual meeting is, so we could get a free trip out of it and hang out together. To sweeten the deal, while you're there you vote on different rules for the lower levels, and every time I got to vote I felt like Olivia Pope from *Scandal.*

That year we got an all-expenses-paid luxury vacation to Colorado Springs, where we could stay at a DoubleTree and get free cookies. All members of USFS are allowed to watch the annual meeting online, so Shawn's job, as the videographer, was to film it for them. I'm sitting in this meeting, kind of spacing out, and all I could think was, "Who is this hot video guy with his cap on backward?" When USFS gives you lemons, make backward-cap lemonade.

Of course, I find a way to get to know this cute guy a little bit, and eventually I found out that he's gay. I also discovered he was in the closet to most of his family. When he tried to come out to them, they sent him to conversion therapy. Now he just kept quiet about being gay. He was born and raised on a small farm and had just moved to the big city of Colorado Springs, but this is the same Colorado Springs that is home of the notorious anti-gay group Focus on the Family. I discovered all this when we all went out to a group dinner and I sat next to Shawn so I could pry and flirt but, you know, mostly pry.

After I took a few trips back to Colorado Springs for training and working with choreographers, Shawn and I started dating. He was the nicest, sweetest guy, and because this was his first relationship, he thought that every idea I had was the best idea and I could do no wrong. After being with Pete, who always told me I was wrong, this was really a great feeling.

That summer, while all this is going on, I'm still working with Denis, but not nearly as much. I didn't need to transform like I did before—I just needed to maintain what was working. I was already a butterfly; I didn't need to turn into a butterfly again. Well, I had stopped highlighting my hair and got my eyebrows waxed, so I was still evolving into a more beautiful butterfly, but in different ways.

I was fully in the driver's seat. When I would meet with Rafael, I would tell him my plan and he would let me know if I needed to change it at all. My skating was getting stronger and stronger, and for the first time I was fully out and had nothing to hide (except for the scar where Ashley's teeth hit me in the forehead).

I decided for that season I was going to skate to Queen's "Who Wants to Live Forever" for my short program and a Beatles medley for my free skate. I sent the tracks to my mom to tell her that was my music for the year.

"You're such a beautiful skater—are you sure this is what you want to do?" she asked. My mom's ideal for my skating career would always be me skating to Josh Groban in the puffy shirt from *Seinfeld* with my natural blond, curly hair.

"Yes, this is what I'm going to do," I told her.

"OK," she said, ending the conversation and agreeing with my choices. It was a new look, but one we both loved.

That summer I also dyed my hair purple, which meant that it now clashed with my red-and-yellow costume, which meant I needed something new to wear to my competitions. Yes, that is the gayest sentence in this entire book.

The violet hair, the pop music, and the new costumes seemed to be helping, because I was being my authentic self out there, which is the one thing in skating no one else could—or would want to—do.

At my first Grand Prix event I came in fourth, which was much better than my tenth-place finish the year before. Then my gay evolving butterfly self and purple hair went to my second Grand Prix in Russia. I was a little bit scared because of how they treat gay people in the country, but it was fine. I traveled there with Rafael's wife, Vera. If you ever travel to Russia, the best way to go is with someone who is Russian. You will have a wonderful time. They know where they're going, they can speak the language, and they know when someone is trying to pull shit on you and won't let anyone mess with you. Maybe we should put Vera in charge of our elections.

I was trying a quad in my program, and I decided during the warm-up that I just really didn't feel like doing one that day, because I knew I wasn't going to land it. In the morning practice, the day of the competition, I had slightly dislocated my shoulder, a new trick I learned in my old skating age. I knew I was going to fall, and I didn't want to risk it. I took the quad out and still ended up getting a personal best score, which landed me in the bronze medal position. My friend Ross Miner, who had been skating with me since we were twelve, was in the same competition and he came in fourth.

Because I was in third, I had to get my costume back on to stand on the podium. I was leaving the locker room, which was right across from the judges' room. I see all the judges standing in the hallway with white faces, and they're looking right at me.

"We're very sorry," one of the judges said, which is exactly the thing you don't want to hear from a judge after a competition. "We had to go back and adjust the scores because we gave Ross a level three on one of his spins, and it should have been a level four. When we recalculated it, Ross came in third and you came in fourth."

Ross was standing with me in the hallway, and he looked at me and said, "I'm so sorry."

"Don't be," I told him. "It just means I was never third. It's not a big deal. You skated really well, and you are actually the bronze medalist. Being third for ten minutes was great, but go get your costume on and get out there on the podium."

Ross got his medal, and later that night everyone from Team USA was out at dinner celebrating. Ross pulled me aside and said, "I really commend the way you handled that today."

"Duh." I said immediately afterward, "I was the rightful fourth-place finisher and you were the rightful third-place finisher. It's really not a big deal. You deserve it and I know you would do the same if the roles were reversed." Remember this because it's going to be important later. (That is what we call foreshadowing.)

As nationals were approaching, I had a conversation with my mom and she said, "I think you should dye your hair back." It was still purple, and I loved my purple hair because it made me uncomfortable. I felt insecure about it every day because I was sure, for the first time in my life, someone was going to come up to me and call me "homo" because of my hair.

That never happened, because I never gave them a chance to

say it. I was confident about it and I owned it. I gave off a "Yeah, my hair is purple. So what?" vibe.

"I think for nationals you should have your natural hair color," my mom said. "You are so many things that I don't think you need to make this statement to stand out."

I told her I wasn't going to do it, but it marked a major shift in our relationship because I thought about what she said and really considered her advice. We were listening to each other and treating each other like adults.

Then I heard from an official who said I might want to rethink my purple hair. "That might be the one thing that pushes the conservative people away," he said. "You skate to the Beatles; you skate to Queen. You're really pushing being modern, and it would be dumb if anyone ever marked you down for something as unimportant as your hair." For the first time ever, the notes from the judges were real and they didn't actually come from my mom.

After that I decided maybe I would make the concession. They were both right. I didn't need the shock of my hair to make me stand out. I was skating the best I had in my career by being totally myself. I could let that speak louder than any haircut, even the crappy *Avatar: The Last Airbender* Mohawk I once got by mistake in a janky mall in China.

Before nationals, I asked Rafael if I could get coaching credentials for my good friend Derrick at the event so he could be with me and support me during the competition. Derrick is a skating coach and would already be there with some of his students; he just needed a different pass. We worked it all out and he was happy to be my support system, and I was glad to have him there on Team Rippon. Derrick is one of the most selfless people I have ever met, and to have him as a friend, I feel so lucky, but to have him be a part of my team made me feel so ready.

I had a good short program, and during the free skate I did exactly what I had trained to do. I knew the scores going into the final skate and thought I might have done enough to clinch first place.

Since I had been doing well, I would feel confident and in control when I finished skating a program, but I never celebrated that much or got emotional. Over the past couple of years, I had been training so intensely that I expected myself to skate well, so when I did, it was just confirmation of what I already thought was going to happen. Then a friend of mine once told me I need to take time to celebrate myself and to have those moments in front of everyone so they will get excited too. That's Hollywood, baby.

When I finished, I thought, "I think I did enough, and I have to show that to everybody. Make a moment out of it." I cried a little bit on the ice, I pumped my fists, and I really took a second to celebrate and almost give everyone permission to celebrate with me, including the judges. I wasn't necessarily *faking* it—I was still emotional enough to cry, but I was making sure that I acted like a best supporting actress accepting her Oscar.

I go to the kiss and cry, and Rafael is standing behind me and Derrick is sitting next to me. The marks come up and it's enough. I'm national champion.

I start to cry for real for real this time, and Rafael punches me in the back and walks in front of me so the camera can't see him anymore. A lot of people watching at home thought he hit me and stormed off because I beat Nathan, who came in third and had just set a record for most quads landed in one program. What they didn't see was Rafael standing in front of me celebrating and screaming, "You did it! You did it!"

It was also great to have Derrick there by my side. Derrick gave me so much and helped me out when I moved to LA with no money. He became the big brother I never had and was the honorary seventh Rippon sibling. I felt like this was a way for me to give back and say thank you. Derrick was already coaching young, really strong international kids. Now he was the coach for a national champion skater.

Derrick is so modest and he would say, "I didn't do anything." But if he hadn't helped me, I wouldn't have been able to skate. He did just as much as anybody else ever did, and he deserved to be there. He had to be there.

After I won, the thing I remember feeling the most was relief. Maybe I was allowed to have my dreams come true after all. It was powerful because I realized I got there because I wasn't trying to be a national champion at all. Being a national champion isn't something you can control. For a long time I thought the right reason to do it was to win—after all, this is a competitive sport. But that wasn't the right reason at all. The only competition should be the one I was having with myself, and when I focused on that is when I finally triumphed. I know I sound like the coach of the Bad News Bears right now, but it really is true no matter how corny it is.

Instead, I focused on the things I could control, like the programs I skated, the way I felt on the ice, how I represented myself, who I was skating for. When I did that, I realized I'm doing it for the right reasons and the success found me.

Some of that success also had to do with coming out professionally. It wasn't so much everyone knowing that I was gay as it was not worrying if people thought I was gay. Having something to hide and worrying about people's perceptions can be such a burden. Once I was able to be honest and be myself, I started making different choices and doing the things I wanted rather than the things I thought people wanted to see. That made me feel smart, creative, powerful, and in control. I didn't feel like a passenger in my own career anymore.

That summer I was invited on the Stars on Ice tour for the first time. The tour was great, and a lot of work, but I got to hear myself announced as "reigning national champion Adam Rippon" every night, which, I'm not going to lie, are the only five words in the English language better than "new music from Britney Spears today."

Everything is going great, but I still had two more years before the Olympics. After I won nationals, Johnny Weir sent me a text that just read, Only two more years. Once he said that, I knew he was right. It seemed both close and far away at the same time, but I knew that if I could just keep hammering away for two years, I could do it. I was laser focused on February 2018.

Going into the next season I don't have purple hair anymore, so I wonder how I can push the envelope a little bit and decided to do my short program to Ida Corr's "Let Me Think About It," which is a straight up EDM dance anthem that you would more likely hear while lying on the floor of Eleven than at a figure skating competition.

I play it for Ashley and she says, "That's too much. You can't skate to that."

"I don't care," I told her. "No one else could and no one else would, and that's why I'm going to do it."

I sent the track to my choreographer, Jeffrey Buttle, and thought there was no way he would take me seriously and let me do it. I flew up to Toronto for him to set the routine with me, and my mom met me up there.

When I got to the rink, I asked him, "Do we have music?"

"Yeah," he said. "Aren't we going to use the song you sent me?"

"Yes," I told him. I was thinking to myself, "Wow, he's really going to let me do this." I was so excited, like I was getting away with something.

There is one lyric in the song that says, "Baby, I'll take you for a ride." At this point in the routine, I stop right in front of the judges, put my arms out like they're on a steering wheel, and give my hips a sexy gyration. As I'm doing this, my mom is on the side of the rink filming me on her phone, like Amy Poehler watching "Jingle Bell Rock" in *Mean Girls*.

This was also the first season that male skaters were allowed to show their shoulders in competition. If you tell any gay male performer that he's allowed to show his shoulders for the first time, he's only going to think one thing: tank top. I got one made—in pleather, naturally—just for this song. But it wasn't just a pleather tank top. The back panel of it was entirely see-through mesh. I wouldn't say it made me look like a whore, but it did make me look like a well-paid go-go boy in West Hollywood.

For a long time I was doing what I thought people really wanted to see. Now I was doing what I really wanted to see, and it was quite different.

The judges didn't necessarily love it though. I had one competition in Paris that was almost a disaster. It was over my birthday weekend (I know you know it's November 11), and I hate competing on my birthday. I feel like my birthday sets the tone for the year, so if I have a bad skate, then I might be cursed for the entire next year.

We flew to France the night of the presidential election. Before we boarded, all the eastern states were turning blue on the news and I thought, "Great, I'm going to land in Paris and Hillary Clinton will be president." Um. Yeah. About that…

The results of the election really got me in a bad headspace because it was the first time I felt that people really went out of their way to vote against someone like me. I felt like there was still so much hate in the world.

To make everything even worse, the morning we landed the team leader came up to me with bad news. "The referee told me that she is going to give you a deduction for your costume," she said. The referee had seen that I wore that costume in a competition a few weeks earlier and decided it was inappropriate. When she saw me wearing it again in rehearsal, she knew what was coming and offered her ruling. "It's because the back is see-through. The rule is that you need to have seventy percent of your body covered."

"That is ridiculous," I said.

"I think you should just do it," she told me.

"I'm not getting a deduction, but I'm also not going to wear a stupid T-shirt. I'll figure something out."

I walk through the rain in Paris to get to the subway and find an H&M. I go to the women's section and buy a size extra-small black T-shirt. When I get back to my hotel room, I have my friend Marissa Castelli come to my room with her scissors. I get the tiny shirt on my even tinier dried-out raisin body and then put my tank top over the shirt and tell Marissa to cut off all the fabric that is sticking out from the tank top. I really trusted Marissa because she was the first person who told me I should wax my eyebrows. She knew what she was doing.

Now the back wasn't see-through, and I still got to wear my tank top. I was willing to play by the rules, but I was going to play by my rules. I skated great later that day, had no deduction, and everything was perfect.

The next day I landed the cleanest quad I had ever landed in competition and ended up getting third at the event. Despite the new president and the equally fascist fashion police at the rink, maybe it wouldn't be such a bad year after all.

I did so well at both my Grand Prix events that I qualified for the Grand Prix Final for the first time. This is one of the most elite events in the skating world, where only the top six skaters from the Grand Prix series are invited. Getting to the final had been one of my goals for a long time, and I finally accomplished it, in a tank top, no less.

When I got to the event, I was one of the oldest skaters there at the overripe age of twenty-seven. My other competitors seemed like kids, and they were all doing four or five quads in their programs. I had one quad that I had just landed in competition for the first time, and I didn't always include it, because it was still iffy.

I fell right back into that place where I didn't feel good enough, where I felt like I was a fraud. I felt embarrassed and like it was a joke that I was there. This was a backslide into my old way of thinking, where I pressured myself to be perfect and come in first or else it wasn't worth it.

I was surprised that I backslid like this, especially because I think it hurt my standing in the event. My secret weapon was always my consistency. I wasn't always the best, but when someone had a bad day, I never did and I could end up beating them. I know at this point in the book it sounds like I had a lot of bad days, but by now I had gotten over that and was always very consistent. But with a field of six, I wasn't thinking about that; I only thought that I was the worst, and that made me have a bad day. A couple of the other skaters had bad days as well, and my secret weapon of consistency failed me.

I ended up sixth, which is last place. When I got home, I really tried to explore why I felt like shit about it. Yeah, I was last, but that meant I was still the sixth best in the world. I was working really hard, doing what I wanted to do, and I qualified for the first time. I forgot to look at that accomplishment and was letting all the other stupid stuff get in my way. Last place at the Grand Prix Final was still better than how I had ever done at the Grand Prix Final—because, like, I had never qualified before.

It was a good reminder, though, that if I was going to keep doing this—and the Olympics were only a year away—I was going to have to do it because I loved it. I was reminded that I should have gone to the Grand Prix Final and just skated like it was an exhibition and enjoyed it and let everybody else compete. I tried to compete, and that is when I always end up failing.

There were now six weeks before nationals, and I was really able to focus on getting over this and training hard. I started skating really well and training a program where I was able to land two quads and another program with one quad. This put me more in the mix with the other top skaters in the world who were doing even more quads.

Every year, two weeks before nationals, officials from USFS come and evaluate the top skaters to see what they can expect at the competition. The first day they were there, I skated really well. That night I got a voicemail from Mitch Moyer, the head of Athlete Development at USFS and the only person other than my mom who leaves voicemails on my phone. He said, "I just wanted you to know that you're doing really well and we'll see you again tomorrow. Stay healthy. Don't get hurt."

The next day I went back to the rink, and I was getting geared up to skate for the officials that were all there. Rafael and I had been working on an exercise off the ice where he would hold his forearm out parallel to the ground and I would grab it and push off to jump into the air as he would launch me up a bit. It was meant to get me used to feeling the air underneath me so that I could get better height in my jumps and land the quads more easily.

Rafael calls me over and puts his arm out for me to do the drill. When he lifts me up, he lifted me higher than I expected and I landed all of my weight on my left ankle. I rolled it and immediately heard a crack.

As I sat there on the floor next to the rink, it was just like when you drop your iPhone in a parking lot. When you pick it up, either the screen is going to be fine and you just got away with murder, or it is cracked to bits and you won't text again for another week.

I looked down at my ankle and it was almost as big as my thigh, and I don't have regular thighs—I have big ice skater thighs, so that thing was huge.

I knew immediately that it was broken and I was totally fucked.

An Edible Disaster

The only reassuring thought I had in the moments after I hurt myself at the rink was that the day before I had gotten a pedicure and had my nails painted. You know how ballerinas have really gross toenails because they're walking on pointe all the time? A similar thing happens to figure skaters from using a skate's toe pick to hit in the ice all the time to execute jumps. I had my nails painted nude to cover up the black and blues underneath. I had never painted my toes before, but I was feeling cute.

As I lay there in incredible pain, the one good thought I could muster was, "At least when I go to the hospital, my feet won't look like a horror scene out of *Black Swan*."

The rest of the scene in the rink was a little bit like a horror movie though. Rafael was standing over me, and he looked about one second away from crying and clearly felt responsible for what happened. The other skaters rushed over to see if I was all right, and everyone was totally white because I was, like, the leader of Rafael's team and they didn't know what to do. Even worse, the US Figure Skating officials were there hunched over me.

"Maybe it's just a little sprained," someone said.

"It's not," I told everyone as I looked down and saw that my ankle had fluctuated in weight faster than Seth Rogen.

It's funny that I wasn't very upset in the moment. I was just determined and snapped into survival mode. I somehow knew that I would be OK. This made perfect sense for my journey, and this was going to be part of the story. I've come so far, then I break my foot, and then I'm going to the Olympics. Maybe we'd still get that NBC producer her Pulitzer.

"I think we need to call the hospital," I said.

Because the USFS officials were there, they were with a trainer from the US Olympic Committee named Brandon. He told us that the USOC had a deal with the UC San Diego Health Sports Medicine, where all medical treatments are free. Our rink was in Long Beach, south of LA, so it's about an hour-and-a-half drive to San Diego. The other closest hospital that anyone would recommend for athletes was in Irvine, so I either drive an hour to Irvine or ninety minutes to San Diego. I chose San Diego, because the allure of free anything is too much for me to resist. Even in pain I couldn't pass up the opportunity to take advantage of a deal.

Before we leave, I call over to Mitch and say to him, "You know I'm the second-best skater in the country, and you know that I'm on track to go to the Olympics. I really hope this will not affect my funding at all. I'm going do everything I can to get back as soon as possible. Here are my next steps..."

As I was trying to give Mitch my five-year plan, he interrupted me and said, "Why don't you go to the hospital first and we can talk about it later?"

Everyone helps me hobble out to Brandon's rental car because I can't put any weight on my foot at all. We get in the car and Brandon says, "Why don't we listen to some comedy?"

My leg is throbbing, my head is throbbing, I'm in so much pain that every second feels like an eternity, and I might vomit at any second. Truly the only thing that could soothe my soul was the voice of Sarah Silverman talking about her pussy. Brandon was really sweet and spent the next two hours in the car trying to do everything to distract me from how badly my ankle feels.

When we got to the hospital, he parked the car and I got out and tried to crawl on all fours into the building like I was some kind of demonic baby. Brandon looked at me like I was insane and then helped me get inside.

As soon as I arrived in the emergency room, a rush came over me like a warm breeze and I didn't feel any pain at all anymore. I just felt safe.

The doctors took an X-ray of my ankle because it was so large and in charge and told me that it wasn't broken. "Well, something is definitely broken," I told them.

"We don't see anything on the X-ray."

"I heard it snap. I know it's broken. Can you do another X-ray of my foot this time?"

"Well, you're already here so we might as well." My neglected foot would finally have its time to shine.

They took another X-ray and then came back later to say, "Yeah, you broke the fifth metatarsal." That's what the rest of us would call the bone in your foot that lines up with your pinkie toe.

Then the doctor said, "There's no way that you're going to be able to skate in two weeks for nationals." Why did she insist on telling me all these things I already knew?

The doctors gave me the choice. I could have surgery and get screws in my foot, which would get me back to skating more quickly, but the doctor told me that nine out of ten times athletes always feel like they have something in them and there needs to be another surgery to take it out. Or I could be in a walking cast for four to eight weeks and not have to have any surgery. The doctor said my foot broke at an angle that she felt confident it would heal properly on its own and that the extra time in a boot would be good for my mangled ankle as well. I chose the cast.

While I was at the hospital, I had a lot of time to think about my plan and also talk to Brandon. I was thinking about my training partner, Nathan Chen, who had recently come back from hip surgery. A year before at nationals in 2016, right after Nathan had just done four quads in a long program, we were all skating in the exhibition, which is called the Skating Spectacular. They empty the arena, turn down the lights, and get out the spotlights so the skaters can show off once the competition is finished.

I always hated it because it's only a couple of hours after the men are done competing, so there is a short turnaround from the physically and mentally exhausting competition and then going out there with our best razzle-dazzle to make the crowds happy.

Nathan went out and tried to do a jump and landed wrong. He hurt his hip so badly he had to be helped off the ice. He had surgery and then went away to the Olympic Training Center in Colorado Springs for training and rehab (like, physical therapy, not the rehab Amy Winehouse said no, no, no to). He came back a few months later not only totally healed but able to do more quads and different quads than he had done before. How do you have emergency surgery and get *better*? I didn't understand it, but I was inspired by it and I was hoping the training center could help me too.

I told Brandon that after nationals were over I was going to move there, live at the Olympic Training Center, and we're gonna get this done there. Also, if an athlete is in the upper echelons of a sport, like I was, everything at the training center is free: housing, food, trainers, physical therapists, even the Wi-Fi. This is a way for me to save a ton of money. I would say it was a deal, but considering all the money I spent to get me good enough to qualify to go, I was probably still in the hole—but it was still better than apples and trail mix.

There was also the hidden bonus of my boyfriend, Shawn, living there, so we would get to actually spend a few months in the same city. Do snuggles help heal a broken bone? Not sure, but I was willing to find out.

The other reason I wanted to go to Colorado Springs was more psychological. I didn't want to stay in California and ever associate my home turf with this period where I was weak.

My car was still at the rink, so after the hospital, Brandon drove me back there with my new boot and my new crutches. (Wait. Were those abandoned crutches at Eleven when I gashed my head on Ashley's teeth an omen all along?) Brandon asked, "Are you going to be all right to drive?"

"Yeah," I told him. He watched me get in the car and then drove away. Once he left I got out of the car and hobbled back into the rink. I went right over to the spot where I had broken my foot earlier that day and had a little ceremony. "I'm unhexing this spot. I'm not afraid of this spot; I'm not afraid of this rink." As Maxine Waters would say, I was reclaiming my time.

The next thing I do is go to the private locker room upstairs. We all have removable name tags in brackets above our lockers where we can keep our things, and I knew I wasn't going to be there for a while. I didn't want my skates getting all dusty and everyone having to see my stuff just sitting there every day. I slid out my name tag, removed all my things, and start carrying them to the car. But it wasn't like I had everything in a box and did it all at once. I'm struggling on my new crutches and had to go back and forth, like, five times to get it all done.

Once my life was loaded up in the back of the Jetta, I found the vacuum and vacuumed my locker and the carpet all around it. I wanted it to look like the different-colored wall after you take down a painting that had been hanging there for a long time. I wanted it to look like someone had died.

Nationals were in two weeks and my mom was planning on traveling to watch me skate, but instead she came to California to drink wine with me on the couch. Every year for nationals the women skate on Saturday and the men skate on Sunday. On that Saturday I would watch the competition on NBC while lying in bed. I was doing that again this year, so it felt familiar, but it also made me think that I was competing the next day. I had to keep telling myself, "No, self. Tomorrow you and your mom are making flatbreads and having Oyster Bay Sauvignon Blanc."

But I never went home and cried about it. That's what I

did in 2014 after not making the Olympics, and I learned that experience did not serve me well. Now I knew instead of feeling bad for myself, I just had to deal with it.

Part of dealing with the injury was realizing that I might not ever make it to the Olympics, and honestly, I was fine with that. If I didn't make it, I would be upset and devastated, but I knew I would survive. I wanted to go more than anything I had ever wanted in my life, but I knew it was circumstantial. I already had done everything I needed to do in skating. At that point, even if I never went to the Olympics, that was OK, because I had learned the lesson of what sport was about.

I had learned it was about personal discovery. I had learned it was about your hard work paying off in the satisfaction you feel. I'd learned all the lessons. I have friends who went to the Olympics, I have friends who are Olympic champions, and they're still the same people. I would still be the same person even if I *didn't* go.

I was not going to let this break me as a person. I will always be a national champion. I'd gone to every Grand Prix event. I'd done everything I needed to do. I was going to give myself a shot and still try to make the Olympic team the following year, but it wasn't something I needed to do. It was not going to define me as a person.

If I'm being totally honest, though, it wasn't all rainbows and unicorns. After nationals ended, my mom went to bed and I went for a walk around the apartment complex where I live. I decided I was going to send an email to Mitch Moyer, who was in charge of the top athletes for US Figure Skating, the one who was standing there when I broke my foot.

"I just watched the national championships and I know I can be better," I wrote him. "I think I should be considered for the world championships. I know it's only eight weeks away, but they told me at the hospital I should be all better by then. I know I'll be fine to compete."

Of course he didn't email me back that minute—he had just finished watching nationals. The next day he wrote back: "Let's just see how your rehab goes." That was my only moment of crazy where I was thinking magically. Looking back now, I must have been fucking crazy or really overserved on the sauvignon blanc. In that moment, though, I was thinking, "I need to be back out there."

This injury right before nationals was going to hurt my chances of going to the Olympics. In order to qualify, there are a number of bullet points the US Olympic Committee and USFS consider. One is how a skater places at 2017 nationals. I'm not going. One is how a skater places at the 2017 Four Continents competition. Not going. One is how a skater places at 2017 worlds. Not going. Anyone who goes to any of those competitions and places well automatically has a better shot of making it to the Olympics than I do.

I was at a huge disadvantage, but I knew there was nothing I could do. Just like Toni Braxton couldn't unbreak her heart, I couldn't unbreak my foot. What I *could* do is focus on doing really well next year. Since I was at such a disadvantage, everything would have to go perfectly that final season for me to qualify.

It was mid-January and I need a little sojourn to the OTC, so I took a few days to drive myself to Colorado Springs. I needed to do something that made me feel strong. I also needed to do something that felt like this was the beginning of my Olympic journey, or at least my journey to be my best, and just showing up at the OTC with my suitcase, a dream, and a fake tan wasn't enough. The drive out there gave me that feeling.

The OTC is nothing fancy. The dorms are old military barracks where each cinder block room only has a sink and there is a shared bathroom for each floor. The cafeteria is, well, a cafeteria. The best part is the gym, which is huge, beautiful, and never had very many people in it, which is just how I like it. To paraphrase

Homer Simpson, I like my beer cold, my homosexuals flaming, and my gyms totally empty.

I was working with Brandon, the comedy-loving Olympic trainer, who was in constant contact with Rafael, who gave him things that he wanted me to work on. I was in the gym every day for, like, four or five hours, just sitting there doing therapy exercises for my ankle because my ankle was still swollen from being sprained so badly.

I was doing everything on one leg. Anything I could do on two legs I would, but I wasn't allowed to do anything too crazy, because I was in the boot and my hips were off. I would sit in the chair where you do exercises for the quads and hamstrings. I worked on my flexibility. I just did anything I could when I was in the gym. I did tons of core. Eight-minute abs? Try eighty-eight-minute abs.

I also didn't want to lose my cardio, because that is the hardest thing to get back. I couldn't be huffing and puffing after each jumping pass. The only cardio I could do was riding the exercise bike. The bikes were upstairs in the gym, so I'd hobble my way up there. The boot wouldn't fit in the straps on the pedals, so I had to MacGyver it together. I would take the TheraBand, those giant elastics people use for training, and I would tie the boot to the pedal of the bike so it wouldn't go flying, and there's some stability because the other foot fit right into the other pedal.

At first, I was doing steady-state cardio for an extended amount of time, and then I started doing intervals and I'm wearing a heart rate monitor and everything. I was doing this four or five times a week.

I would also prop my iPad up on the handlebars of the bike and rewatch episodes of *RuPaul's Drag Race*, particularly season four, the one Sharon Needles wins, because it is, objectively, the best season. Also season five too because, "Back rolls?" I love that it's campy and fun, but it's also so real for the people going through it.

It was an escape from what was going on because I was upset that I couldn't skate. But watching *Drag Race* reminded me that the contestants still put on a brave face and a glittery gown and win, even after going through all sorts of awful things with their family and with society at large. If they could do it with nothing but sequins and highlighter, I could do it through focusing on getting better—and probably some sequins and highlighter too.

All this training put me in the right mind-set. There were Olympic countdown clocks everywhere: in the therapy room, the sports medicine room, the cafeteria. A few days after I arrived, the clock said 365 days. I remember looking at that clock and thinking very clearly, "Everybody else going to the Olympics still has to go to nationals. They still have to go to worlds. They still have to do all the summer shows. What they don't have is 365 days to focus on the next year, and I do. This is my advantage."

I started to love life in Colorado Springs. The time with Shawn was great for our relationship, and I had other friends who lived and trained there as well, so I could still have a social life.

Also while I was there I went to see the nutritionist. Whenever I'd seen one before, I would always lie to them and tell them I was eating a lot more than just Dave's Killer Bread, I Can't Believe It's Not Butter, and the occasional bowl of Honey Nut Cheerios. This time I decided to end the charade and come clean like Hilary Duff.

I told her what I was really eating in a day but I also said, "I don't have an eating disorder. I've just been eating badly and trying to be thin." She told me the first stage, like with any addiction, was admitting I had a problem. Slowly, I was able to because, if I'm honest, eating the way I did might have helped cause me to break a bone while doing a simple jump at the rink.

She taught me there is a way to be thin but to also eat enough to be healthy and make sure my body was getting all the nutrients it needed. I would see her once a week and tell her what I was eating, which was still hardly anything. I would tell her stupid things I made up, like I wasn't eating red meat because it made me too bloated and I wouldn't be able to jump, or that eating a whole container of hummus in one sitting was normal. I made up my own reasons. Just like the White House, I was creating my own fake news.

Once, she asked me why I wasn't having any dairy. I couldn't come up with a good excuse. The best reason I could come up with was that a baby cow drinks milk to grow up to be a big cow, and I really didn't want to become a big cow—I already had been a big cow before I moved to California. "Right now your body is trying to rebuild tissue, to fix this bone," she said. "You need as much calcium as you can get."

"Fine. I won't drink milk, but I'll have yogurt," I said, making up yet another arbitrary rule.

She looked at me as if she wanted to say, "You're an idiot." Touché.

After weeks of this dietary cat and mouse, she said, "What's going to be the best way for you to get over this?"

"I think the best way for me to get over it is if you give me all the pamphlets, and I'm going to read them because I am anal like that," I said. "Then I can create my own rules just because I love structure. Then I will follow the rules."

She agreed to that and gave me little worksheets and every pamphlet in her office. Each visit we'd go through them together, and I learned more about nutrition week after week. Now I knew how to build a plate, so if it was a day that I had a hard workout, I would put a carbohydrate on one side with a little bit of protein and then more vegetables. If it was a lighter day, I could have more vegetables to cover the plate and fewer carbohydrates.

I was good with my nutrition but also still a dried-out raisin and not a grape on a stick. This was the right way to eat, and I wasn't getting that rush of blood to my head every day when I would have my one hit of I Can't Believe It's Not Butter. Wow, that really does make it sound like I was an addict.

Finally it had been eight weeks from my injury, and I was excited to go get my boot off. I'd been testing my foot a little bit in my dorm room and it didn't hurt when I tried to put some weight on it, so I was excited to get back to skating.

I went for my eight-week X-ray. The Olympic countdown clock was at 309 days. The doctor showed me the film and I said, "That's great, but where's the one from today?"

"That is the one from today," she said. It still looked almost exactly like the one from right after the break.

The doctor zooms in on the break and says, "It's on the right track. Calcium deposits are coming in and they're filling the gap."

"What do you mean it's on the right track?" I said. "Somebody told me—I don't remember her name, or where she's from, or what her credentials were—but she said eight weeks and it's eight weeks. I was told eight weeks!"

"Well, we're gonna get another X-ray in four weeks but until then, you need the boot again."

I wanted to say, "Are you fucking kidding me?" because that's how I felt, but I probably said something like, "Thank you for your time," because my mom raised me to be respectful like that.

I had Amazon Primed myself a new pair of sneakers to the OTC, and now I needed to sheepishly put the left shoe away and shove it back into my backpack. I would only be wearing one right shoe and my awful boot leaving the office today.

I went back after four more weeks, and the countdown clock was at 281 days. Less than 300! It was the same thing all over again. I was originally told eight weeks! I had to go back four weeks later and finally the doctor cleared me to get out of the boot, sixteen weeks after my injury, which was double what I was promised. The clock is now at 253 days and I am freaking out. Will it be enough time? I didn't know, but it was all the time I had.

In April, not long after I got my boot off, I got a call from the organizers of Stars on Ice, asking if I'd be able to go on the tour that year.

"I don't know how much I'll be able to do yet, but it will probably have to be a little limited," I told them. "I'm going to perform, I'm going to spin, I'm going to do everything I can and give it one hundred percent." They were cool with that and booked me for the tour, which was in five weeks.

This would be my first time back performing, and it wouldn't be under the pressure of competition. I knew I was going to be nervous after not having been on the ice in so long, so I think it was for the best it was in front of an arena of screaming fans rather than a panel of judges. This way I could get the nerves out without my scores being on the line.

I worked out some modified versions of my programs from the year before that wouldn't be as strenuous, and I decided after all the therapy and doctor's visits that I was now a certified medical professional, and I cleared myself to start skating again.

I went to my last appointment in the sports medicine office and told the doctor, "I went skating today."

"You did what?" she said.

"Was I not supposed to?" I asked, feigning innocence.

"No, you're not allowed to yet."

"Well, I didn't do anything bad," I said in my most adorable, supersweet, cherry-on-top voice.

"Whatever," she said. "You're fine." So that's how I got back to skating earlier than I should have, pushing the limits as usual. Dr. Adam Rippon had a nice ring to it.

The Stars on Ice tour goes off without a hitch, except for the one time that I took an edible. I've only gotten high three times in my life (and all when I was over twenty-one and in states where it was legal, so don't @ me), and they were always with edibles.

The first time I was at home in California with a friend who had some powdered donuts that were filled with THC. He cut one into quarters and we both had a piece. "That's enough," my friend said. "It's your first time and it takes a while to get into your system."

We started watching *Burlesque*, as soon-to-be-stoned gay men do, and after about thirty minutes, I'm still not feeling anything. "Let's eat another quarter," I said.

"I don't think we should do that," my friend said.

"Come on, it's not working." So we both eat another quarter.

After another thirty minutes, he's passed out on my living room floor and I'm still watching the movie, waiting for the edible to kick in. I went into the kitchen, and the rest of the donuts were sitting on the kitchen counter. "You've already eaten half a donut," I thought to myself. "You're supposed to have a whole donut per person. That makes sense." I cut one of the donuts in half and ate it.

I sat down in front of the movie and still nothing. "I must have a high tolerance," I thought. "It's my thick Irish blood." I was watching a scene where Christina Aguilera comes out in a green dress, and I suddenly realized that I was crying. No, I wasn't crying; I was sobbing uncontrollably. "She doesn't even know how beautiful she is," I said out loud even though the only person in the room was snoring into the carpet.

Then it dawned on me that I was stoned. I went into the bathroom and looked into the mirror and my eyes had no white in them at all. They were just green, black, and red. I saw my reflection and started laughing uncontrollably like the Joker after he just blew up Gotham City. I sat down to finish the movie and passed out right there on the couch in some sort of crazy blackout. Not the best, but it got worse the next time I tried.

That was with my boyfriend, Shawn. He had some gummies and wanted to watch *Sausage Party*, the animated movie. We took them an hour before starting the movie. As soon as we put it in, Shawn said, "I'm high."

"Great, I'm not," I told him. About an hour into the movie,

I was still not feeling it. I got up to go to the bathroom and decided to pop another gummy. The movie ended and I still wasn't feeling it, so I took *another* gummy.

Shawn was passed out on the couch, so I woke him up and said, "Let's go to bed." As he's rousing himself, I close my eyes for just a moment and then open them quickly. "How long was I asleep for?" I ask him.

"What?"

"I was just asleep. How long was I asleep for?"

"You weren't asleep. You just closed your eyes for a second and freaked out."

Then, all of a sudden, I felt like the couch was going to swallow me whole, like I was going to sink into it and never return. I was also having trouble remembering how to breathe. I had to keep reminding myself, "Breathe in. Breathe out." Great, I thought; I had ruined the cognitive function of breathing. You don't realize how useful it is until it's gone.

"Maybe we should eat something," Shawn said.

"Yeah, let's eat something."

There was a frozen pizza in the freezer so Shawn got it out and turned on the oven. Being tired and stoned, he turned on the burner instead of the oven. I saw that and thought, "It's not safe here. He's going to take my head and smash it onto the burner." I was getting super paranoid. Maybe I wasn't stoned—maybe Shawn poisoned me and I was dying.

"I'm not hungry anymore," I told him. I was afraid he's going to blow me up with the stove or something. "Let's go to bed."

We went to bed and as I was lying there next to Shawn, I thought, "It's funny that most people don't know when they're going to die, but I know for sure that I'm going to die tonight." I thought pot was supposed to make you more relaxed; it just turned me into even more of a drama queen.

Shawn could tell I couldn't sleep, because I was freaking, so he put on another movie—this time it's *Avatar*, which I was seeing in 3-D even though I didn't have any glasses on or anything. I kept telling myself to just focus on the movie without freaking out. Then I started crying silently to myself because it was so beautiful. Christina Aguilera I could understand, but *Avatar*? I was also getting really sleepy, but I knew I had to stay awake until Shawn fell asleep or else he was going to kill me. Finally we both passed out, and when I woke up in the morning, I thought, "God, I am never doing that again."

Well, I never told that story to any of my friends who were on the Stars on Ice tour. We had a stop in Colorado (where weed is legal!), and one of my friends bought some weed chocolate. Four of us (all of age!) decided to have some before we got on our plane to our next stop.

There was a Quiznos in this airport, which is one of my favorite food groups, so I made everyone go to get sandwiches. The three of them were sitting at a table laughing their faces off as I was getting my sandwich, and it hadn't hit me yet.

Then, when I sit down, they're still laughing and I get paranoid once again. I think that everyone in the restaurant knows what we did and is pissed about it. I think my friends are acting so obnoxious, but they're just chatting and laughing like it's no big deal. I decided I have to act super proper so no one notices, and I started eating my sandwich like a dainty lady with my pinkies out because that is what a proper person would do.

We got on the plane and I was in the first aisle seat after first class, so everyone getting on the plane kind of had to look at me as they made their way to the back. I was still paranoid so I decided I had to act super normal. What would a normal person do in that situation? Oh, of course he would sit there with a huge maniac smile on his face and greet every single person as they walked by. "Hello." "Hello." "How are you?" It was like I was a stoned Walmart greeter.

The guy sitting next to me tried to strike up a conversation and I said to him, "Isn't this the nicest plane? These seats are so soft.

What is this? Is this leather? Does everyone know that Alaska Airlines is so luxurious? I'm only flying Alaska from now on."

We all hear the announcement that the door to the plane is now closed, and I feel like I'm trapped. I look around and realize that the floor of the plane is actually filthy. My seat isn't leather—it's vinyl and the stuffing is kind of coming out of it. I got really worried, thinking the plane wouldn't even be able to fly (was I even on the right plane?) and that we were all going to die. Yes, it got there again this time, and I hadn't even taken way too much.

I put on my headphones and concentrated on my music and made it through the forty-five-minute flight by white-knuckling my armrests. The scene at the airport was a mess, as the four of us were too stoned to find the baggage claim or figure out what bags were ours. With the help of everyone else on the tour—who had no idea what we had done—we got it together enough to make it to the hotel. I took a shower and passed out.

When I woke up the next morning, I thought, "This time I'm really, really, really never going to do it again." I've tried some killer combination jumps in my career, but no combination is deadlier than Adam and edibles.

The tour was over, and I went back to Colorado Springs to pack up my stuff and move back to California and start training again. As I was getting ready to do this, I was thinking a lot about Shawn.

The thing that worried me was that he was starting to come out, and he really wanted to show his family, "I'm out and this is my boyfriend." I didn't like the thought of that, because I felt like his parents would think it was only a phase and I had just tricked him into being gay like some sort of homosexual wizard. He had to come out because he wanted to, not because he thought it was the right thing to do for our relationship.

Shawn is only a year younger than me, but he didn't seem as much of an adult as I did. I felt like I had done so much more. I came out to my family and I came out publicly. I went through all this already and had my life somewhat in order. It just felt like we were at different points in our lives. I didn't think we were on different levels—we were just on different tracks. Shawn reminded me of myself when I first met Scotty.

I had to worry about myself and getting to the Olympics, and I didn't think I could handle being worried about Shawn too. He thought he needed someone to hold his hand and teach him what it was like to be an out gay person, and I never thought he did. I didn't want him to lose who he was. This was his journey, and just like Rafael had taught me, he would be stronger if he did it alone.

But breaking up with him seemed wrong because he was always so sweet and so kind. "He didn't do anything wrong and nothing's wrong with our relationship," I thought. "This is such a selfish and awful thing for me to do, but I have to do it." I figured I'd wait until I got home and had some time to think about it before I made up my mind.

The day I left I drove to Denver to meet my friend Douglas at Denver Pride. We got brunch before I was to hit the road to head back to California, and before I left, I asked him what I should do about Shawn.

"You already know what you have to do," Douglas, always blunt, told me.

"I hate that answer," I told him. "But I'm going to think about it as I drive."

I drove four hours to Breckenridge, where I thought I would stop, but I wasn't tired. I was in the car, not even listening to music, just thinking of returning home and what to do about Shawn. I decided to keep driving.

When I finally got tired a few hours later, I pulled off the highway and went to a Holiday Inn two hours past Breckenridge in some mountain town. The receptionist told me the hotel was full because there was some event happening in the area and that all the hotels within a hundred miles were booked. She told me the closest hotel room was probably Vegas.

I drove all the way to Las Vegas, which was fourteen hours away from Denver. It's about 4 a.m. when I pull over to get gas in Vegas. It's only four hours from LA, but I figured I'd get a hotel and rest before getting home. As I'm at the gas station, I see these two people who are so drunk that they are literally crawling across the oil-stained concrete of the gas station, the only thing dirtier than the dance floor at Eleven after I had bled all over it. There was no way I could stay here.

That was it—I was just going to drive all the way home. After eighteen hours in the car, I felt like I couldn't go right back home. I needed something to cap off the trip, so I drove to the beach. I got a Starbucks iced coffee, walked over to the pier, and sat on a bench, just looking out at the morning sun over the ocean.

I knew what I had to do. I had to break up with Shawn.

"You didn't do anything wrong," I told him when I called him. "It's just where I am right now. I know that I need to be completely focused on what I'm doing, and I'm really sorry. It's really selfish but I only have this one chance."

We were both crying on the phone. He told me he understood. "I know this is important and you only have one shot," he told me. It made me cry even more that he was being so supportive. How could I let a boy this sweet go? It was about as good of a breakup as anyone could ever have, and Shawn and I are still friends.

After some much-needed sleep, I went back to the rink the next day with my skates, equipment, and everything else I had taken out of my locker. I had left the countdown clock back in Colorado Springs, but now it was in my mind: 197 days to go. One of the skaters was already in the locker room when I arrived. He was happy that I was back and feeling better. "It was so sad when all of your things were gone and you took your name tag out," he told me.

"I wanted that," I replied with a smile that said I was maybe half joking. I filled my locker up and thought about how I got exactly what I wanted: to never feel handicapped for even one second on my home turf at the rink and to come back stronger than when I had left. Then came the moment I had been waiting for, which the whole ritual of cleaning out my locker was really about—I slid my name tag back where it belonged. I knew I was back and in exactly the right place.

The Text That Changed My Life

In the season leading up to the Olympics, there was no way I was letting anyone hurt my chances of qualifying, and that included Rafael. As soon as I put my name tag back on my locker and got back to training, one of the first things I did was take control of my coach's schedule.

Rafael's passion has always been teaching. As great of a coach as he was, sometimes he would put off giving his students answers on what his schedule might be. That was because he hates traveling and he would often get sick if he was traveling too much. He also hated that while he was off traveling to a competition with one student, which would be a minimum of four days, there were all his other students back at home that he wasn't teaching. A lot of the time you'd ask him if he was going to a competition or not and he'd say, "We'll talk about it later," and none of the skaters would ever get an answer. There was no way that was happening this year.

I went to every single skater he worked with and I said, "Tell me all the competitions you're entered in." I wrote all the skaters' competitions on a schedule. Yes, that might seem a little direct, but I was the oldest skater he worked with and had been working with him long enough that everyone treated me like the team leader. Also, everyone was happy that they'd finally get a firm answer if he would be there or not.

Rafael needed to stay healthy, and I wanted him to go to

the competitions he needed to go to. If I was going to one and I didn't feel like it was important, I'd make sure he was home resting and taking care of himself. This was an important year for me, and the last thing I needed was for him to get sick or stress himself out too much. But if he had multiple students at one competition, of course it made sense for him to attend.

I walked into the rink and I said, "Rafael, this is your schedule. This is where I think you should go. If you think this is good, I'm gonna tell everybody this is where you'll be this year. And if they're going to a competition that you're not, that they should make plans to bring a different coach with them."

He said, "That sounds great." He was always waiting for someone to do the dirty work, and I have always been happy to get dirty.

One of the competitions he didn't need to go to with me was the Finlandia Trophy, so I brought Derrick as my coach. The Finlandia Trophy is an annual event in Thailand. Just kidding; it's in Finland—duh. It's a lesser competition, but I always loved it because it's in a big arena and the crowd gets really pumped for it, so even though it's not that big of a deal, it still feels very glamorous. I thought this would be a good first competition back after my injury because the pressure wouldn't be on as much as it would at some other competitions, and I'd get some practice before the Grand Prix.

Right before I was going to go compete in the free skate, the fire alarm went off. Derrick and I (and the entire arena) needed to leave the building. I stayed outside in the rain and in my costume, taking selfies in front of the fire truck that came to put out the grease fire that was happening in the kitchen. It was nothing serious, but to think that I almost lost my life to chicken tenders is too real. Once we got back inside, the competition finished, I placed third, and I was officially on my comeback journey.

While I was in Finland, I decided to open up Tinder, because what else are you supposed to do when you have so much free time in a new country? It was time to talent scout. I did it out of boredom, like my version of playing *Candy Crush*. I'm swiping away—a few left and a few right—but finally match with this impossibly handsome, impossibly tall Finnish guy named JP.

At this point I had a decent number of followers on social media because I'd been skating so long. I didn't have as many as, say, the Kardashians' gardener, but I had way more than just your average dude on Instagram. JP, not a skating fan, decided I was cute but told me later he thought I was a wannabe influencer who looked like I dreamed of one day selling Flat Tummy tea, SugarBearHair, or maybe, if I was lucky, having my own discount code named after me. He was cute and his English was just slightly off in the most adorable way, so we keep this chat up well after the competition.

Going into my two Grand Prix events, I knew that my biggest competition to go to the Olympics was Jason Brown. Barring injury, act of God, or kidnapping, Nathan Chen was for sure going to the Olympics, so the fight was really for the second and third slots on Team USA. Jason placed second at nationals the year before, when I broke my foot, and then went to worlds and came in sixth. That meant he had two criteria better than I did because I had to sit out those two events.

We were both at the same Grand Prix event in Japan, and I knew it would really help my chances of making the Olympic team if I beat Jason. I didn't know if I could beat him, but I knew it would be a big statement if I did. Nathan was the A Team, and Jason, several other skaters, and I were the B Team. I needed to break out from that pool and be the best of the B Team, because the best of the B Team still makes the Olympics.

When looking at Olympic criteria, if one skater has beaten another skater head-to-head in a competition, that puts him ahead. If I beat Jason there, it would mean that even without going to nationals and worlds the year before, I would still have an opportunity to come out ahead of him.

We are very similar skaters. Jason is a beautiful technician, and if I don't have the best spins in the world, then Jason does. He is more flexible than me, he has more transitions in his skating, and our technical elements are roughly about the same. The only thing that separated us is that I could do a quad at this point, but I couldn't always land it in competition.

When I did land a quad the year before, I was doing a quad toe loop, which is the easiest quad jump. However, to execute it, I have to toe into the ice with my left foot, which is the one I broke. After my recovery, it hurt too much to do this jump. I'd have to transition to doing a quad lutz, which is the hardest quad jump that anyone has landed in competition. It would mean the point value of my program would go up, but I had yet to land it in front of the judges.

Jason did well in the short program, but with a slight mistake, and I skated clean. Still, Jason beat me and I was in fourth place right behind him. I could tell the judges were pushing one American and it wasn't me, because my scores seemed kind of low. I had no filter at this point so I asked our team leader, "Why are my component scores so low?" The second mark was called the component score, which is the score given for performance and skating quality, so it's the most subjective. I was skating the same program I had the year before and skating it just as well but getting lower marks. It didn't make sense to me.

The team leader comes back and says, "You're not going to like the answer."

"What?"

"They said you haven't been to the world championships in a few years so they don't know how to base your skating."

"That's fucking bullshit," I said. "I was at worlds two years ago, and I was at the Grand Prix Final last year doing the same routine. That is lip service. You can tell whomever you asked to go fuck themselves."

This might seem like a diva moment, but I think of it

differently. This was me standing up and saying I deserve better. If the judges had told me that my program was too slow or didn't have enough steps in it, I could have changed it and fixed it. Figure skating is a subjective sport, but I was not going to accept an answer that had no basis in reality.

I can't get mad about it though. I can't control the judges. The only thing I can control is my free skate. I went out on the ice, landed my quad lutz, and showed the judges they made a mistake the day before. I knew if I wanted to make the Olympics I had to skate like I was already at the Olympics, so I went out there and showed them the performance of a lifetime. My marks still weren't awesome, but it was enough to come in second and ahead of Jason. Mission accomplished.

My next Grand Prix is Skate America, which was held in Lake Placid, New York, that year. That was really special for me because not only did my mom come but my brother Brady, who lives in New York, came up to watch me too—the first time he'd seen me skate since I was ten and my mom had taken the whole family to watch me skate in Hershey, Pennsylvania. We all spent so much time playing in the pool that the next day my legs were tired and I performed horribly. Damn that Ramada Inn pool! I was excited to show Brady that my skating had improved in the last eighteen years.

I skate the short program at Skate America and I come in second, behind Nathan. After complaining about my scores in Japan, suddenly the same routine is being scored significantly higher. Apparently it pays to diva out every now and again.

A couple of months before this competition, I tripped on the ice at practice and put my arm down to catch myself, dislocating my shoulder. I felt the same flushed feeling I felt when I broke my foot, but I sort of knew what was wrong. I just lifted my arm up, and it fell back into place.

Ever since then, I couldn't really raise my hand above shoulder height without it hurting. There's a move named after me that I invented called the Rippon Lutz, where I do a triple lutz with both arms raised over my head. Because of my shoulder injury, I couldn't do it anymore, so I have bequeathed it to junior women around the world who absolutely love it. Seriously, every junior ladies skater from Russia does a Rippon Lutz, so my legacy lives on.

In the warm-up before I was to compete, another skater dislocated his shoulder and had to withdraw from the event because he was in so much pain. As soon as that happened, I had this awful feeling. "It's in the air," I thought to myself. "The dislocations are in the air." I told myself to get that out of my head, that they're not contagious like the flu or something.

I went out to skate my program, and there were all these dead bugs on the ice. Somehow these huge fucking hornets got into the arena and their corpses were lying all over the rink. I've dealt with all sorts of plagues while skating before, but bugs were a first. I knew that if I skated over one, my blade was going to slip and I would fall over. I was trying to get to the Olympics and I was not taking any chances, so I got a tissue and I picked up the dead bugs off the ice.

After getting into my starting pose and mentally getting ready to perform, the referee blows the whistle at me and calls me over. I skate over to her and she says, "There are still some more bugs on the ice."

I am here to skate and am trying to do everything I can to show everyone that I deserve to be on that Olympic team, and now this lady has the audacity to be like, "You missed a few," right before my skate?

A skater only has thirty seconds after his named is called to start his program or else he's disqualified. They had already called my name so I said to her, in a tone that was so dripping with sass it left a puddle on the ice, "I'll do it but you have to give me thirty extra seconds." She agreed and I picked up the remaining bugs, because apparently that was the kind of skater I had become. One who barters with the referee.

I skated over to Rafael on the side of the ice and he whacked me on both shoulders as a sort of "Go get 'em," and I went back to the center of the ice, ready to start my program. I went into the first jump, the dreaded quad. I came down short and put my hand down to catch myself. I could feel that familiar flush feeling as my shoulder dislocated.

I stalled a little bit on the ice and everything rushed through my mind at once. Should I go over to the referee? No, because she's a bitch who just made me pick up bugs. Also, if I stopped, I'd get a deduction for stopping and they'd only let me start again from where the music ended, and I'd lose my first element.

I was also thinking that I could do it and if I stopped, I might not medal. I didn't come all this way to lose, and honestly, I wanted my coins. I was holding on to my shoulder, and I looked up at Rafael and he's motioning for me to stop.

I threw my arm back, and I felt it thud back into place. I shook it out, and I started skating around and I look Rafael dead in the face, as he's motioning furiously, "Stop! Stop!"

No way, ho. I kept going and skated the rest of the program perfect. I end up second in the competition.

Afterward, an NBC reporter asked me what I was thinking in that moment when I dislocated my shoulder. "You know what?" I told her. "I want my money. I want my check. I'm going to finish this program and I'm going to be awesome, and that's what I did." That statement was enough to make me a little bit of a meme, at least on gay Twitter and on a gay blog that called me their "sassy spirit animal."

I went into nationals and I was feeling really good, prepared, ready. I told Tara Lipinski before the competition, "I want this to be my coronation." Every queen needs a crown, right? I was excited because for the first time heading into nationals before an Olympics, I thought I could actually do it. You could call it cocky, but I called it confident. And also I loved the reaction I would get from everyone I did an interview with when I would say something so forward. They weren't used to someone being so honest and candid. I also lived for when I would get a laugh out of someone. I felt like the Amy Schumer of sport.

For the short program, I was still doing my EDM routine from the year before. I went for my six-minute warm-up. I'm a little shaky and I feel like I might have diarrhea. I said to myself, "You know what? Fuck it. If I don't make the Olympics, I don't make the Olympics. But I never want to look back at this event and think I should've tried harder or that I held back. I'm just going to go out there and do what I've done every single time. I'm going to enjoy the moment as hard as this is, and if I mess up, I mess up."

It might have been the best short program I ever performed in my life, and I end up with ninety-plus points, which without a quad is almost impossible. I end up in second place right behind Nathan and way ahead of the next skater.

The next day was the free skate, and all I needed to do was skate decent. I was skating to a Coldplay song, "O (Fly On)," and the program was about a bird with a broken wing that learns how to fly. It could have been about two songbirds being threatened by a hawk, but I didn't want it to be too meta. Anyway, I was feeling confident and wearing a top that was a copied design from a sex harness I saw outside of Chi Chi LaRue, a sex shop in West Hollywood named after a famous gay porn director. I took a picture of it on the mannequin and sent it to my friend Braden and his girlfriend, Jill, who were both as excited as I was about the concept. I was ready to do this.

I go into my first jump, which is the quad, and I fall. It was not really a big deal. I knew I could get up and skate clean. I make it through all the major jumping passes and do all the toughest jumps in my program. "I did it," I think to myself. I was already picturing myself in the Olympic village and lost focus.

When I went into my last two easy jumps, I turned both of the triples into singles. I knew that I would never be as explosive a jumper as Nathan, but I thought if I could prove that I was super consistent that I would make it to the Olympics. Now, when the consistency mattered most, it failed me. It was the worst I had skated in years.

Four years ago, when I had skated so poorly at nationals, I felt the Olympics slip away from me and was devastated. This time I was so much more advanced not just as a skater but as a person that never for a second did I think I wasn't going to the Olympics or get down on myself. I lost focus but I didn't give up for a second. I gave 100 percent on everything, and I told myself if I did that, I would be happy with myself. I made a mistake. People make mistakes, and I'm going to be all right.

Off the ice, Rafael is devastated for me because he has seen me do that program perfectly a million times. I know my mom is going to be upset too, so I text her as soon as I get off the ice. I'm not sure what happened, I wrote. I made a mistake. I'm just human, but no matter what happens, I'll be OK.

She wrote back simply, I love you, and that was the first time that I started to get a little bit emotional.

I watch the final skaters, and the results were surprising, except for Nathan coming in first, which was no shock. Jason has a rough skate and ends up in fifth place. Vincent Zhou, the reigning junior world champion, ended up coming in third, just before me. Ross Miner, my friend who I swapped third and fourth places with at the Grand Prix event two years earlier, skated his heart out and placed second. It was the first competition he'd medaled at since that third-place finish at that Grand Prix two years ago. (See? I told you remembering that would be important.)

Once the final figures are in, my mom starts texting me furiously with all the stats and all the criteria, trying to figure out if I'm going to make the Olympics or not. It looks like I should make it. Even though Ross came in second, I still beat him in head-to-heads, both at the Finlandia Trophy and Skate America. I'd also beat Jason in head-to-heads twice now, even though he has the third-best criteria after me. I'm not really worried, but I know they've picked the Olympic team based on national performance before, and if they do this time, it means I end up the first alternate.

I thought back to where I was a year ago—sitting on my couch drinking wine and having flatbreads with my mom. I did everything I could, and I have so many good experiences from skating and all that. I've learned a lot, I've grown up a lot, and I've learned the right lessons. I know the Olympics is just a competition and that it's not going to change any of that, but I want to go so badly I can feel it all through my body.

We find out if we make the Olympic team or not by text message. It should probably be a little bit more official than the medium that gave birth to the poop emoji, but that's the way they do it now. Welcome to the twenty-first century.

I'm waiting in my hotel room with my mom, Derrick, and Ashley, who I have shared a hotel room with at nationals for the last several years. The night before was the women's free skate, and Ashley also ended up fourth in her competition. It was just Ashley and me the night before when she found out she wouldn't be going to her second Olympics. She got back to the room late after she was finished, and when she came into the room, we hugged very tightly and cried. I was so sad for her, and the next night, here we were again, just waiting.

We're all sitting by the phone, waiting for a stupid text message. It felt like that four-hour Salem witch trial documentary my mom made me watch was shorter than this wait. It came around 1:30 a.m. It said, Congratulations on your selection to the 2018 Winter Olympic Games. This is the first time I cracked and started crying. My mom was crying, Derrick was crying, Ashley was crying, the guy who brought us room service was crying. Everyone in the hotel was crying, because the world was celebrating that I made the Olympics. Well, it wasn't that extreme, but close.

I think more than anything my mom was crying because she

was proud of the man I had become. She wasn't thinking, "We barely made it"; she was thinking, "You did what you needed to do, and you were right." She was really proud of me for making this experience my own.

I wasn't jumping around and screaming; I was just grateful and quiet. Ashley was happy for me, but I was sad for her that she didn't get to go and we didn't get to go together. But I was going with my friend Mirai Nagasu, who also made the team and had been getting drunk with me to the *Les Mis* soundtrack on her roof four years ago. There were a lot of emotions that night.

The next day I found out the Olympic team is Nathan, me, and Vincent. Jason, who was fifth, is the first alternate, and Ross, who was second, gets to be the second alternate. I walked around the whole next day with my tail between my legs, because I felt embarrassed about my performance, but I know that I earned the spot based on how they said you should earn it.

I ran into all the judges, people I had known and competed in front of for years. They would say, "Congratulations, we're so happy for you," and I would start crying. I saw the next one, "Congratulations, so happy for you," start crying. I'm saying hi to everybody and crying.

We had a press conference with the Olympic team, and I got a little emotional. During the press conference was the first time I heard that I was the first openly gay man to qualify for the Winter Olympic Team. I didn't know that before, but I was excited by it. Hey, I just wanted to go to the Olympics. I would have been the first openly whatever-you-want as long as it meant I was going to the Olympics.

(My friend Gus Kenworthy would qualify for the Olympics for the second time a few weeks later. But this was his first Olympics being out, so I'm the first only because of scheduling. Together we were the first openly gay men to go to the Olympics, and I'm happy to share that honor with him, but like all twins, one of us had to be born a little bit earlier.)

I was a mess that whole day, and we still had that Skating Spectacular, which, for the first time ever, was the day after the men competed. Not only was I in the Skating Spectacular, but Ross was in it too because he came in second. We're about the same age, so I know that just like this was my last chance to make it, it was his too.

I saw Ross backstage at the arena and I went up to him. I said, "I don't really know what to say, but I'm sorry." We hugged and I wish I could have done something to take his hurt and disappointment away, because I certainly knew exactly what he was feeling in that moment.

After our hug he said, "You know how much it sucks. But it wasn't your decision. It wasn't anyone's fault. It just sucks."

"I know; I'm really sorry it went down this way," I told him, and I honestly felt that way. I didn't want to crush anyone else's dream to have my own. On some level I feel like the way that I acted in Russia when our results got flipped saved our friendship, though, because he showed me even more grace than I showed him two years before. He put whatever he was going through second so that he could be a good friend to me in that moment, and I'll never forget that. Ross is one of the coolest and best people I've gotten to meet in skating. The emotions can get really high, but we genuinely have always cheered for each other. I'll always be grateful to call him my friend.

That day I was even grateful to skate in the Skating Spectacular. As I showed the crowd my best moves in a sheer black top that no one could yell at me for because there were no judges, I was happy to be there just entertaining that crowd, doing what I love the most, because I knew in just six weeks I would be on the athletic world's largest stage.

Hello, Fame; It's Me, Adam

As a kid, I was a celebrity in my own mind even though nobody knew who I was. Since I was twelve years old, I trained myself not to smile with my eyes so that I wouldn't have crow's feet and ruin this famous face that no one outside of the Rippon household could recognize. I've completely taken my eyes out of the equation since I was twelve. I've been Joan Crawford for over fifteen years.

I've been pretending I was famous as a joke since I was a teenager. I've been walking around in the airport with sunglasses on for over a decade as if the paparazzi are going to come around the corner and confront me at baggage claim about my recent paternity scandal. (Am I the father? Am I the mother? Who knows?)

I do it because it's ridiculous–obviously no one knows who I am. When I'm with my friends, it embarrasses them and I think it's so funny. I'm not doing it seriously. I know people aren't going to say, "Oh, are you that guy I've never seen before?"

Not only is it my favorite joke, but it's been a coping mechanism because when I was young, I was so unpopular, and I was not embraced by so many people. It's a way for me to laugh at myself before anyone else can laugh at me.

I always felt that if nobody was going to be a cheerleader of mine, I had to be my own, even if I was taking it to an exaggerated extent.

Heading up to the Olympics, I had a publicist named Lynn who was a woman who did publicity for Stars on Ice for about fifty years, and I had an agent who did my contracts for skating shows and would book some interviews for me. After I qualified, Lynn asked me, "What press do you want to do?"

"I want to do everything," I told her.

When I qualified, I told myself I was going to have the full Olympic experience, because it was only going to happen once, unless I really got into archery around forty and went to the Summer Games, like Geena Davis. Part of that experience was meeting as many people as I could, talking to every journalist I could, and getting my story out there. I've had this pent-up stand-up routine inside of me for years, and I was ready to unleash it on the world.

I vowed I was going to use the same philosophy that made me a successful skater: I would just be my authentic self, and people could take it or leave it. I also knew, to some extent, that I could control the message. I knew I was never the most athletic skater with the biggest jumps, but I decided that I had the best spins in the world. I started saying this in every interview when I had the chance, and pretty soon, I started hearing it come back to me. Other people would write that I had the greatest spins in the world. It wasn't a lie—my spins were (and continue to be) amazing—but it was like I used The Secret to bring that into existence.

My other superpower was I treated everyone like they were already my friend. I never had to win anyone over or prove myself to anyone, because in my mind, they were already in love with me. During my last season at competitions, I would skate by the judges and greet them and ask how they were doing. This wasn't illegal, necessarily, but it was completely against the custom for how skaters were supposed to act. There was a total Chinese wall between athletes and judges, and here I was poking my pretty little head over it to give them a wave.

I was tricking everyone into thinking that I was a fucking superstar. When you act like you know who you are, people don't disagree with you. I knew who I was, and I was famous since the time I was twelve.

So I was doing all of this press before the games—it was just fun. Being one of the first gay men to be in the Olympics helped because it was a new story. I moved my practice time later in the afternoon, and every morning I would do some press. One day it would be *People* magazine, and the next it would be a gay blog that I had never heard of. I didn't turn anyone down.

It was fun, and I made people laugh. I was able to have a good conversation with everybody, and I love talking with people so I had a great time. Every outlet was getting a different quote, because I would never do the same shtick twice.

One reporter asked me, "What's the difference between a gay athlete and a straight athlete?"

"There isn't any difference," I said. "Except I have better eyebrows." That quote got a fair amount of play because it was funny. I'm supposed to just say that we're the same, because we are, but no one is going to remember that.

I'm a smaller-framed, kind of effeminate guy, and I'm actually saying things like this where I normally wouldn't be allowed to say them. You're supposed to be under the radar and say, "Oh, I'm just happy to be here," and clutch your pearls. I would say I was happy to be there and then add, "But I'm also so pretty."

Because of all this media attention, Reese Witherspoon tweeted that I was the only reason to watch the Olympics. Yes, Reese Witherspoon, the star of *Cruel Intentions* and someone so beautiful that I would cry if I saw her in a movie after I had eaten too many edibles.

After getting this attention, one day we were all in the gym warming up, and I walk over to the mirror and I'm fixing my eyebrows when I should be warming up. My training partner Mariah Bell said, "Adam, you're going to be so famous."

"I don't even know if I want to be famous," I said, giving my eyebrow one last tweak to perfection.

"You don't want to be famous?" Ashley asked me. "Look at you right now in the mirror playing with your eyebrows."

Preening aside, I really wasn't sure if I wanted to court fame, because people whose only objective is to be famous turn me off. Yes, I wanted to be myself and get my story out there, but I think that fame should be a reward. It's nice to gain fame, but I wanted it to come as a repercussion of excellence. I wanted it to come because of all the hard work I put in to be one of the top skaters in the world.

If I just wanted to be famous, being a figure skater sure is a strange and expensive route to take. I could have just given an awful audition on *American Idol*, latched myself on to a scandal, or showed off my abs on Instagram and gotten a million followers. The last one I'll still do, but it's because I'm vain, not because I want to be famous.

One day I got a call from Lynn and she told me that a reporter named Christine Brennan, who I had known for a while, was working on a story for *USA Today*. She wanted to get my thoughts on Vice President Mike Pence being named as the head of the US delegation to the Olympics.

I had done some research on Mike Pence before the presidential election, and I thought he had an awful record on gay civil rights. He said in 2006 that gay couples would lead to "societal collapse." As governor of Indiana he had opposed a law that would ban discrimination against LGBT people in the workplace. He opposed the repeal of Don't Ask, Don't Tell. He even made a remark that some construed as him supporting conversion therapy for gay people. I was not a fan.

Christine wanted to give me a chance to think about it and get my words together, because as an athlete going into the

Olympics, my response would be amplified. We arranged a time for a call and I went outside of the rink so that I wouldn't be disturbed on the phone.

The rink where Team Rafael trained used to be a Ralphs grocery store. It was in the same shopping plaza as a Kohl's, a bowling alley, and a Taco Bell. The glamorous world of figure skating. I drove over to the Taco Bell parking lot so that no one from the rink would see me talking on the phone in the car like a crazy person. Also, if I couldn't eat at the Taco Bell, I at least wanted to be around to smell it like greasy aromatherapy.

We started with a few easy questions about how I was feeling going into the Olympics, and then she asked what I knew she came for. "What do you think of Mike Pence being named head of the Olympic delegation?" she asked.

I promised myself I would always be candid in all my interviews, so that's what I did. "You mean Mike Pence, the same Mike Pence that funded gay conversion therapy?" I said. "I'm not buying it."

Of course, I had more to say. "If it were before my event, I would absolutely not go out of my way to meet somebody who I felt has gone out of their way to not only show that they aren't a friend of a gay person but that they think that they're sick. I wouldn't go out of my way to meet somebody like that."

If that didn't make my stance clear, here is one more quote Christine used in her article: "I don't think the current administration represents the values that I was taught growing up. Mike Pence doesn't stand for anything that I really believe in."

With that off my chest, I sat in my car and took in the sweet smells of Taco Bell beef.

The next day the piece came out, and I got an email from Lynn with a link that said, "Great article by Christine."

I was happy we were all on the same page. I went to practice and put my phone on airplane mode so I could play the music from my program without being disturbed by phone calls or texts. While still on the ice, I turned my phone on and I had three missed calls from my agent, two missed calls from US Figure Skating, and a call from the US Olympic Committee.

"Girl, I think you're in trouble," I said to myself. There are voicemails both from Barb Reichert, who is in charge of communications for USFS, and my agent. They both say essentially, "I have some news; give me a call."

I call my agent first and he tells me that Mike Pence's office reached out and wants to talk to me. My initial reaction was, "That's amazing." In this country we grow up with great respect for the office of the president and the vice president, so if one of them wants to speak to me, my reflex is that I should do it, regardless of which party they might be.

I think that this might be my chance to make a difference and maybe change his mind. I tell my agent to find out if this is a phone call or if it's a face-to-face meeting, and to let me know.

Then I call Barb, who just happens to be a lesbian. "It's pretty incredible that you've heard from the vice president of the United States," she said. "I think you should think about what you want to do, and you should talk to your friends. You should talk to people you trust, and I will support you one way or the other."

I still had a lot of training that day, including a session with my choreographer, Cindy Stuart, the woman who had helped me when I was choreographing for Ashley. She also happens to be a lesbian. (Figure skating: It's not just for gay men.)

Cindy and I worked for maybe thirty minutes, and I said, "I can't focus right now. Can we chat?"

I told Cindy what was going on and she said, "I know a few people that you could call who are really involved in different LGBTQ alliances. You can find out their opinions. You should also just talk to somebody who's been in politics before, and I know a few people that I can give you their contacts."

She put me in touch with the husband of Randy Gardner, a former national and world pairs skating champion, who is involved in politics. He told me, "You need to step out of where you are right now, and you need to see this situation for what it is. Think about it objectively. You don't know this person, but this person is just like you. What would be the advice that you would give them?"

I knew the advice I would give this person would be, "Fuck this guy—he's only looking for a photo op." This was not an attempt for him to reach out to the LGBTQ community; this was him trying to shut up a gay athlete before he goes to the Olympics. This is an opportunity only for him. It will leak that the office reached out, and he can just say, "Oh, I talked to Adam, and we're all good."

I had found out that it would just be a phone call with Pence, so I knew it would be leaked. If Jared Kushner's WhatsApps with the Saudi prince are getting leaked, I'm sure that Adam Rippon's private phone call from an AT&T iPhone 8 are going to get leaked too.

I wasn't even the one this guy needed to talk to. He needs to have a call with that black trans woman who doesn't feel comfortable walking down the street and isn't allowed to go to the bathroom where she wants. He needs to call that young gay boy or gay girl who doesn't feel comfortable going home, because they know that their parents are going to put them in conversion therapy if they come out.

I called Barb and I said, "I've thought about what I'm gonna do."

"Yeah?" she asked.

"I think it's truly an honor to hear from the office of the vice president, but you can tell him to go fuck himself," I said.

"Good for you," Barb added.

Then I did my next interview with a reporter and he asked, "So, is your butt real?" And I thought, "Back on track."

I didn't want all this Pence drama to detract from the most important thing leading up to the Olympics: training. I was training ten times harder than I had trained for anything in my life, and I didn't want this media circus to distract me.

When an athlete makes it to the Olympics, it's because they did something right, and the six weeks between qualifying and the games is not the time to say, "I'm going to have a new diet. I'm going to start a new routine." You've got to focus, and you've gotta do everything you can to be in the best shape of your life.

However, I started working with a different trainer because I wanted that brand-new feeling. I found a trainer named Steve Zim, who bills himself as a celebrity trainer. I went to him and told him to help me look good, because I knew that if I looked good, I would feel really good.

Let me tell you, Steve was not cheap, but I was only going to the Olympics once, and this was only for two months, so I happily forked over the cash. He really pushed me in the gym and made sure I was doing what I needed to, so it was worth every cent.

I also knew that I would be skating three times in PyeongChang—twice in the individual competition and once for the free skate in the team competition. I didn't want the audience at home to think that they'd seen my programs before, so I needed a third costume. Yes, I did it for the fans. So selfless.

I called up Braden Overett, who made my costumes for the last few years, and told him I wanted to be a beautiful white bird in a slutty bird costume. It would be me in my highest bird form. He came up with a beautiful white shirt with an explosion of blue Swarovski crystals all around it, which looks a bit like a blue jay flew through a pride float. I decided I liked it so much I wanted to wear it for my first skate in the team competition. All my costumes for the Olympics were skintight and mesh—a white shirt for my team event, a harness-inspired shirt for my short program, and a beautiful all-blue and fully crystaled shirt for my individual free skate, which I would lend to you, but it's now in the Smithsonian.

The rest of the gear I wore while in Korea came when I went to

Seoul for athlete processing. All the athletes went through Seoul and got a basic orientation about how to act and what is expected of them. We also got the outfits we would wear for the opening and closing ceremonies, what we would wear on the podium should we medal, and suitcases and suitcases full of swag. I got enough Olympic gear that it could sink a small boat.

I got a ton of T-shirts, sweatshirts, and everything you can imagine with the Olympic rings on them, which are irreplaceable. I also picked up an Olympic ring, which looks sort of like a giant class ring. When I was in California filling out all the Olympic paperwork, I was sitting across the table from Rafael. We had to pick if we wanted the basic ring, which was sterling silver, or pay $1,000 to upgrade to the gold ring with diamonds in it.

Rafael got up from the table, walked around it, and stood behind me. "You have to upgrade to the nicest ring," he said. "If you don't have the money, I'll give it to you, but you have to get the nicest ring." He was right—I did, and I even had the money to buy it.

After that Nathan, Rafael, and I all traveled to Chuncheon, a city about two hours from both Seoul and PyeongChang where US Figure Skating had a rink it was using for practice. There was a rink where we could practice in the village, but we would only get about forty-five minutes a day, there were tons of other skaters trying to use the ice at the same time, and the press was always there watching. It wasn't the ideal situation for rehearsing for this make-or-break moment.

I practiced for a day in Chuncheon, and I told Rafael I was going to go to the opening ceremonies and come back, and that I would be going back and forth multiple times between my events.

"You need to go to the village," Rafael told me. "Nathan is going to do his own thing here, and I'm going to stay here, but you need to go and experience the Olympics." He told me that I should be working out in the gym instead of skating every day and to take advantage of those crowded practices if I needed it. He wasn't going to let my skating go to shit, but he also knew how important this was to me.

I left Chuncheon and never went back. For the PyeongChang Olympics, there were two main clusters for sporting: the mountain cluster, which was in PyeongChang itself, and the coastal cluster about an hour away in Gangneung. All the rink-based sports, including figure skating, were in Gangneung, and there were two separate villages for the athletes in their respective clusters.

In both the mountains and on the coast they built huge towers for the athletes that would be turned into apartments as soon as we moved out. In fact, all the apartments were already sold—all they were waiting for was moving day.

I shared a three-bedroom apartment with my friend Mirai Nagasu, the ice dancing pair Madison Hubbell and Zach Donohue, and Vincent Zhou, who got his own room because he was only seventeen at the time. When we moved in, it was sort of like living in a model home. All the carpets, walls, and cabinets were covered in plastic so that they would look brand-new when the real owners eventually showed up. There were no appliances in the kitchen, and the sinks only worked in the bathrooms.

The sense of community in the village was amazing, but I could see the comedy in training for this event my entire life and I'm literally living in an unfinished bedroom.

Everyone always talks about how there is all this sex happening at the Olympics, but sadly for everyone, I didn't see any. A tragedy. I think that everyone is so focused on their own performance, especially at first, that there is hardly any room for Grindr or Bumble or just picking up random bobsledders the old-fashioned way, when they're eating a Sausage McMuffin in the village McDonald's.

I was on the lookout for those famed Olympic condoms you hear so much about in news reports. Supposedly they go through, like, 100,000 a day or something crazy like that, and I couldn't find one of them. I thought they would make the perfect souvenir back home because they're cheeky, they're easy to pack, they're free, and you can't buy them in stores.

After about a week of looking everywhere for an Olympic rubber, I finally found some. I was called for random drug testing one afternoon when I was in my room (and by "my room" I mean a nice Korean family's future apartment), and they told me I had to go to the medical tent to get a blood test.

I went into the medical tent and that is the first time I saw the condoms. There was a small basket of little purple condoms that literally said, in English, "Generic Condom" on the wrapper. I was furious. After all that hype and all the rumors, all I saw was a small Michaels craft store basket of "generic condoms." I mean, I still emptied the whole thing into my bag, but I was livid.

The gym in the village, of course, was gorgeous and I went every day. It wasn't as empty as I would have liked, but everyone there was so focused that no one bothered anyone. I kept running into this super jacked German guy there, and one day he came up and started talking to me.

He was a trainer for one of the teams, and we started talking a little bit and then he mentioned his "husband." I thought, "Oh, he's gay or at least he got tricked into marrying a man."

Then he said, "You know, all this stuff you're doing is really cool. It's really, really nice. Somebody like me really appreciates you using your voice."

That moment meant a lot to me, and it meant that regardless of what Mike Pence wants, the Olympics are going to be full of gay people for years to come. And if anyone was going to try something, I knew just the German trainer to call to kick their ass.

Other than Gus, I only ran into one other gay athlete. He was another American, and he approached me and told me that he appreciated what I said about the vice president and thought I was brave for coming out. He said he thought about coming out publicly but didn't know if he should.

Like a one-man It Gets Better campaign, I shared my coming-out experience with him and told him how it had been overwhelmingly positive.

"I don't know if I should," he said. "I don't know if my teammates know. I don't try to hide it, but I'm not sure if they know."

I wanted to tell him if he doesn't know that they know, then they probably know. It doesn't take Harriet the Spy to figure these things out, especially around people you see every day, like your teammates. But I didn't say that. I just gave him support and told him that I would always have his back if he needed it and that he could get in touch with me anytime.

I didn't run into Gus, because he was staying up in Pyeong-Chang where the skiing events were being held, but I knew he was going to be at the opening ceremonies. Strangely enough, that was the first time we ever met in person.

He came out a few months after I did, but it was a totally different thing: I was rebuilding my career; he had already won an Olympic medal. I was in a sport that everyone thought was super gay; he was in a sport that everyone thinks is fueled by testosterone and Red Bull. I came out in a tiny little corner of *SKATING* magazine; he came out on the cover of *ESPN* magazine to tons of press.

When I saw his magazine cover, I followed him immediately. I try to follow and read about as many openly gay athletes as I can because there aren't many of us, and I think it's really cool when we can support each other.

I was following Gus for months, and as the Olympics approached, we kept getting lumped in articles together as the two gay guys who might be going to compete in Korea. Eventually he followed me back and DMed me to ask if I had qualified yet. I told him I hadn't but that I would know in a few months. He told me he hadn't yet either and was having a tough season.

We messaged each other back and forth to keep track of how the other was doing and commenting on this journey that so few people have, and even fewer gay people have. Once we both made our respective teams, we were trying to figure out when we would meet, and it seemed like the first time would be the opening ceremonies.

The night comes and it's controlled chaos. There are three hundred American athletes and we're all in the same area, but everyone is wearing the exact same outfit so trying to find Gus was like trying to find a needle in a gaystack. (See what I did there?) We were trying to find each other over text, and it was like something out of the end of a rom-com when Meg Ryan finally finds Tom Hanks at the top of the Empire State Building.

We locked eyes and it was like seeing an old friend that I hadn't seen in forever. We hugged. We kissed. I introduced him to everyone on my team, and he introduced me to all the skiers. We start talking and joking around and then he asked, "Do you want to walk in together?"

I felt my chest get tighter because it was such a powerful moment. It was like I was being asked to the gay platonic prom that I never had.

I couldn't believe I was not only out but allowed to totally be myself, which is the best and only way you should represent your country at the Olympics. Then I got to walk in the opening ceremonies with somebody else who's also kind of been on the same journey as I have, someone who felt totally uncomfortable being who they were but came through the other side of that to find success. That moment is mine and his moment is his, but we both got to share it with somebody else who totally understood. That experience was for little Adam, who never thought that what was going on would be possible.

Right before I first found Gus in the crowd, I was standing

with my friend Evan, the ice dancer. "Are you going to meet Gus?" he asked.

"Yeah. I just need to find him," I said.

"I have my really good camera. I need to get a good picture of you guys," he said, sounding like my stage father. "You're going to be so famous with these Olympics—I just know it." Evan was beaming.

I had acted famous from the time I was a little kid—what was weird was that it was finally starting to come true.

I Did It for Leslie Jones

When I didn't make the Olympics in 2014, Derrick was incredibly supportive, which shouldn't come as a surprise, because Derrick has never been anything but incredibly supportive. As a skating coach, Derrick had one student who was as supportive of him as he was of me.

This girl, Kana, was in love with Derrick, and all her art projects in school were always inspired by him, and she would bring them to the rink during their lessons and give them to him. She would give him these adorable notes that would say things like, "I'm never going to have another skating coach except you."

Derrick must have told her that I was going through a rough time, because one day she showed up with two magnets she made, one for each of us. One had a drawing of a little black boy and a little blond white boy that were supposed to be Derrick and me and said "Best Friends." The other one she told Derrick to give to me, and it said "Future Olympian" and had the Olympic rings on it.

This was at the time when I didn't even know if I was going to keep skating. When Derrick handed it over, he said, "I don't even know if I should give you this, but Kana wanted you to have it."

He absolutely should have given it to me, because it was just what I needed. She didn't see me as someone who failed to go to the Olympics twice. She didn't see me as someone who was probably too old to make it the third time. She saw me as somebody who's really good, someone who could go to the Olympics one day. She was so optimistic, and that was the attitude I needed to have. I kept the magnet on the fridge, where they still live even though I am now a past Olympian.

When I got to Korea, I thought about that magnet because it said "Future Olympian," which was a goal that I had made come true. It didn't say "Future Gold Medal Winner," because I sort of knew that wasn't going to happen. The best I had ever placed at worlds was sixth, and all the same skaters who had beaten me before were going to be at the Olympics. They were all doing multiple quads in their programs, and I could only do one, which I was able to land about 60 percent of the time on my best day. Mathematically I didn't have the points I needed to win gold.

Growing up in America, where we have so many athletes who are so good, we're sort of raised with this mentality that gold is all that matters. Thanks to all the disappointments and triumphs I had over my long career (and skating years are like dog years, so I'm about 137 at this point), I knew that gold didn't matter. I knew that winning didn't matter. I knew that qualifying was the goal, and I did it.

Everybody has to have a game plan of what it is they want out of the Olympics, and my game plan was that I wanted to skate clean. I wanted to be perfect, and I wanted everybody at home to say, "Oh my God, you got ripped off and you should have won," even if that wasn't truly the case. Everyone in the general public is going to remember me for these skates, and the way I wanted to be remembered as a skater was someone who skated perfectly every single time. With that in mind, I decided I wasn't even going to try the quad. I was going to stick to triples, land every one, and have Leslie Jones screaming in a Twitter video when I did, which, if you follow her on Twitter during the Olympics, was the easiest goal for me to achieve.

We found out we would be competing at ten in the morning.

The earliest I had ever competed before this was at noon for a Sunday matinee, but usually we would compete later in the evening. That way we could practice in the morning, rest for most of the afternoon, and then be ready to give our best at night.

Competing at 10 a.m. is crazy—it meant we had to be up at 4:30 to practice at 6:30. But they selected the times so that we would skate live during prime time in the US. That's when I realized that the Olympics is not set up for athletes to have the best competition they can. It's set up to give the best show to the people at home. That was fine with me. For the past year I had been skating like I was in an exhibition, so I was ready to do that again. If a show is what you want, then a show is exactly what I'm going to give you.

Still, there was a shot I could get a medal in the team competition, where the US is a medal favorite, according to Vegas oddsmakers (because they are *very* interested in figure skating bets).

The medal wasn't my focus though. My focus was taking all the opportunities the Olympics provided and soaking in the whole Olympic experience. The magnet Derrick gave me was right—getting there was the prize.

For all the things he had done for me—large and small—I knew that Derrick needed to go with me to the Olympics. I talked to Rafael about listing Derrick as my coach and how important it was to me. Of course he understood, and he would be there as Nathan's coach, so it's not like I'd be there without him. I felt like I needed all the people in my corner I could get.

My mom was the other big part of my journey, so she would obviously make the trip. Derrick's mom, Dallas, who was like a second mother to me and had also gotten close to my mom, came as well. She shared a room with my mom, and they stayed for the whole three weeks of the Olympics. They always shared a dream—to see their sons at the Olympics—and they got to realize that dream together.

Two of my siblings also came—Brady and Dagny, my sister who was so happy she had a gay brother that she cried. Dagny ended up getting sick with the flu the day before they left. Between all their flights and ground travel to get to the Olympic village, it was going to take them twenty-four hours to get to Gangneung. "You have twenty-four hours to get well," my mother told her before they left. She was afraid if she had the flu they weren't going to let her into Korea or that they might quarantine her. "You are nineteen," she told my sister. "That means you are an adult, and I will leave you in Seoul if I have to."

If there is one trait all the Rippon kids share, it's that we know not to mess with our mom. Dagny started popping Motrin every four hours to get her fever down and made it through customs with no problems. (Though someone should make a sitcom about her being stranded in Korea since the Olympics and never making it home.)

Thank God my mom got there when she did, because the Mike Pence stuff started to flare up again. Christine Brennan found out that Pence's office had asked to have a call with me and that I had declined the offer. This happened the day after the Olympics started. When she approached me for a quote, I knew I couldn't get in the middle of this again. I was gearing up for the team competition, and I didn't want everyone else on the team getting asked about this and having to take sides.

When she requested a comment for the story, I said, "I have to focus on the competition. There are people all around here who have the answers and you can ask them. They know." I knew full well that my agent and the people from US Figure Skating could tell her what happened, and I didn't want to be in the middle.

Christine got her confirmation, but then the vice president's office denied that it ever happened. That's so unlike the Trump White House to just make something up. How strange!

When they denied it, it made the story grow even more, and it got picked up everywhere, including the *New York Times*, which published its story on the first day of the team competition. They called me "a charismatic 28-year-old figure skater, newly minted gay icon and social media darling," and if it's in the *Times*, then you know it has to be true.

When my mom first arrived and got out of the taxi in front of where she was staying, which was a hotel that the figure skating and hockey teams bought out so friends and family could stay there, my agent was standing right there. "I'm glad you're here," he told her. "You're on CNN talking to Chris Cuomo in ten minutes." My mom had just spent the last day traveling with a sick daughter. She hadn't read the news or checked Twitter or anything. Now she only had ten minutes to figure out what the hell was going on.

The same day this story breaks, Pence decides to @ me on Twitter and says, I want you to know we are FOR YOU. Don't let fake news distract you. I am proud of you and ALL OF OUR GREAT athletes and my only hope for you and all of #TeamUSA is to bring home the gold. Go get 'em!

Yeah, it's great that he would stand with me at the Olympics, but I knew as soon as we all got home and the attention was off he wouldn't be standing with me anymore. In fact, he'd be actively standing against me.

When a reporter asked me about all this stuff, I did what I promised myself I would do and was totally candid. "I don't want my Olympic experience to be about Mike Pence," I said. Then I dropped the mic, skated away, and showed that reporter that I am the best spinner in the world.

The Hill, a DC newspaper that covers politics, took that quote and ran with it, which is where Donald Trump Jr. saw it. His response to the quote was, "Really? Then perhaps you shouldn't have spent the past few weeks talking about him. I haven't heard him mention you once???" Seriously, dude? He literally just @-ed me on Twitter. The whole Trump family is just lovely.

It's a tale as old as time: An Olympic athlete gets heckled by the first family of the United States during his competition. This was not what I wanted at all. When all this started going again, especially after Trump Jr.'s quote was widely ridiculed, it was February 14. I decided it was the perfect day to remind everyone how pretty I am.

With everything going on in the media about me this Valentine's Day I don't want people to get distracted and forget how beautiful I am (on the outside), I said on Twitter. And that, ladies and gentlemen, is all I have to say about that.

This was all happening around the time of the team competition, which, honestly, I think was great for me. Michael Terry, the media relations person for USFS who was dealing with all the athletes at the Olympics, told me his brother said, "This is the first time I'm going to be watching figure skating, and it's because of Adam Rippon. I want him to do so well after all of this shit with the vice president."

By this point a lot of people had heard about me, and the team competition was the first time they were going to see me skate, and I wanted it to be perfect just to make Pence and company look like fools for heckling me. To me it was a moment to represent so many other things rather than competing.

For the team competition, each country puts their best skaters in men's, women's, pairs, and ice dance disciplines and adds all their scores together. There is a short program and a free skate for each discipline. However, a country can make two substitutions and have a man, woman, pair, or ice dancing couple stand in for either the short program or free skate for their lead man, woman, pair, or ice dancing couple. They're like pinch hitters (which aren't nearly as fun as being switch-hitters).

As the highest ranking of all the disciplines, the ice dancers, Maia and Alex Shibutani, got to pick first, and they decided they wanted to skate both programs to have more time in front of the judges. Nathan selected next, and his team decided he would skate in the short program only. He had a great chance to medal in the individual competition, and he was focused on that. The team chose the short program so he would have more time to rest before the individual competition.

My free skate wasn't as physically demanding as Nathan's, so I wouldn't need as much time to rest. Also, I was such a consistent skater that the only mistakes I had really made in the past couple of years were the ones I had made at the last nationals. They knew I could be counted on to deliver.

Bradie Tennell, the lead women's skater, also only wanted to do the short program, so Mirai was also going to do the free skate along with me. With both subs accounted for, that left Alexa and Chris Knierim to skate both programs for pairs.

Bradie is our first skater, and she does really well but is in a deep field, so she gets fifth place. The Knierims did better than anyone expected them to do, which brought us up a bit. The Shibutanis are our strongest team, and they place second.

The biggest surprise was Nathan, and it wasn't a great surprise. The Olympic nerves got the best of him, and he didn't deliver the performance everyone expected and comes in fourth out of ten men. It's not a disastrous performance, but it certainly lowered our medal potential. At the end of the first day, we're in third place, but everyone expects that the Italian team will overtake us the next day and we'll go down to fourth.

The practice rink for the skaters is in the basement of the arena where the team competition is going on, so I didn't get to watch Nathan's short program, because it was happening when I was downstairs training. Suddenly I see Nathan, still wearing his costume, come down and get back on the ice to start practicing not ten minutes after finishing upstairs.

Rafael, who was coming downstairs to watch my practice, was with him and let me know that Nathan didn't skate as well as he had wanted. I was worried about him because I knew how hard he could be on himself—something I used to be as well, much to my own detriment. To make it worse, I was worried he felt like he had screwed everyone out of a medal.

Because Nathan had always been like a younger brother to me, I went up to him when he was done practicing and said, "You need to get this out of your system. What happened, happened. You need to focus on the individual competition. It's over. There's nothing you can do, but don't let it get in your head." I never had someone telling me that when I had bad skates when I was younger, and I thought that maybe if I had an older brother figure tell me to take it easy, I might have learned some lessons a little bit sooner.

That night, in our room, Mirai and I were getting our things together to both compete the next day. I was moving very gingerly because I was afraid I was going to injure myself. In the back of my mind was this weird fear that I would break a leg and not get to compete in the Olympics after all.

"We're not going to medal," Mirai said as we were getting ready.

"I think we have a really good shot. But I don't think we should worry about it," I said.

"I don't know," she said, clearly discouraged.

"You know you've been skating well. That's what you should focus on," I told her. Then I reminded her where we were four years ago, getting fat on In-N-Out burgers and drinking screwdrivers on her roof. I told her what I had been telling myself for weeks: A medal isn't important.

The next day, when I get into the center of the ice to compete, it's looking fairly likely that we're going to lose the medal, and I remember thinking, "That's not my problem. My problem is that I need to focus so that I skate well for my team. I can help raise their spirits if I go out and skate perfectly."

After my name was called and I was in my starting pose, so many thoughts were going through my head at the same time—it felt like what people say happens right before you die. It's like my entire life was flashing before my eyes.

I was very nervous because it was like more than a medal was at stake. I could feel it in my soul. I also felt that maybe I was going to poop myself like I did on my way to train with Sofia that one time. It seemed like this one skate would determine whether I would be taken seriously for the rest of my life. I had already said so many things to the press and had so many funny quotes that if I didn't skate well, I thought everyone would think I was a farce.

People would write to me and tell me that the only reason I was put on the team is because I'm gay. On social media the haters would say, "You even say it yourself that your teammates were seventeen and eighteen and you're twenty-eight. People felt bad for you and they put you on the team because they wanted to really push a diversity card." This was my chance to prove that I am a serious athlete, which also, for the record, is exactly how I was selected for the team in the first place.

I remembered that disastrous nationals when I didn't make the Olympics in 2014; I remembered forging out on my own and being so poor I couldn't eat; I remembered coming out of the closet personally and professionally and what a struggle and triumph it was. I thought about every competition I won and every competition I lost. I thought about all that led me to this one moment where I needed all the tools I had acquired on this journey to give the performance of my lifetime.

Then I thought about Leslie Jones. "I bet Leslie Jones is watching," I told myself while I held my opening pose. "If I fuck up, she's going to put it on Twitter and I will be devastated." Then I thought that the vice president is watching. Reese Witherspoon is watching too, and I can't disappoint her. What if Britney Spears is watching? She could be. Everyone could be watching. Everyone *is* watching.

As the music started, I reminded myself what I always say in practice: Take it one thing at a time, give every element 100 percent, and you'll be great.

That is exactly what I did, and as I got to the last jumping pass, I knew I was doing it—I knew I was giving the performance my team needed. Then I remind myself not to lose focus, because if I don't make that last jump, I might as well tell the referee to stop the music, skate up to the judges, and stab myself in the neck with my skate and end it right there. I've learned a lot in my life, but I've never learned not to love a dramatic exit.

I put my spins at the very end of my program because I've heard that I'm the best spinner in the world, and I want to leave the judges and the audience remembering my best element. I was spinning for my life, and as I was finishing my program, I remembered to make it a celebration. I pumped my fist and showed everyone that I'm really happy, but inside I felt drained. Not just tired from skating but from everything that led up to this moment.

I get off the ice, and Mitch Moyer, the USFS official who was there when I broke my foot, was standing on the side of the rink. He said, "Just remember where you were a year ago, and here you are at the Olympics and you are perfect. That was amazing."

The scores come in and I'm third. I skated my best for my team and that was all that mattered to me. Later that night I checked Twitter, and Leslie Jones was *not* happy with it. She didn't understand how some of the guys ahead of me fell but I skated clean and was still in third. Thanks, Leslie—that is just what I wanted everyone to think.

My performance changed the whole mood of our team because in the next event Mirai went out there and became the first American woman to land a triple axel in the Olympics. She skated the rest of her program perfect and better than she's skated ever in her entire life.

That is when I really couldn't control how I feel. As she finished her program, I just started sobbing because I know what she had been through and I know what I had been through. We shared so many of those experiences together, and it hit me that we both skated so well. I was having a Kelly Clarkson "Moment Like This" meltdown in our team box at the Olympics.

Mirai places better than anyone anticipated and came in second in her event. After that only the ice dancers were left. If the Shibutanis performed as well as they always did, we were guaranteed to come in third.

They made it through the last section of their program, and they looked over to us in the team box. They're still competing, and we all know we're going to medal. It was this crazy, amazing feeling that I couldn't possibly describe. It was like getting a pony for Christmas but also having an orgasm at the same time, but that orgasm lasted for about thirty minutes until the last skaters competed and we knew for sure that the bronze medal was ours.

In classic Adam style, I also thought about what I got to wear. At athlete processing, we got a Nike outfit that we would wear only if we medaled. I thought, "Wow, I get to wear that outfit. Only medalists get to wear that outfit."

Then we were on the ice actually getting our medal, and I couldn't believe what was happening. I was so happy not just to medal, but to have done it with these people—people like Mirai and Nathan who I had known for so long—and to be linked in this way forever.

As the medal was going around my neck, I knew it put me into a different caliber of athletes. I knew it was going to change things because I wasn't just an Olympian—I was a medalist. To me it didn't matter if I medaled, but I knew that to everyone in the public, having a medal—any medal—makes you more legitimate in a certain way. I will be announced as an Olympic medalist for the rest of my life. Third place is good enough.

After the medal ceremony, Derrick was freaking out, and we took a million pictures. Of course my mom, his mom, and my siblings were also so excited. I got really calm because I knew I still had my individual skates to do. I was most likely not going to get another medal, but I knew that they were going to show me on TV. I knew that people knew who I was, so I still needed to have people forget that I wasn't going to medal by skating perfectly. Yes, I was going to be a scam artist right up until the last second.

Going into the individual skates, I was nervous but not as nervous as I was for the team skate. I needed to back up my big mouth with big skating, even more so than big results. I couldn't control the results. I already know from the scores I'm getting that the judges weren't doing me any favors.

I felt like these three skates were sort of like a pop album. My team skate was the single that everyone was paying attention to. That went well. These individual skates were the B sides to prove that I was more than a one-hit wonder—I am someone to be taken seriously.

Usually, the person like me is supposed to just be stupid and pretty and nothing more. I knew that, and I knew that's why it was so important for me to be really good. I wanted to be stupid, pretty, *and* a good athlete.

There was one week between the team competition and the men's competition, and I took the entire week just to train. I wasn't doing any interviews. I focused on preparing and practicing every day. After a few days, Rafael said, "Why don't you take a day off?"

"Well," I said, questioning his advice, "what if I come in, but I won't jump or anything? I'll just skate around."

"Sure," he said, knowing full well that I was going to do it anyway. At this point, he might as well just agree with me.

Before the short program, I was totally prepared, and I went in and skated cleanly again. After the short program, I was in seventh and the highest-ranked American going into the free skate.

The morning of the free skate, I went to the practice rink and ran through everything enough times that I was confident I was going to do well. There were ten minutes left on the rink where I could do whatever I wanted or get off the ice. I looked around and stared at the ice and I made sure I saw the Olympic rings. It's like when you are hiking and you approach a mountain, you want to make sure that you can take in the big picture for a second and make sure to get it all in your mind all at once so you'll never forget it.

"I did it," I thought to myself. "I'm here. I did everything I needed to do. I just need to skate one more time."

It was a strange moment for me because it felt bigger than anything I've ever done, but on another level, it just felt like every other competition I've ever been to. The arena felt the same. The backstage felt the same. I was seeing all the same skaters I've been seeing for years. I'm doing the same programs I had been practicing for what seemed like an eternity. But the audience was different. The scope was different. My impact, it turned out, was very different.

I landed the last jump of my last performance at the Olympics. I realized I had skated another clean program, and in all my gay drama, I felt myself starting to cry. "Don't do it," I thought. "Don't you dare ugly-Kim-Kardashian cry at the Olympics."

After the free skate, I come in tenth. I am so proud to say that I placed in the top ten at the Olympics. When I got home, there was, like, a whole spread in the *National Enquirer*, the bastion of journalism that it is, saying how there was a whole conspiracy keeping me from winning a gold medal. When I went on *Ellen*, she told me, "I think you should have won." Mission accomplished.

Once my competitions are over, I got a chance to start enjoying the Olympic village more. One night the Czech house was having a party, and I went with a few of the other skaters. The US men's hockey team was there. They all knew my name and they all wanted to take a picture. "My girlfriend loves you," they would say. "She said she would kill me if I saw you and didn't take a picture."

It was like *Freaky Friday* to me. When I was a shy little kid with teeth as big as Hilary Duff's before she got her veneers filed, all the macho guys on the hockey team intimidated me. Now they all wanted to take my picture and I was trying to be their friend. If I had a dollar for every girlfriend selfie I took with an athlete, I would have made back all the money I had spent on training to get myself to the Olympics in the first place.

At the same party we saw a few other athletes who were standing by themselves, and I told my friends I was going to go talk to them. "Oh, I wouldn't do that," someone said. "I think they're kind of religious, and I don't know how they feel about gay people."

"Watch this," I said as I walked right up to one of the guys and said, "What's up with your haircut?"

Like I said before, my superpower is that I think everyone is my friend and that's the way I treated them. I brought them right down to my level and acted like we already had a bond and we established one. It works every time, even with people who might not normally accept someone like me.

I think being gay is a fun fact about me. It's like any other bit of biographical trivia: I'm from Pennsylvania, I have five siblings, I get Brazilian blowouts, and I'm gay. They're all fun facts. (The fun fact of being gay might influence the fun fact of getting the blowouts, but who's to say?)

When I treat being gay like that, it doesn't keep me from talking to someone at a party, having a good time with them, or even establishing a friendship. And it doesn't keep them from associating with me. Fun facts have a way of doing that.

I didn't have too much time to party, because as soon as I was done competing, almost every day was filled up with working, doing interviews, and meeting people. The *Today* show broadcasts live from the Olympics, so they would go on at 11 p.m.

in Korea. I sort of fell in love with Hoda Kotb and Savannah Guthrie, and they wanted me on *Today* every day.

There was a lot of media that wanted a little bit of the Adam show. I think it's because I was treating them like my friends too. I always had something funny and candid to say, and I wasn't afraid to go there, wherever "there" might be. I don't think a lot of media people are used to getting that from athletes.

There were a lot of other athletes that were getting tons of attention before the games and raking in tons of sponsors, but that wasn't me. Other than vice president–gate, I wasn't getting all the focus until I was at the Olympics.

Once people looked into my story, they could see that I broke my foot a year before the games, I missed out on making the team two times before, the two people that I went to the Olympics with were seventeen and eighteen, and I was still able to win a medal. I was skating the best I ever had at the age of 137 (in skating years).

I think people really connected with all that. And I was doing Invisalign, so my teeth were straight and perfect.

I didn't want to just share the sassy side of me, though, the sort of brilliantly calculated idiot I had been for years. I wanted the world to see I put all of my own shit behind me and used it to help catapult me to where I was. I wanted to show people I learned to take the bad situations and realize they weren't just bad—they were the starting line to get to somewhere else.

The message must have been working, because at one point NBC made me the offer to be a correspondent for the rest of the games. Sadly I had to turn it down because then I would have gone from being an athlete to being a member of the media, and I would have to give up my housing in the Olympic village. There wasn't a hotel room, Airbnb, or FEMA trailer in PyeongChang for me to rent if I got kicked out of my pre-owned apartment.

And it was important for me to be there as an athlete. I knew I would have the rest of my life to be a reporter, media personality, or celebrity influencer (call me, #FlatTummyTea), but this was the only time I was ever going to get to be an Olympic athlete.

That was especially true because I knew as soon as I was done competing, it was time for me to hang up my skates, at least competitively.

Right before I left to fly back to LA, I saw Rafael. He said, "OK. So, you should get back on the ice and you should start skating again because worlds are coming up."

"Whoa, whoa, whoa," I said. "I know we have worlds coming up, but I don't think I'm going to go." But I told him I would think about it.

It's not unheard of for those who do well at the Olympics to skip worlds that year unless they have something to prove. Nathan, who placed fifth at the Olympics, didn't think he skated as well as he should have. He went to worlds, got to show everyone how incredible he is, and won.

I wasn't going to win worlds. I had three perfect skates on the biggest stage figure skating ever sees. What if I went to worlds and screwed something up? I wanted everyone to remember those perfect skates.

Also, I needed to focus on the next chapter. If I'm done, I need to get my shit together and think about what I am going to do now. I need to figure out how to start approaching life after skating.

I wasn't sure how I was going to break the news to Rafael. I felt like I was disappointing him a little bit. I probably make him sound like he's stern and serious and always telling me I'm fat, but we had so much fun at these competitions. We had been through so much together, and no one showed me support like he did. From the first moment when he told me he wouldn't take money from my mother but would wait for me to pay him, he was always there for me, doing more than he ever needed to.

I also think it's a testament to him as a coach that he took me on as I was older and on somewhat of a downward trajectory and turned my skating and my life around so I was at my best when I was twenty-eight.

He would show that he cared about me in ways that only he could. During practice he would always tell the other skaters, "Watch Adam. Do what he's doing. You need to practice like he's practicing." In the end, in Rafael's eyes, I could do no wrong.

Right before getting on the plane to go home, I knew I had to tell him officially that I wasn't going to worlds. I texted him to let him know.

When the text went through, I could see the three dots on the iPhone, meaning he was writing back. English is not Rafael's first language, and all the texts I ever got back from him were either "Yes," "No," or "OK." I had no idea what was taking him so long to compose.

His response came through and it said, OK. I'm going to miss you. That's about as emotional as he's ever going to get.

I flew home to LA with my suitcases and suitcases full of Olympic memorabilia and one case of generic condoms. When I finally got back to my apartment, I saw that magnet still there on the fridge. "Future Olympian," it read.

It made me think of Scott Hamilton, the figure skating commentator who was on NBC during every Olympics I ever watched growing up. He would always say, "At the end of tonight, somebody's life is going to be completely different and somebody's world is going to be completely spun on its head. And when they go home, their life is never going to be the same."

He was always talking about the person who wins Olympic gold. Now I felt like he was talking about me. I hadn't come in first, but my life was completely different and my world was spun on its head. Good thing I'm still the best spinner in the world.

Get Ready, World

I have never been busier in my life than the weeks after the Olympics when I got home. I went to meet one of my idols on *Ellen*. It was Ellen. I went on *The Late Show with Stephen Colbert* to meet another one of my idols. It was Reese Witherspoon. (Sorry, Stephen, I love you too.)

I brought my brother Brady and my friend Sarah, who both live in New York, with me to *Colbert*. Reese was unbelievably kind and amazing, and she not only wanted to meet me but she wanted to meet my whole family too. Reese's security walked up to them and said, "Reese wants to meet the siblings," so Sarah said she didn't think she could go.

"This is my sister," Brady lied to the bodyguard, totally being the best wingman in the world so that everyone got to meet Reese. I just have to figure out how to break it to my mom she's now the mother of seven.

Mirai and I also got invited to the Oscars, which was shortly after the Olympics. We did a segment with *Access Hollywood* where they took us to get something to wear on the red carpet and then they were going to show us attending the event. I'm figuring they're going to take me to Men's Wearhouse or something, but instead we went to the studio of the fashion designer Jeremy Scott, who designs for Moschino and who I totally love. He had never dressed anyone for the Oscars before, so I was going to be his first.

When we arrived with the cameras, Jeremy had a few outfits picked out for us.

One was a loud, fully metallic gold suit with no shirt underneath it and just a harness. The next one was basically a shirt that didn't tuck in, so it was like a napkin tied around the neck, and that had a sleeveless blazer to go with it. Then there was a purple suit with glittery green flames shooting up it. You know, the sort of understated style I'm really known for.

After the cameras were turned off, it was time for me to really pick out what I was going to wear. The idea of wearing a harness was so titillating, but I didn't think of the sexual aspect of it—I just thought of it as cool straps. I knew a harness look would be badass, but it was with the gold suit, which I didn't want to wear. I didn't want to offend him after he styled all these looks himself, but I asked Jeremy, "Can I maybe move some of the pieces around?"

"Sure," he said. "Do whatever you think is good." He couldn't have been more welcoming or easy to work with.

I tried on the harness with a different blazer and pants, and the stylist said, "Adam, you have to wear a shirt. It's the Oscars, for God's sake." Apparently they have a sign on the Dolby Theatre that reads NO SHIRT, NO SHOES, NO SERVICE. So we also picked out a shirt to wear under the harness.

We were all getting ready at a hotel near the theater, and the stylist pulled out the harness look and some backups. "You don't have to wear this harness if you don't want to. If you do, it's really going to change your image." Everyone said if I wore it, people would think I had some grit and edge to me.

"I don't think anyone is going to notice," I told the stylist. "It's not like I'm Jennifer Lawrence. No one is going to care if I'm there."

We go to the Oscars and the Vanity Fair party afterward, and I'm getting a lot of compliments on my harness, but nothing too out of the ordinary. When you're in a room full of people that were all dressed by professionals, everyone looks amazing.

The next morning I woke up and looked at social media, and I understood what a big impact my harness had made. Tyra Banks was talking about it. I was still in the running to be America's Next Top Model. I was also on a lot of best-dressed lists and a few worst-dressed lists. Either way, people were talking about me, which I thought was fun.

What I really loved about that outfit, though, is that it proved to me the lesson I learned in my skating career was also true in the "real" world. I thought that outfit was cool and really expressed me, so I went with my gut and did something fun and got rewarded for it. The same thing happened with skating, where I stopped doing what everyone thought I should be doing and started to do the things I thought were great. Now I knew that lesson was something I could carry with me into the next chapter of my career.

I was getting a lot of offers too: endorsements, reality shows, speaking engagements, high school productions of *Grease*. Anything you could possibly imagine. When I was in Korea, I was just using my sports agent who I had used for ten years. After I started getting so much press attention and so many people wanted to work with me, it became too much for him to handle, so I got new representation. That was another thing I learned in skating—finding a team I could trust and who would support me the best they possibly could.

When I met with my new agents, they told me I should meet with everyone who wanted to meet with me and decide what I wanted to do and what seemed right for me. I did just that—I met with absolutely everyone to hear them out.

It was never my objective to be or try to be famous, but I also knew this was a great opportunity to do one of the things I always wanted to do, which was let people know I could be funny. I really feel like my best self when I have everyone entertained and laughing. Skating is this amazing thing, but to be out and engaging with people, having them feeling good and making them laugh—that is what I feel my true passion is.

In those weeks following the Olympics, I discovered that skating was just a thing for me to be able to perform and express myself. Getting exposed to this world of entertainment opened my eyes because being an entertainer was a dream I was embarrassed to talk about. I didn't want to be an up-and-coming actress. I spend twenty years of my skating life working hard, failing, and waiting for a big break. Do I really want to do that again, waiting for a break to be a movie star?

I also knew that it might not happen in the entertainment world. I didn't want to miss those chances, and there was always a part of me that knew if the moment passed me by, that I love teaching and working with skaters. I could go be a coach in a heartbeat. There was really no bad option for the next stage of my life.

When I was doing all this media, I treated each appearance like it was an audition or a job interview. I would watch old interviews the hosts had done, and I would see who their favorite guests were. I would write four or five jokes for each appearance and try to get at least two of them into the conversation. I didn't want it to look too obvious, like I was straining to get to the punch line, but I wanted to have material prepared. See? That was another thing I learned from competing—to do the hard work in the dark so I could shine in the light.

Another opportunity that came my way that I wasn't really expecting was that nice gentleman named JP who I met on Tinder in Helsinki during the Finlandia Trophy, months before the Olympics. We kept messaging on Tinder even after I went home from Finland, and then we transitioned to sending messages on Instagram. He'd message me, and I would wait a day or two to respond as *Cosmo* taught us, because we don't want to look too desperate. He would do the same. And this went on for about a month.

Finally I decided to test him. I responded to one of his messages with a video message. I remember I looked in the mirror before I started to record this message, and I looked busted. I was very glossy from wearing all my night creams, but I also remember thinking, "Who the fuck cares?!" The only way for him to pass this test would be to send a video back. I still hadn't heard him speak or seen what he really looked like in the flesh, and I was very curious. He passed the test.

We upgraded to sending videos every day. Then his started getting longer, sometimes like ten or twenty minutes long. This is when I was training and was at the rink all the time where the service is awful. They'd be so long I'd have to wait until I got home to load them. But I watched every day and then sent him messages back about everything that was going on in my life.

It was so weird because I was starting to feel close to him and really connect to him even though I'd never met him in person before. Then it started to affect my skating, but in a good way. When I was going to my Grand Prix and other events, I knew I had to do well because I had to tell my fake Finnish boyfriend how I did at the competition, and I didn't want to tell him I came in sixth or tenth. I wanted to tell him that I came in first or second. My fake Finnish boyfriend needs to think I'm a good skater.

Even though we would talk every day, I didn't have any expectations that this was a real thing. I kept saying to myself, "You're never going to meet him. You're never going to meet him." The only people I told about JP were Ashley, because we're best friends, and Mariah Bell, who was obsessed with the fact that I had this Instagram boyfriend I had never met. When talking to Mariah one day, I decided that if I didn't qualify for the Olympics, then I was going to treat myself with a trip to Helsinki to meet JP. Well, we all know how that turned out.

When I qualified for the Olympics and for worlds, the plan changed and we were going to meet at worlds, which that year were in Milan. He was going to come down after the competition, and we would just hang out in Italy.

At this point we're sending multiple long messages to each other every day. The only time the conversation really lapsed was when I was at the Olympics. I was so busy with competing and swatting down the Trump family on social media I didn't have time to give him really long messages. But still, every day, JP would send me, like, a twenty-minute video about what he was up to.

After a while, I knew that I was getting millions of new social media followers and that I was in the news even in Finland, and JP still hadn't said anything about all the attention I was getting. He just carried on like everything was normal and never even mentioned the Olympics. I was thinking, "I wonder if he even knows what is actually happening?"

Then, the next day, he said in his message, "I know everything is changing and there is a lot going on right now, and I just want you to know I know that." That was really his only acknowledgment of the level of insanity in my life, but I knew he knew and he knew that I knew he knew and we knew that she knew that they knew that my fake Finnish boyfriend was getting realer by the minute. In fact, this made me like him even more because he was no more or less interested in me now that things were taking off than he was when I was back home training in obscurity.

After the Olympics, I wasn't going to worlds anymore, so Milan was off. JP told me his dream was always to move to LA but he had never been, and if I had some time, he could come to me. He said he had some friends here he could stay with. He booked a trip to come, and I knew if things went bad, at least he could go stay with his friends and I would be off the hook.

We wanted our first few days together to be on neutral territory, so I planned a trip to San Diego for a couple of days. When I was headed to the airport, I told my agent, Justin, what was going on. He said, "You're going to pick someone up at the airport you never met before? You need to text me every hour so that I know you're safe."

I picked JP up and the first thing I thought was, "God, you are really tall." We went for our first date where all of the really classy ladies take their internet boyfriends: Cheesecake Factory. Then we headed down to San Diego, and while the conversation was a little awkward at first on the two-hour drive, it soon picked up and it was just like we were sending video messages back and forth but actually sitting next to each other. He ended up spending the whole ten days in LA at my place, and we've been seeing each other (and video messaging because he lives in Finland and I travel all the time) ever since. My life has always had a flair for the dramatic, so it makes sense that I have a foreign boyfriend who goes between Helsinki and LA and that we travel halfway across the world to spend time together.

After we were getting cozy in San Diego, the one commitment I knew I had for sure was with Stars on Ice. They had asked me after nationals if I would join the tour, and it was always one of my dreams to go on the tour right after being at the Olympics, so I said yes in a heartbeat.

I also started talking to the producers of *Dancing with the Stars* about appearing on that show, another thing that I always wanted to do. But I wasn't sure I really wanted to be on a reality show at this point. I was getting a lot of offers to do silly things, like go out and spend a day working in different professions or just say mean things about people on camera, and that's not something I ever wanted to do. I don't mind making fun of myself, but I didn't want people laughing at me for being dumb. Also, I'm sassy, but I'm not very good at being mean. I had people make fun of me as a kid, so now I'd much rather make fun of myself than what someone is wearing on the red carpet.

The other problem is that the six weeks of the Stars on Ice tour lined up perfectly with the six weeks that I would have to be rehearsing for and performing on *Dancing with the Stars*. But I had watched a documentary about Joan Rivers (RIP), and she said in it that she always says yes to everything. Joan would not only do *Fashion Police* and stand-up sets all around the country, but also fly out to a mall opening in Indiana to cut the giant red ribbon. She always said yes and was a multimillionaire. I decided that I was going to be just like Joan Rivers but, like, alive.

I said yes, and I'm glad I did *Dancing with the Stars*, but I could never do two such huge things at the same time again. I was only getting three or four hours of sleep a night. I was rehearsing four hours a day with my partner, Jenna Johnson, on top of rehearsal for Stars on Ice, doing those shows, and staying until the last person left the meet and greet each night.

After the Stars on Ice performance on Sunday night, I would take the red-eye overnight back to LA to tape the show with only the sleep I had gotten on the plane to get me through. Then that night I was back to the next tour stop.

I was giving it my all, though, practicing my ballroom steps backstage at Stars on Ice. It got to a point where I was so exhausted I just needed to conserve as much energy as possible. When rehearsing for Stars on Ice, I stopped doing all my jumps, because I needed that energy for when the audience was there. I skated clean every night and went on to win *Dancing with the Stars*.

Though all I wanted to do was sleep, I never bitched about it. I told myself that I'll never be coming off an Olympic Games, on a skating tour, and competing on a reality show all at the same time again, so I better soak it up and soak it in. I let myself be tired, but I didn't let myself be anything but grateful. I knew that being this tired came from all the hard work I had done to make it to the Olympics. I earned being this tired, but I did not earn getting bitter.

Once Stars on Ice was over, I knew that I needed to take a step away from skating to focus on some other things. I didn't think I really needed to officially retire with a press release or anything. I thought people would know that I was done, especially because

I was so old the competitive figure skating world was about to put me in a boat, set it on fire, and push it out into the ocean like a Viking funeral. Still, in my own mind, that chapter was closed the minute I landed the last jump in my last program at the Olympics.

One of the reasons I needed to stop being a competitive athlete is because I was still on the list for the US Anti-Doping Agency, or USADA as we called it. This meant every month I had to send them a detailed account of where I would be every single day, because they could come by and randomly drug test me at any minute. You have an hour from when they call you to meet them at your house or else you miss the test. A missed test means a failed test, and just ask Lance Armstrong what happens with a failed test.

When the USADA agent would come to my house, he had to watch me the entire time he was there, and I had to pee in front of him (for male athletes it's a guy, and for female athletes it's a lady), and you have to show him from "nipples to knees," so everything in the middle section of the body has to be exposed. This was to make sure I wasn't grabbing any fake pee or trying to mess with the results of the test.

Once, Patrick Chan, a fellow skater and world champion, asked me if I ever had to poop in front of the drug-testing agent. "No!" I shouted, laughing at him. He revealed that on at least one occasion he had to do this. He said he told the agent he had to go number two before he could go number one and asked if he could have some privacy so he could drop the deuce. The agent told him no, so he had to take a shit in front of this guy.

I teased him for years about this, because I did drug tests every few months and never even had the urge to poop, so I thought this was hilarious. It was also funny because I started to have a friendship with the drug-testing agent for Southern California. His name was José, and I programmed his number into my phone so I wouldn't ignore him when he called, like he was a telemarketer or something.

He would call, I would meet him at the house, we would chat for a bit and have a cup of coffee together—you know, something to get the juices flowing. I would ask José all about his kids, and once, after he had knee surgery, I even helped him up the stairs into my apartment for the test. I was about as close as someone could be with his drug-testing officer.

Once, about two years before the Olympics, José came to my house, and as we were having our cup of coffee, I realized, "Oh no. I have to take a shit." And I could feel from the rumbling in my bowels that it wasn't your average shit—it was going to be a wet diarrhea. There is no way that I could shit in front of my good friend José.

I decided that I was going to pretend to be doing chores. I was walking from room to room, organizing things and moving things around while we continued to talk. I was trying to give off this air like it was no big deal. I'm just working around the house. Then I said, "I have to go put this away." I ran into the bathroom, pushed out the diarrhea as fast as I could while also choke holding my dick so no pee came out. As soon as the door closed, José is like, "Adam? What's going on?"

"Sorry," I shouted while still holding my penis like a garden hose. "The door closed by accident." I cleaned up and went back out to the kitchen where José was sitting and said, "OK, I'm ready to pee now."

As soon as José was out the door with my urine in a cup, I called Patrick and said, "I just barely got out of taking a shit in front of the USADA agent."

"You deserve that," Patrick said.

"I know. I'm calling you to apologize."

Just after the Olympics, I was at the rink visiting Rafael one afternoon and I get a call on my phone. It was José. In all the craziness after the Olympics, I never took myself off the list for USADA screenings. Now I had to show up to my house to do a drug test, because I didn't want to miss it, fail it, and have everyone think that I was using drugs this whole time.

Nathan was also at the rink, and one of his sponsors was Powerade. He had a million giant bottles of the electric-blue sports drink all over the locker room. I asked him if I could take some so that by the time I get to my house I'd be able to pee for José. He gave me two, and I start chugging them in the car on the ride home.

I met José and we talked about the Olympics. I got the medal out and showed it to him, and we took pictures with it. I showed him the Mirrorball Trophy from *Dancing with the Stars* because his wife is a huge fan. We sent her a picture of José holding it. We were having a great time together, and I knew it was probably my last time seeing him, so we were enjoying ourselves.

Suddenly the Powerade wasn't settling so well in my stomach, and I could hear it giving out some awful gurgles. Oh no. Not again. I have already danced this dance with the devil. Why is it happening again?

José and I were on the couch, and as he's talking I'm having a self-talk with myself. "Adam, I know that there's a lot of stuff in you right now, and I know that it needs to come out. I need you to use those visualization exercises you've learned and mentally redirect everything that wants to come out of the back right now to come out the front so that you can pee in front of José." I was doing everything mentally that I could. I felt like I was North Korea telling the world they didn't have nuclear testing sites, when we can all see them on Google Maps.

I got up to go to the bathroom to try to pee, and I could feel it in my bones. It was coming out. There was nothing I could do about it. There was no way around this.

"José, I have something really bad to tell you," I said.

"What?" he asked.

"I need to go to the bathroom."

"Good. That's why I'm here."

"No. I need to take a shit and there's nothing I can do about it."

He started laughing and said, "I've been to a million houses before. I've drug tested a million people when they've been awful sick where they pee and then they throw up at the same time. I've seen it all. It's fine."

"We've known each other for a long time, and this is probably my last drug test with you and I'm going to need to look you in the eyes while I do nipple to knee like a dog and take a shit in front of you."

He was still cracking up laughing about all this (as I'm sure Patrick Chan would be too), but I was mortified—and maybe a little excited to tell the tale one day.

I sat down on the toilet and the door is open and José was kind of standing in the doorway, because he needed to watch me pee. It's sort of a chicken-or-egg situation at this point, where I didn't know if I was going to poop or pee first. I was trying to pee so I can close the door and shit, but it was not working. I realized that the shit needed to come before the pee. The shit would unlock the door of the pee.

"I'm shitting, José," I said, because the only way I could get over this moment was to keep saying, "I'm shitting," out loud. José has the door open, but at least he's giving me the courtesy of looking away.

"OK, now I'm going to pee," I said. I took the cup and José watched me pee into it while sitting on the toilet like we're cellmates in the worst prison in the entire world.

I handed him the cup and then said, "Can I have a moment to myself?" I cleaned up, washed my hands, and went back out into the living room. I couldn't believe I just had to do that. I was karma's bitch. José was still laughing about it as we said goodbye, a friend until the bitter, bitter end.

As soon as he got in his car and drove away, I called US Figure Skating and asked, "How the hell do I get off the USADA drug-testing list? It needs to happen *today*."

While I'm glad I'll never have to go through drug testing again, I do sometimes miss my life as a skater. As challenging as it was, it gave me a huge amount of structure. Not only was I training every day and working out at the gym, but the season had a certain flow to it. I was always at the same competitions at the same time of year. And when the competitive season was over, there were new costumes to get, new routines to choreograph, new music to find. I knew the pattern in and out.

I've never been busier since leaving skating, but almost everything I've done has been a onetime thing. I'm never going back to *Dancing with the Stars* (though I would in a heartbeat). Even when I get assignments for *Good Morning America* or *Nightline*, I'm going to a new place and interviewing a new person every time. It's not the rigor of doing the same routine so many times that it's tattooed on the inside of my brain.

That structure was pulled out from under me as soon as I retired. I love the ride I'm on now, but after living the first thirty years always knowing what is around the corner, I have to admit that I'm a little bit scared.

It wasn't the competitive aspect of skating that I craved; it was the desire for excellence. That is something I will always strive for. It's the Winnie Cooper in me always wanting to be perfect, always trying to figure out ways I can do something better. I honed that on the rink, but it will be handy in any arena.

When I was a kid, my mom would say to me, "All you have to do is try," and I wanted to tell her, "That is such bullshit." Like so many other things my mom told me, I grew to realize it was true. If you don't try, you don't even go anywhere. If you try and fail, at least you can go back and analyze what happened, what you can do differently. If you try again and you fail, you can analyze more. And if you try again and you fail again, then you need to go home because you probably look like a mess.

I've had disappointments and setbacks, and I've been upset by them, but I had to learn not to dwell on them. If you think of every mistake as falling into a hole, then you need to climb out of that hole just to get to where you were before. If you keep falling in holes and getting back up, you're just living on a plateau.

I think of every mistake as a launching pad. It's going to lead me somewhere else, somewhere higher, someplace I might not have been able to see before.

Yes, that means there are going to be a whole lot of launching pads in this new phase of my life. Give me six months and I might have even launched myself into space by then. But now I have the confidence to ask for help if I need it, and the confidence to give my best and not be upset if it's not perfect.

When I was working on a segment for *Good Morning America*, I called one of my agents and said that all the people who toiled away in small local markets trying to get to a national platform probably hate me because I didn't do any work to get there. I felt like I was just walking down the street and someone said, "I like your outfit. Wanna be in *Vogue*?"

That agent told me, "That's not true at all. What do you think you were doing on all of those cold mornings in rinks in random cities all over the country? The opportunities you have now are from all of the hard work you put in to go to the Olympics. That's the same as their hard work. You might have gotten a break in a different way, but it might have been an even harder way. You shouldn't be embarrassed by that. And if you don't keep working now that you're here, you won't be asked back, and that weather guy from Duluth is going to get your shot after all."

An athlete's life is a very selfish life. Everything is focused around how the athlete feels, what he needs to do his best. When I was an athlete, I had to put everything and everybody second.

What I do now is totally different. I'm not out there being judged on my own; I'm working with a million different people. I'm meeting new people all the time and seeing not what they can do for me, but what I can do for them. After all those years in the rink, I'm ready to meet the world. The world better get ready for all this, because like Lauryn Hill once said before she went to jail, "Ready or not, here I come, you can't hide."

Acknowledgments

First and foremost, I would like to thank the people. Also I would like to thank Meryl Streep, because that is what everyone does when they win an Oscar.

None of this would have happened without Suzanne O'Neill and everyone at Grand Central Publishing, especially Nidhi Pugalia. On a hot New York day, the first time I met Suzanne I knew I wanted her to be my editor and I can't thank her enough for taking a chance on this small-town boy with a big dream.

Everyone at Grand Central has been a dream and I can't thank these guys enough: Jimmy Franco, Jordan Rubinstein, Brian McLendon, Tiffany Sanchez, Mari Okuda, Albert Tang, Karen Kosztolnyik, Ben Sevier, and Michael Pietsch. A big shout-out to Eliza Rivlin for doing the legal read and keeping me from getting sued.

When I met my book agent, Mel Berger, he looked exactly like I thought a book agent from New York should look. He wasn't scared when I walked into his office and said, "Are we really going to write a fucking book?" For all that, he is a star.

I want to thank my mom for having me, believing in me when I didn't believe in myself, and for doing all the insane shit that is in this book. Also, thanks for still driving me to a skating lesson after I shit myself. That took courage.

This past Christmas my dad gave me a baseball that he got when he went to see a game with his father. He wasn't hoping that I would still become a baseball player, he gave it to me because it was sentimental to him and he wanted me to have it. It was a big deal. It just reminded me how far we've come and how lucky I am to have a dad like that.

A big thanks to all my brothers and sisters for supporting me when we were growing up and when our mom was always away. You were always happy when things went well and were always there for me when things didn't.

Susan, you are the best publicist, and thanks for not firing me as a client when I never return your text messages and haven't read emails you sent to me a year ago. I'll get to them. I swear.

I had some of the best coaches in skating and I would like to thank them all for all the hard work they put into helping me achieve my dreams, pushing me, helping me to be my best, and for not charging me for shame.

Derrick did more than lend his old costumes when I was poor. Thanks for becoming part of my family, always being there for me, and being my best friend. I feel really lucky to have a great group of friends who have always and continue to be so special to me, whether it's to spend a few extra days in Minneapolis antique shopping with Molly or an impromptu staycation in Scottsdale with Douglas and Bianca. Also thanks to Ashley and Mirai for taking a chance on me when I was really low. I'll never forget the way you treated me.

I would also like to thank Ms. Britney Jean Spears for her continued work of enlightening the world and Reese Witherspoon for enlightening my life.

When the opportunity came to write a book, I thought, "Well, I've written emails before, and a book is just like a really long email." I was sadly mistaken, because now I write very long emails but just about the book. So thank you, Brian Moylan, for being my writing coach. Also thanks to the makers of Spindrift for fueling our work sessions with your delicious water. And thank you to Google Docs for unknowingly participating in one of the most important works of literature of this and future generations.

I want to thank JP for listening to me read this entire book at least four times and forgiving me when he told me how his day was and I would say, “Yeah, but what do you think about the chapter I read to you last night?”

And, of course, I have to thank my fans new and old for their support, for laughing at me and laughing with me. I hope you laugh as hard as I did at myself while reliving all my trials, tribulations, and triumphs.

About the Author

One of the world's most dramatic figure skaters, Adam won the hearts of America and the world at the 2018 Winter Olympics. Known for his refreshing candor and wit, he rose to fame on the global stage, which has provided him a platform to speak out in support of LGBTQ rights and the freedom to be oneself, making him a role model and icon to millions.

Adam has been recognized for his advocacy work by the Human Rights Campaign with their Visibility Award and the Matthew Shepard Foundation and has supported GLAAD's Ambassador Program and hosted the Trevor Project's TrevorLIVE. He has also been named to the *TIME* 100, *Forbes* 30 Under 30, and *Out* magazine's Power 50, among others.